For My People

The Bishop Henry McNeal Turner Studies in North American Black Religion

Editor:

James H. Cone,
Union Theological Seminary, New York

Associate Editors:

Charles H. Long,
University of North Carolina, Chapel Hill

C. Shelby Rooks,
United Church Board of Homeland Ministries

Gayraud S. Wilmore,
New York Theological Seminary

The purpose of this series is to encourage the development of biblical, historical, theological, and pastoral works that analyze the role of the churches and other religious movements in the liberation struggles of blacks in the United States and the Third World. What is the relationship between black religion and black peoples' fight for justice in the U.S.? What is the relationship between the black struggle for justice in the U.S. and the liberation struggles of the poor in Asia, Africa, Latin America, and the Caribbean? A critical investigation of these and related questions will define the focus of this series.

The series is named after Bishop Henry McNeal Turner (1834–1915), whose life and work symbolize the black struggle for liberation in the U.S. and the Third World. Bishop Turner was a churchman, a political figure, a missionary, a pan-Africanist—a champion of black freedom and the cultural creativity of black peoples under God.

*The Bishop Henry McNeal Turner Studies
in North American Black Religion, Vol. 1*

JAMES H. CONE

For My People

Black Theology and the Black Church

ORBIS BOOKS

Maryknoll, New York 10545

Fifth Printing, September 1990

The Catholic Foreign Mission Society of America (Maryknoll) recruits and trains people for overseas missionary service. Through Orbis Books Maryknoll aims to foster the international dialogue that is essential to mission. The books published, however, reflect the opinions of their authors and are not meant to represent the official position of the society.

"For My People" was originally published in the book *For My People*, copyright © 1942 by Margaret Walker, published by Yale University Press; used by permission.

Library of Congress Cataloging in Publication Data

Cone, James H.
  For my people.

  Includes bibliographical references and index.
  1. Black theology. 2. Afro-American churches.
1. Title.
BT82.7.C67   1984   230′.08996073   84-5195
ISBN 0-88344-106-3 (pbk.)

To The African Methodist Episcopal Church,
the community where I first heard the gospel preached,

and

to black Christians everywhere
in hope that we will remake our churches according to
the liberating heritage of
Allen, Varick, Tubman, Sojourner, Martin, and Malcolm.

FOR MY PEOPLE

By Margaret Walker

For my people everywhere singing their slave songs repeatedly:
   their dirges and their ditties and their blues and jubilees, praying their prayers nightly to an unknown god, bending their
   knees humbly to an unseen power;

For my people lending their strength to the years, to the gone
   years and the now years and the maybe years, washing ironing
   cooking scrubbing sewing mending hoeing plowing digging
   planting pruning patching dragging along never gaining never
   reaping never knowing and never understanding;

For my playmates in the clay and dust and sand of Alabama back-
   yards playing baptizing and preaching and doctor and jail and
   soldier and school and mama and cooking and playhouse and
   concert and store and hair and Miss Choomby and company;

For the cramped bewildered years we went to school to learn to
   know the reasons why and the answers to and the people who
   and the places where and the days when, in memory of the
   bitter hours when we discovered we were black and poor and
   small and different and nobody cared and nobody wondered
   and nobody understood;

For the boys and girls who grew in spite of these things to be man
   and woman, to laugh and dance and sing and play and drink
   their wine and religion and success, to marry their playmates
   and bear children and then die of consumption and anemia and
   lynching;

For my people thronging 47th Street in Chicago and Lenox Avenue in New York and Rampart Street in New Orleans, lost disinherited dispossessed and happy people filling the cabarets and taverns and other people's pockets needing bread and shoes and milk and land and money and something—something all our own;

For my people walking blindly spreading joy, losing time being lazy, sleeping when hungry, shouting when burdened, drinking when hopeless, tied and shackled and tangled among ourselves by the unseen creatures who tower over us omnisciently and laugh;

For my people blundering and groping and floundering in the dark of churches and schools and clubs and societies, associations and councils and committees and conventions, distressed and disturbed and deceived and devoured by money-hungry glory-craving leeches, preyed on by facile force of state and fad and novelty, by false prophet and holy believer;

For my people standing staring trying to fashion a better way from confusion, from hypocrisy and misunderstanding, trying to fashion a world that will hold all the people, all the faces, all the adams and eves and their countless generations;

Let a new earth rise. Let another world be born. Let a bloody peace be written in the sky. Let a second generation full of courage issue forth; let a people loving freedom come to growth. Let a beauty full of healing and a strength of final clenching be the pulsing in our spirits and our blood. Let the martial songs be written, let the dirges disappear. Let a race of men now rise and take control.

Contents

Acknowledgments

I could not have written this book without the assistance and encouragement of many people. Much of the material in this book was presented as lectures at universities, seminaries, colleges, community groups, and churches in the U.S., Europe, Africa, Asia, Latin America, and the Caribbean. I am deeply grateful for the global interest in black theology and for the translation of my writings into many languages. Many persons of various races and cultures throughout the world, Christians and non-Christians, have supported me in my research and writings.

I must offer a special word of thanks to the Union Seminary community for their support of my teaching and research on black theology. Several faculty and graduate students read all or part of my manuscript and offered helpful, critical comments. They include: Donald Shriver, Cornel West, Roger Shinn, James Forbes, Gerald Shephard, Kelly Brown, Dennis Wiley, Josiah Young, Benjamin Chavis, Alonzo Johnson, Dwight Hopkins, Sherrill Holland, Bennett Ramsey, Lois Kirkwood, Nancy Duff, Howard and Jualynne Dodson, James Washington, Rienzie Perera, Jacob Thomas, and Ho-Suk Hahn.

The first draft of my manuscript was written in London, England, and the first critical reading was given by Makeda K. Coaston. Her excellent editorial skills and keen intelligence improved my manuscript immensely.

As was true with my previous books, Lester B. Scherer, my friend and critic of many years, has given unselfishly of his time, debating the issues with me and working on the precision and clarity of my writing style.

No one has influenced my thinking on black theology more than Gayraud S. Wilmore. He read my manuscript and corrected several factual errors and misleading interpretations. I will always be deeply appreciative for his friendship and for his critique of my perspective on black theology.

Charles H. Long and C. Shelby Rooks are special friends who also have been very supportive of my work for many years. They gave my manuscript a critical reading, correcting some misleading statements and offering their judgment regarding the strengths and weaknesses of my interpretation of black theology's history and of my suggestions for its future development.

I must offer a word of appreciation to several bishops and many ministers and laypersons of the African Methodist Episcopal Church for their encouragment and support of my teaching ministry. Even when they have disagreed with my critical perspective on the A.M.E. Church, they have defended my right to speak and to write from my theological convictions.

A similar word of thanks is also appropriate regarding many black clergy and laity in other denominations. I have received much love and support from many sectors of the black Christian community.

I also wish to offer a word of thanks to William Jerman for his excellent copy editing and to John Eagleson and Philip Scharper of Orbis Books for their support of black theology.

No one has been more supportive of my work than my family—Michael and Charles (my sons), Robynn and Krystal (my daughters), Charles and Cecil (my brothers), and Lucy Cone (my mother). Without their love and encouragement, I would never have written this book.

Although many persons encouraged and assisted me in many ways, I am alone responsible for any failures in the content of this book.

Acronyms

AACC	All-Africa Conference of Churches
AME	African Methodist Episcopal (Church)
AMEZ	African Methodist Episcopal Zion (Church)
BCCC	Black Catholic Clergy Caucus
BEDC	Black Economic Development Conference
BMCR	Black Methodists for Church Renewal
CORE	Congress of Racial Equality
EATWOT	Ecumenical Association of Third World Theologians
IFCO	Interreligious Foundation for Community Organization
NAACP	National Association for the Advancement of Colored People
NCBC	National Conference of Black Churchmen
NCC	National Council of Churches
NCNC	National Committee of Negro Churchmen
NUL	National Urban League
PIE	Partners in Ecumenism
PUSH	People United to Save Humanity
SCLC	Southern Christian Leadership Conference
SDS	Students for a Democratic Society
SNCC	Student Non-Violent Coordinating Committee
SSBR	Society for the Study of Black Religion
TIA	Theology in the Americas
WCC	World Council of Churches

Introduction

The "Black Power Statement" of the National Conference of Black Churchmen (NCBC), in 1966, initiated the development of a theological consciousness that separated radical black Christianity from the religion of white churches. It set in motion a series of events that led seminary professors and other members of the black clergy to create what has since been called black theology.

Between 1966 and 1984 black theology went through many changes, from hostile rejection by both white and black churches to tolerance by many whites and increasing acceptance by many blacks. It is now time to make a critical assessment of its origin in the 1960s and its development throughout the 1970s, in order to chart the course of its future in the 1980s and beyond. Unless we look honestly at our past, it is unlikely that we shall know what to do in the present for the shaping of a creative black future.

I want to point out that this book is not, as such, a history of black theology in North America. Rather, it seeks to give a theological interpretation of the civil rights movement and of other race-related issues stemming from it. By the same token, it must explore the civil rights movement of the 1960s and '70s as the matrix of black theology. Theology, in turn, reviewing that history, adds—discovers—another dimension that secular involvement and scholarship, by themselves, would overlook.

When I speak of "theology" or "the theological dimension" in this book or in my previous works, I am not saying only that the black struggle for justice and freedom within the American cultural and political systems is a matter of "ultimate concern." It is that, to be sure; but I am writing—intentionally and explicitly—as a Christian theologian. Although, therefore, the language of "ultimate concern" might define a generalized sense

1

of the importance of sacred meanings—meanings that brought together a large number of concerned blacks and whites, with whom I make common cause—I must make my own concerns and motivations crystal clear, and adhere to them unswervingly. As a theologian I perceive in the history of the black struggle for liberation the working of the will of God—the God revealed to Abraham, Sarah, Isaac, and Jacob, the God who sent Jesus Christ into the world for its redemption. It is the same God whose presence became known in the history that recalls the names of Paul of Tarsus, Augustine of Hippo, Martin Luther, John Calvin, and, closer to our time, Bishop Richard Allen, Sojourner Truth, and Martin Luther King, Jr. My work is defined by this tradition, and this tradition gives a specificity and concreteness to my understanding of history.

As a work of theological interpretation, this book is, of course, addressed to the theological community. But in a special way it is addressed even more to all those persons whose lives helped shape, and were themselves shaped by, the civil rights movement—as also to their present and future successors. It is of the very nature of the theology we are forging that it cannot be merely a "science" or an "intellectual discipline": the theological task is worked out in dialogue and cooperation between and among individuals and groups who are dedicated bearers of the Christian faith.

Although this book is addressed to all persons who are interested in the Christian gospel and the human struggle for justice, it is *primarily* addressed to the black church in particular and the black community in general. As a people we have reached a critical juncture in our history: we must decide what kind of future to make for ourselves and how and with whom to make it. Will it be a future that is derived from the values of white, capitalist America and its European allies, or will it be formed from the liberating values of our own history and culture and of other oppressed peoples who are struggling for freedom throughout the globe? Will it be a future that is tied to the values of white religion, which enslaves the poor, or will it be defined by the liberating elements in black religion and the religions of the poor in all communities?

The complexity and the urgency of the problems that we blacks must face require that we pause for a moment to evaluate our past and present struggle for justice and the gospel's relation to it so that we can see more clearly what must be done to make a humane future for our children. I do not claim to have all the answers to our problems. I only hope that I can raise the right questions and point us in the direction where answers might be found. In the sense that the black church and community have shaped the issues that I address, this book is "for my people."

Chapter I

The Origin of Black Theology

All people need power, whether black or white. We regard it
sheer hypocrisy or as a blind and dangerous illusion the view
that opposes love to power. Love must be the controlling
element in power, not power itself. So long as white church-
men continue to moralize and misinterpret Christian love,
so long will justice continue to be subverted in this land.
> National Committee of Negro Churchmen,
> "Black Power Statement," July 31, 1966[1]

The idea of "black theology" emerged when a small group of radical black clergy began to reinterpret the meaning of the Christian faith from the standpoint of the black struggle for liberation in the United States during the second half of the 1960s. To theologize *from within* the black experience rather than be confined to duplicating the theology of Europe or white North America was the main objective of the new black theology. It represented the theological reflections of a radical black clergy seeking to interpret the meaning of God's liberating presence in a society where blacks were being economically exploited and politically marginalized because of their skin color.

What does it mean to be black and Christian? If God is the Creator of all persons and through Christ has made salvation possible for everyone, why are some oppressed and segregated in the churches and in society on the basis of color? How can whites

5

claim Christian identity, which emphasizes the love and justice of God, and still support and tolerate the injustice committed against blacks by churches and by society? Why do blacks accept white interpretations of Christianity that deny their humanity and ignore their own encounter of God (extending back to Africa) as the liberator and protector of black victims of oppression? These are the questions that challenged the black clergy and black theologians to reflect more deeply about the meaning of God in a society that had no place for blacks to be fully human. In this chapter, I shall describe the origin of black theology, including the events that gave birth to it, the organizations that promoted it, and the stages of its development.

THREE CONTEXTS OF THE ORIGIN OF BLACK THEOLOGY

The origin of black theology has three major contexts: (1) the civil rights movement of the 1950s and '60s, largely associated with Martin Luther King, Jr.; (2) the publication of Joseph Washington's book, *Black Religion* (1964); and (3) the rise of the black power movement, strongly influenced by Malcolm X's philosophy of black nationalism.

Civil Rights Movement

All those involved in the creation of black theology were also deeply involved in the civil rights movement, including the protest demonstrations led by Martin Luther King, Jr. Unlike most other contemporary theological movements in Europe and North America, black theology did not arise in the seminary or the university. In fact, most of its early interpreters did not even hold advanced academic degrees. Black theology came into being in the context of the struggle of black persons for racial justice, which was initiated in the black churches, but chiefly identified with such civil rights organizations as the Southern Christian Leadership conference (SCLC),[2] the National Conference of Black Churchmen (NCBC),[3] the Interreligious Foundation for

Community Organization (IFCO),[4] and many black caucuses in white churches.[5]

From the beginning, black theology was understood by its creators as Christian theological reflection upon the black struggle for justice and liberation, strongly influenced by the life and thought of Martin Luther King, Jr. When King and other black church persons began to relate the Christian gospel to the struggle for racial justice in American society, the great majority of white churches and their theologians denied that such a relationship existed. Conservative white Christians claimed that religion and politics did not mix.[6] Liberal white Christians, with few exceptions during the 1950s and early '60s, remained silent on the theme or they advocated a form of gradualism that denounced boycotts, sit-ins, and freedom rides.[7]

Contrary to popular opinion now, King was not well received by the white American church establishment when he inaugurated the civil rights movement with the Montgomery bus boycott in 1955.[8] Because blacks received little or no theological support from white churches and their theologians (who were preoccupied with Barth, Bultmann, and the death-of-God controversy!), blacks themselves had to search deeply into their own history in order to find a theological basis for their prior political commitment to liberate the black poor.[9] They found support in Richard Allen (founder of the African Methodist Episcopal [AME] Church in 1816),[10] Henry Highland Garnet (a nineteenth-century Presbyterian preacher who urged slaves to resist slavery),[11] Nat Turner (a slave Baptist preacher who led an insurrection that killed sixty whites),[12] Henry McNeal Turner (an AME bishop who claimed in 1898 that "God is a Negro"),[13] and many others.[14]

When blacks investigated their religious history, they were reminded that their struggle for political freedom did not begin in the 1950s and '60s but had roots stretching back to the days of slavery. They were also reminded that their struggle for political justice in the United States had always been associated with their churches. Whether in the independent northern churches (AME, African Methodist Episcopal Zion [AMEZ], Baptist, etc.)[15] or in the so-called invisible institution[16] among slaves in the south (which merged with the independent black churches after the

Civil War) or as members of white denominations,[17] black Christians have always known that the God of Moses and of Jesus did not create them to be slaves or second-class citizens in North America. In order to forge a theological witness to this religious knowledge, black preachers and civil rights activists of the 1960s initiated the development of a black theology that rejected racism and affirmed the black struggle for liberation as consistent with the gospel of Jesus.

Joseph Washington

When black preachers and lay activist Christians began to search for the radical side of their black church history, they also began to ask about the distinctive religious and theological contributions of black persons. It was generally assumed, by most whites and many blacks as well, that black culture had no unique contribution to make to Christianity in particular and humanity in general. Indeed white liberal Christians understood integration to mean assimilation: that blacks would reject their cultural past by becoming like whites, adopting European cultural values. The assumption behind the white definition of integration was the belief that African cultural retentions among North American blacks were completely destroyed during slavery.[18] Therefore, if blacks were to develop a cultural knowledge of themselves, they had to find it in their identification with white American values.

Joseph Washington, a black scholar, wrote his *Black Religion* in the context of the hegemony of integration in black-white relationships in America. Contrary to the dominant view, Washington contended that there was a unique black culture, a distinctive black religion that can be placed alongside Protestantism, Catholicism, Judaism, and secularism. Black religion is not identical with white Protestantism or any other expression of Euro-American Christianity.

Washington, however, was not pleased with the continued existence of black religion, and he placed the blame squarely upon white Christians. He contended that black religion exists only because blacks have been excluded from the genuine Christianity of white churches. Because blacks were excluded from the faith of white churches, black churches are not genuine Christian churches. And if there are no genuine Christian churches, there can be no Christian theology. Blacks have only folk religion and folk theology. In Washington's own words:

> Negro congregations are not churches but religious societies—religion can choose to worship whatever gods are pleasing. But a church without a theology, the interpretation of a response of the will of God for the faithful, is a contradiction in terms.[19]

Although *Black Religion* was received with enthusiasm in the white church community, receiving major attention from white scholars,[20] it was strongly denounced in the black church community.[21] Black Christians did not deny that white churches were Christian and had excluded them from their community; but they vehemently rejected Washington's claim that exclusion from white churches and seminaries also meant exclusion from the spiritual and theological riches of the biblical faith. They refused to accept his assumption that whites had a monopoly on what the true church is, and how theology is to be defined. Indeed, black theology, in part, was created in order to refute Washington's book.[22] The black clergy wanted to correct two flagrant misconceptions: (1) that black religion is not Christian and thus has no Christian theology, and (2) that the Christian gospel has nothing to do with the struggle for justice in society.

The black clergy contended that Washington had everything backward. It was black religion that was truly Christian, and it was Christian precisely because it had identified the gospel with the struggle for justice in society. White churches were hypocritical: they said one thing but did another; they preached love but ignored justice, and then developed a theology that justified it.

The black clergy intuitively knew that a people's Christian identity did not depend upon its intellectual ability to engage in such theoretical discussions as the relationship between faith and reason, religion and science, theology and philosophy, or being and nonbeing. Such discussions may be interesting for white scholars and even useful in the educational programs of white churches; but they do not necessarily constitute the area in which the central meaning of the faith is identified. Black Christians believe that the God of Moses and of Jesus is first and foremost the God of love and of justice who is "ever present in time of trouble."

In the process of developing a theological alternative to Washington's thesis, some black Christian thinkers began to view white churches as un-Christian, because they concluded that faith without obedience defined by the struggle for justice is in fact not the genuine biblical faith.

Black Power Movement

After the March on Washington in August 1963, the integration theme in the black community began to lose ground to the black nationalist philosophy of Malcolm X.[23] The riots in the ghettoes of U.S. cities were shocking evidence that many blacks agreed with Malcolm X's contention that America was not a dream but a nightmare.[24]

However, it was not until the summer of 1966, after Malcolm X's assassination (February 21, 1965), that the term "black power" began to replace the term "integration" among many civil rights activists. The occasion was the continuation of the James Meredith "march against fear" (in Mississippi) by Martin Luther King, Jr., Stokely Carmichael, and other civil rights activists. Stokely Carmichael seized this occasion to sound the black power slogan, and it was heard loud and clear throughout the U.S.A.[25]

The rise of black power had a profound effect upon the appearance of black theology. When Carmichael and other radical black activists separated themselves from King's absolute commitment to nonviolence by proclaiming black power, white Christians, especially members of the clergy, called upon their black brothers and sisters in the gospel to denounce black power as un-Christian. To the surprise of white Christians, the National Committee of Negro Churchmen (NCNC; later to become the NCBC) refused to follow their advice and instead wrote a "Black Power Statement" that was published in the *New York Times,* July 31, 1966.[26]

The publication of the "Black Power Statement" may be regarded as the beginning of the conscious development of a black theology in which black ministers separated their understanding of the gospel of Jesus from white Christianity and identified it with the struggles of the black poor for justice. This theological initiative was unprecedented in the history of mainline black churches or among blacks in white churches. Although black Christians always contended that the racist behavior of white churches was un-Christian, they also assumed that the *theology* of whites was essentially correct.[27]

The "Black Power Statement" represents the beginning of a radical theological movement toward the development of an independent black perspective on the Christian faith. The black clergy, in its response to black power, was suggesting for the first time that white Christianity and the theology that justified it were bankrupt. Black leadership believed that the time had come for black Christians to make their own interpretation of the gospel by separating black religion from white religion, and then connecting the former with their African heritage and their contemporary fight for justice. Black church leaders would soon openly denounce white racism as the Antichrist and would become unrelenting in their attack on its demonic presence in white denominations. It was in this context that the term "black theology" emerged.

THE ROLE OF THE NATIONAL CONFERENCE OF BLACK CHURCHMEN

In order to give practical guidance to a newly discovered theological idea (namely, that blackness, justice, and power were not antithetical to the Christian faith), members of the radical black clergy created ecumenical organizations and black caucuses in white churches and other religious groups. Among them were the Alamo Black Clergy of the San Francisco Bay area, Black Methodists for Church Renewal (BMCR), the Interreligious Foundation for Community Organization (IFCO), and the Philadelphia Council of Black Clergy. Reacting to the conservatism in black denominations, a similar radical caucus, called the Sons of Varick, also emerged in the AMEZ Church.

Although several radical black organizations influenced the development of black theology, the impact of the National Conference of Black Churchmen (NCBC) on its origin was unique.[28] The NCBC began as an ad hoc group of black ministers who initially called themselves the National Committee of Negro Churchmen (NCNC). They had come together and written their statement entitled "Black Power" because they were "deeply disturbed about the crisis brought upon our country by historic distortions of important human realities in the controversy about 'black power.' "[29]

They claimed in that statement:

> The fundamental distortion . . . in the controversy about "black power" is rooted in a gross imbalance of power and conscience between Negroes and white Americans. It is this distortion, mainly, which is responsible for the widespread . . . assumption that white people are justified in getting what they want through the use of power, but that Negro Americans must, either by nature or by circumstance, make their appeal only through conscience. As a result the power of white men and the conscience of black men have been corrupted. The power of white men is corrupted because it meets little meaningful resistance from Negroes to temper it and keep white men from aping God. The conscience of black men is corrupted because, having no power to implement the demands of conscience, the concern for justice is transmuted to a distorted form of love, which, in the absence of justice, becomes chaotic self-surrender. Powerlessness breeds a race of beggars. We are faced now with a situation where conscienceless power meets powerless conscience, threatening the very foundation of our nation.[30]

After defining the issue in terms of the "conscienceless power" of whites and the "powerless conscience" of blacks, the NCNC statement proceeded to address four groups: the leaders of America, the white clergy, black citizens, and the mass media. In each case, they emphasized the need of blacks for power and they connected it with the Christian faith.

The "Black Power Statement" by members of the radical black

clergy created nearly as much controversy in white churches as secular advocates of black power did in white society. The white clergy was caught off guard and found it difficult to believe that its trusted black colleagues were now associating themselves openly with the "un-Christian" idea of black power. Whites asked their black colleagues whether they had forgotten about the Christian ideas of love and nonviolence that were so clearly expressed in the biblical portrayal of Jesus and in the speeches and actions of Martin Luther King, Jr.

Because black ministers were responding to the crisis initiated by urban riots and the rhetoric of black power, they were neither organizationally nor theologically prepared to answer the concerns that whites would address to them. Their belief that white Christianity was bankrupt and that black religion was prophetically relevant for the present situation was based more upon their instinctive acceptance of the black experience than upon disciplined theological reflection. They were not ready to debate the issues in the halls of white academia or in white-controlled church conferences. The chief concern of black ministers was not their acceptance by white ministerial colleagues; rather, they desperately wanted to be accepted by their own people, and the identification of black Christianity with the religion of white churches prevented that. Black ministers were searching for ethical guidelines to questions not found in the theological deliberations of white American theologians and preachers. As Gayraud Wilmore put it, they were asking:

> What is the responsibility of the churches of the oppressed when the oppressed revolt? How much of the truth should one tell the police when the children of one's own parish are liable to police brutality and summary arrest? What should be the Christian position regarding violence against property as a tactic of insurrection in the face of extreme deprivation and exploitation by the white power structure—city hall, the banks, the landlords, the police?[31]

A theology created for comfortable white suburbia could not answer questions that blacks were asking in their struggle for dignity in the wretched conditions of the riot-torn ghettoes of U.S. cities. Black church leaders had to create their own theological perspective from within the context of the ghetto, using whatever resources they knew from black history and culture. They knew that they could not condemn their own people, even though they "did not condone the violence and criminal behavior of the street people." However "they understood its causes only too well and were caught up in it as leaders whose first impulse was to look to the safety and welfare of their people."[32]

Although the writers and signers of the "Black Power Statement" had no intention of forming a permanent organization, the controversy and confusion that followed its publication forced black ministers to organize so as to think through the practical and theoretical implications of their theological claims about black power. The formational meeting was held in Dallas, Texas (October 1967). It is significant to note that a theological commission was formed whose chief task was to provide theological direction for a black perspective on the gospel that was being developed from black history and culture as interpreted by the contemporary black demands for justice and power.

Between the summer of 1966 and the fall of 1969, the NCBC held three major convocations (in Dallas, St. Louis, and Oakland) and wrote several statements, responding to the political crises of the time and also laying the foundation for the subsequent development of black theology. During this three-year period there was a rapid movement from integration to militant black separatism, from King's idea of the beloved community toward Malcolm X's nationalist philosophy. This movement can be noticed in the change of name from National *Committee* of *Negro* Churchmen to National *Conference* of *Black* Churchmen, "conference" suggesting a permanent body and "black" a change in identity.

The decisive turning point in the movement toward black separatism occurred at the National Council of Churches (NCC) conference on "The Church and the Urban Crisis" in Washington, D. C. (September 1967).[33] The younger black members of the NCBC were so angry and frustrated with white NCC members that they insisted that the conference divide itself into black and white caucuses, with each making its own separate statement regarding the urban crisis. White church persons did not wish to separate into caucuses, because black separatism was seen as a complete denial of Jesus' gospel of reconciliation. But the members of the radical black clergy were adamant in their determination to write a separate statement that would reflect their discovery of the religious meaning of black power. Whites were trying to apply outmoded neoorthodox and liberal theological ideas to a completely new political situation, but blacks were searching for a new theological basis for separating from middle-class whites and affirming unqualified solidarity with the black poor. In their statement, they said:

> We . . . find ourselves profoundly distressed, disturbed, frustrated, and in a state of utter disquietude about the nature and mission of the church in a time of revolution. We have come to realize that black power is an expression of the need for black authenticity in a white-dominated society, a society which has from its earliest beginnings displayed unadulterated racism. We affirm without fear of repudiation the meaningfulness of blackness and our identity as black churchmen. We confess the guilt which is ours for past actions and inaction in failing to be instruments for the expression of the will of God as black churchmen. We therefore propose now to speak and act, out of our own shame and guilt, concerning the lack of the church's responsiveness to the needs of black people seeking to be free and human in a dehumanizing world.[34]

With this introduction members of the black clergy expressed their identification with the forces of liberation in the black community and separated themselves from white Christianity. They then proceeded to call upon the white churches to make the elimination of racism their "number-one priority" by "affirming the legitimacy of the black power movement and to be open to the word that God is speaking to us through the issues it raises."[35]

Black ministers also gave an urgent message to black churches. Recognizing that their radical affirmation of blackness in religion would not be widely accepted among the leadership of mainline black churches, they reminded the black Christian community that the founding of the independent black church was the first authentic expression of black power. "The historical step to separate from the white church was the first clear call for black power," they said.[36]

However, radical black ministers knew that they and other black ministers had not remained faithful to their liberating heritage. They knew that their indictment of white ministers for their racism would have no credibility without indicting themselves for attempting to become like them. That was why they said:

> We confess that in recent times we have not lived up to our heritage, for we have not celebrated, preserved, and enhanced the integrity of blackness. Rather we have fallen prey to the dominance of white society and have allowed the truth, meaningfulness, and authenticity of the black church to be defamed by our easy acceptance of its goals, objectives, and criteria for success. Therefore, the black church has unwittingly become a tool for our oppression, providing an easy vehicle for escape from the harsh realities of our own existence. This of necessity makes it impossible for us to be instruments of liberation which is our calling as Christians and particularly black Christians.[37]

The radical black clergy believed that the appearance of black power offered it the occasion not only for uncovering and fighting the demonic presence of racism in the white church; black power also provided the black church with the sacred opportunity to reclaim its true mission of liberation:

> We rejoice in the black power movement, which is not only the renewed hope for black people, but gives the black church once again its reason for existing. We call upon black churchmen everywhere to embrace the black power movement, to divest itself of the traditional churchly functions and goals which do not respond to the needs of a downtrodden, oppressed, and alienated people.[38]

The urgency of the times and the excitement of being called out by God to participate in the liberation of black persons from centuries of white racist oppression took hold of this small group of radical black ministers and completely reoriented their priorities. They believed that they were living in the midst of the in-breaking of God's kingdom as defined by the black revolution, and that God had chosen them to be an instrument to announce its coming. Reflecting back, Gayraud Wilmore writes:

> We were smitten with a sense of *kairos*. We knew that this was a turning point in the quest for black Christian unity, in the evolution of an independent and creative black theology and in the witness of the black church for liberation from oppression and the suffocating embrace of white Christian liberalism. As few as we were, we had the morale of a legion. The atmosphere was full of the electricity of psychic revitalization and commitment. We believed that God had brought us to this hour and that although there was an immensely difficult struggle ahead, we were right and because of the NCBC the black church would never be the same.[39]

After the September 1967 NCBC meeting, communications between the radical black clergy and the liberal white clergy became inceasingly more difficult and often impossible. Whites were not accustomed to hearing blacks tell the truth in clear, forceful, and uncompromising language, especially their black clergy colleagues.

A similar problem emerged among conservative black ministers as well, because many had worn masks so long that they had forgotten their true identity. In order to prepare for a defense and implementation of their emerging radicalism in religion, members of the black clergy met in Dallas to establish the NCBC as a permanent ecumenical organization that would be the vanguard in the struggle for black liberation in the church. Members of the NCBC were not only determined to make the black church more relevant to the black liberation struggle, but were equally determined to create a black theology that would be supportive of it. Although I was not present at the early NCBC meetings and thus did not participate in the writing of its early documents, I read them closely and was inspired by their messages.

More than any other organization, the NCBC was responsible for providing the context for the development of black theology.[40] And more than any other individual, Gayraud S. Wilmore was responsible for providing the theological knowledge and vision upon which black theology was based. That was why he was chosen to be the first chairman of the NCBC theological commission and was the chief writer of most of its statements. Although I wrote the first two books on black theology and have been at the center of many of the debates regarding its meaning, it was Wilmore's theological expertise and imagination that laid the foundation for the early development of black theology. He is the one most responsible for the positive response of the NCBC to my writings and those of Preston Williams, J. Deotis Roberts, and C. Eric Lincoln. He has also been our most creative critic. Without his presence in the NCBC and his constant encouragement and criticism of other perspectives on black theology, the NCBC would soon have disintegrated and black theology would have had no organizational embodiment.

Albert Cleage's role in the development of black theology should also be acknowledged. He too was an active member in the early formation of the NCBC and had been closely associated with the life and thought of Malcolm X. He renamed his church the Shrine of the Black Madonna and began his efforts toward the development of black Christian nationalism.

Among the black clergy, Cleage was the most radical in his nationalism and eventually became too much of a separatist for most NCBC members. But before Cleage left the NCBC, he played a significant role in laying the foundation for black theology. His book *The Black Messiah* (1968) was an important publication event for the black church.[41] Although it was homiletical and not technically theological, it was the first significant text of the 1960s that joined Christianity and black history as defined by the ideology of black nationalism.

According to Cleage, the people of Israel was a black nation and Jesus was their revolutionary black Messiah. His interpretation of history and theology was too sectarian to gain wide acceptance among members of the black clergy who had studied historical criticism in white universities and seminaries. But Cleage inspired us all, even though we could not accept his most radical conclusions.

THE ORIGIN OF THE TERM "BLACK THEOLOGY"

Although the "Black Power Statement" was written in 1966 and the NCBC became a permanent organization a year later and issued several theological statements in response to events of the time, the term "black theology" was not coined until the end of the 1960s. It is not sure who was the first to use it, but most agree that it was first used in the context of the NCBC theological commission as the theological counterpart to black power.

The earliest reference to the term that I located was found in *Time* (November 15, 1968) in an article entitled "Is God Black?"[42] It was a report on the second NCBC convocation, in St. Louis. A much more informative report on the same convocation that connects black theology with the origin of the NCBC is found in Grant S. Shockley's article "Ultimatum and Hope" in *Christian Century* (February 12, 1969). Shockley uses the term "black theology" in his interpretation of the organizing meeting in Dallas, the NCBC statement on "The Urban Mission in a Time of Crisis (April 5, 1968), and the St. Louis Convocation. In my discussion with Leon Watts and Gayraud Wilmore, both of whom were present at Dallas and St. Louis, they are not sure when the term actually emerged in the NCBC. What is clear is that the idea of black theology (i.e., an interpretation of the faith in the light of black history and culture and completely separate from white religion) was present with the origin of the NCBC. On this point, it is significant to note that the term "black theology" was used several times in Gayraud Wilmore's theological commission project report in the fall of 1968.[43]

My *Black Theology and Black Power* (April 1969) was the first publication that used the term "black theology" in an attempt to develop a constructive theology.[44] Although Cleage's *Black Messiah* was published in the fall of 1968 and Joseph Washington's *Black and White Power Subreption*[45] in 1969, neither used the term "black theology." In his discussion of radical black theologians (including Cleage and myself), Washington used the term "black power theology."[46] My first essay, "Christianity and Black Power" (1968),[47] did not use the term "black theology" either. As I remember, the term "black theology" occurred to me while reading NCBC statements and during the writing of my first book-length analysis of the relationship between Christianity and black power—the title of my first article and the working title of the first book. In the process of trying to write a constructive theological alternative to white theology from the standpoint of the black revolution in the cities, the phrase "black theology" seemed appropriate as a description of what I was advocating.

The phrase "black theology" came into being as members of the black clergy "searched for a theological basis upon which to stand."[48] The term was created in response to black power "at a time when the credibility of the Christian faith was being severely tested in the black ghettoes of the nation."[49] Black ministers were forced by the black revolution to "re-examine their beliefs."[50] It was in the process of reassessing the "ground on which we stand" that the term "black theology" began to appear as the most appropriate description of our views.[51]

As early as the first convocation, in Dallas, "The report of the theological commission . . . was drafted by a small group charged with bringing before the membership the main lines of theological inquiry which might, at some future time, provide the basis for theological consultations—both among black scholars and theologians and their white counterparts."[52] They spoke of developing a "Barmen Declaration" analogous to the confessing church during the Nazi regime of Germany. For the first time since the late nineteenth century, the black clergy became specifically concerned about the development of a theology for blacks who were struggling to be human in an inhuman world of white racism. As Wilmore said in "Theological Commission Project" (1968):

> The point is not that black churchmen are enunciating in these documents [the early NCBC statements] what white churchmen have not said or cannot say. That may or may not be, but in either case it is askew of our main concern.

What is important is that churchmen who share a common
pain and humiliation under the heel of white oppression,
who share a common pride and self-awareness, who share a
common commitment to militant if not radical resistance to
dehumanization and deracination, have lifted up certain
ideological and theological fragments, themes and discern-
ments which, when taken together and ordered in a rational
conceptual framework, provide a clarification of the motivation for black mobilization and renewal and give us a
point of departure for a new dialogue and confrontation
with both conservative "whitenized" black Christians
and liberal but paralyzed white Christians, whose accom-
modations to the religious and secular status quo have
all but robbed American Christianity of its vitality and
credibility —especially among the poor, the black, and the
young.[53]

About twenty black scholars were invited to respond to a list of
questions that had been framed by the NCBC theological commission and to evaluate four representative articles: Vincent
Harding, "The Religion of Black Power";[54] Gayraud Wilmore,
"The Case for a New Black Church Style";[55] Preston Williams,
"Black Church: Origin, History, Present Dilemmas";[56] Henry
Mitchell, "Black Power and the Christian Church."[57] Although
these articles did not use the term "black theology," they laid the
foundation for the intellectual development of black theology
and stimulated much interest in the study of the black church and
black religion.

After the publication of several books and articles on black
theology, black religion, and black power, conferences were held
in order to share our work and explore the precise meanings of
black theology that several theologians had suggested.

The Journal of Religious Thought, published under the auspices of Howard University, devoted a special summer issue
(1969) to a symposium on "The Black Revolution: Is There a
Black Theology?" It included articles by Frank T. Wilson, J. Deotis Roberts, Rosemary Ruether, Preston Williams, Richard I.
McKinney, and Leon Wright, dealing with various aspects of the
question of whether there is a black theology.

It is interesting that the older, more established black scholars—Frank Wilson, Richard McKinney, Leon Wright—were much more skeptical in their answer to the question. They seemed more concerned about the universal character of the Christian faith that the particularity of black theology seemed to deny.

As McKinney said: "Central to the ethic of the Christian message is the ideal of *universality*, a universality that cuts across all lines of race, nation, class or even family ties. . . . It is clear that Jesus was much more concerned with justice than with race."[58] In contrast to this universal Christian message, McKinney claimed that black theology "is calculated to alienate non-Blacks from Blacks. American society is polarized enough as it is. To have one group of Christians promoting primarily the supposed 'blackness' of Christ is to foster a division in the 'body of Christ' that will require a long time to heal. What is claimed as the 'true Christianity' is thus limited to a given cultural group, with those on the outside perhaps only tolerated, provided they subscribe to the new interpretation."[59] By defining God as "primarily pro-Black," black theology "negates the fundamental conception of a deity who is impartial to all his creatures."[60] In McKinney's view " 'Black Theology' appears in essence to be the substitution of one racism for another."[61]

J. Deotis Roberts and Preston Williams[62] came to the defense of the black theology movement by connecting it with the black struggle for an authentic integration of blacks and whites in American society, an integration that Williams called, in another essay, "ethnic pluralism."[63] Roberts focused on the rise of black caucuses in white churches and other institutions, and Williams's paper was essentially an ethical and theological justification of the rise of the NCBC. Both Roberts and Williams were representatives of the new breed of black theologians who associated themselves with the NCBC and assumed the theological responsibility to develop a black theology that would affirm the uniqueness of black religion and a rejection of white racism. Roberts insisted that theology must "become consciously anthropocentric" and "problem-oriented" and thereby develop a black perspective that could effectively "address the masses of Black disinherited ghetto-dwellers and their rebellious children."[64]

In another conference, held at Georgetown University (May 2-3, 1969), the theme was "Black Church/Black Theology." The major addresses were made by Albert Cleage, Joseph Washington, Walter Yates, J. Deotis Roberts, and Preston Williams. Unlike the papers presented at the Howard University symposium, all the Georgetown papers were committed to the development of a black theology. The issue was not whether there was a black theology but whose version of it would emerge as dominant. Cleage, of course, was the most radical and others fell in the general context of advocating ethnic pluralism with varying emphases on black nationalism. The papers of the conference were later published under the title *Quest for a Black Theology*, with an additional essay by Bishop Joseph A. Johnson entitled "Jesus, the Liberator."[65]

In June of 1969 the NCBC called a conference of black theologians and preachers that was convened by its theological commission in Atlanta at the ecumenical black seminary, the Interdenominational Theological Center. The "Black Theology Statement" emerging from that conference was the first NCBC published comment on the subject.[66] Between April 1969 (the publication of *Black Theology and Black Power*) and June of the same year (the NCBC theological commission statement on black theology), the term "black theology" became commonplace among most members of the radical black clergy and theologians.

There was no debate about the possibility of a black theology or about its legitimacy. All black ministers and theologians associated with the NCBC insisted that the black power revolution of the northern ghettoes demanded a relevant black theology or they would lose their credibility in their own community. Gayraud Wilmore wrote of the unrest in the black ghettoes:

[It was creating] a rising crescendo of voices from both the pulpit and pew demanding that [unless] black churchmen . . . begin to speak and act relevantly in the present crisis, they must prepare to die; that unless they "do their thing" in some kind of symbolic and actual disengagement from the opprobrium of white racist Christianity, they have no right to exist in the black community.[67]

The term "black theology," therefore, did not emerge from the ivory tower of black university and seminary professors. It emerged as the black clergy was compelled by the urgency of the time to make theological sense out of the struggle for black freedom. To advocate a *black* theology meant that the black clergy wanted the whole world to know that it was searching for a radically new theological starting point that would clearly distinguish its perspective from the alternatives provided by whites and adopted by conservative blacks. Black church leaders sensed the *need* for a new beginning in theology that would affirm the dignity of black persons and expose the racist white churches as un-Christian. But they did not know how to go about it, and most lacked some of the courage necessary to break completely with what they had been taught in seminaries. Metz Rollins, the first NCBC executive director, said it well:

> Long segregated, separated, treated with scorn and disgrace, the black church and the black churchmen of the predominantly white churches are now coming into their own. No longer content to play second-fiddle, to be treated like stepchildren or wayward dependents by the white church and its leadership, the black church has nurtured an acute awareness of its own unique gifts, its own peculiar understanding of the gospel of Jesus Christ, and a new appreciation for its own hallowed and tortured history. . . . In a period of black awareness and black consciousness in the larger black community, black churchmen are insisting that the witness of the black church is meaningful only as it becomes a militant advocate of the cause of justice and dignity for black people.[68]

THREE STAGES OF DEVELOPMENT

Gayraud Wilmore has divided the development of black theology into three stages, to which I shall have more than one occasion to refer in my analysis.[69] The first stage begins with the publication of the "Black Power Statement," July 31, 1966, and continues to the NCBC issuance of "The Black Declaration of

Independence," July 4, 1970.[70] This is the stage of the emergence of black theology from the civil rights and black power movements as black ministers debated integration, love, and nonviolence with their white counterparts. In this stage, black theology is almost completely defined by radical black NCBC ministers, most of whom were in white denominations.

Some of the chief figures in the early development of black theology were Metz Rollins (Presbyterian and the first NCBC executive director), Leon Watts (AMEZ and the first NCBC associate executive director), Will Herzfeld (Lutheran), Lawrence Lucas (Catholic priest), Herbert Bell Shaw (an AMEZ bishop and chairman of the NCBC board of directors), and M. L. Wilson (pastor of Convent Avenue Baptist Church in New York City). There were also a few seminary professors involved (most of them participants in the NCBC theological commission), but they were not the prime movers. With the NCBC definition of black theology as an attack on the white church, the persons best suited for that task were black preachers in white denominations.

It was not until the second stage that seminary professors began to make significant contributions in the task of defining black theology. With the reelection of Richard Nixon by a great majority in 1972, and with the Vietnam war replacing racism as the chief issue in American society, the NCBC moved into a period of decline and its theological commission lost vitality. The NCBC could not prevent its decline: radical black ministers miscalculated the opportunism in their own ranks and the ability of whites to divide them against one another. Some black ministers were promoted to prominent positions in white church bureaucracies and other radicals were effectively isolated. More will be said about these issues later; however, it is important at this point to indicate some of the reasons for the transition of black theology from one stage to another.

When black students at white seminaries began to press for radical changes in the curriculum and the composition of faculty and students, the Society for the Study of Black Religion (SSBR) was organized in order "to engage in scholarly research and discussion about the religious experiences of blacks" and "to encourage the teaching and discussion of the black religious experience in the curricula of college and seminary departments of religion and theological seminaries . . . in the United States and elsewhere.''[71]

In its second stage, black theology became an academic discipline, and the SSBR became the primary arena in which debates about black theology took place among black scholars. The issues involved the relationship between liberation and reconciliation, black religion and black theology, and the problem of theodicy.[72]

As the clerical attack by black theology on the white churches declined, SSBR scholars initiated their challenge to racism in white seminaries and university departments of religion.[73] What the NCBC was to white churches, the SSBR was to white seminaries and their faculties. But the black SSBR scholars were not nearly as radical as the NCBC clergy. They did not take great risks; it seems that the self-interest of many black professors (in terms of tenure and promotion) controlled the style and definition of their challenge to racism in the seminaries. Black professors did not experience the same kind of urgency and excitement in their calling as was found among black clergy radicals. Black professors "played it cool" and did not rock the boat too much, protecting themselves against future reprisals by their white colleagues.[74] Thus black theology and religion took on a more conservative bent, serving almost exclusively the needs of its black professional advocates (primarily professors but also students) in white academia.

Not everyone was pleased with the new focus of black theology, because its prophetic thrust was being blunted, and the SSBR, unlike the NCBC, was becoming too much of an academic society, like the American Academy of Religion, with little focus on practical and urgent issues in the black community. "Scholarship for the sake of scholarship" seemed to define most SSBR activity, and some of its members wondered how such an approach differed from white scholarship. As I saw the issue then and now (although not so clearly *then*), the problem of the second stage was not the academic focus of black theology, but rather the *accountability* of black theologians: for *what purpose*, and for *whom*, did they do theology? We did not explore these questions in sufficient depth and with adequate care.[75]

I am as much responsible as anyone else for the degeneration of black theology into an academic discipline cut off from the life of the black church and community. Gayraud Wilmore warned us about this danger but we did not listen to him. I myself was too much focused on the internal debates of black theologians. Those debates were useful in sharpening our critical tools for the intellectual development of black theology. But we conducted those debates too much outside the life of the black community, thereby making black theology an abstract, academic discipline in the worst sense. Such debates may have been important to us and may have helped theology get academic respectability in white academia, but I cannot say that they were useful in assisting the survival and liberation of blacks during the Richard Nixon and Gerald Ford era of the 1970s.

It was because many of us were so dissatisfied with the academic sterility of black theology that the third stage of black theology was initiated in the mid-1970s with a focus on global issues in relationship to black communities in the U.S.A. Although some references were made to Asia, Africa, and Latin America in earlier NCBC documents (especially in the 1976 "Black Theology Statement"),[76] it was not until the Atlanta black theology conference of 1977 (sponsored by the recently organized Black Theology Project of Theology in the Americas [TIA] and the NCBC) that the decisive turn to the Third World was made.[77] For many black theologians, the TIA Black Theology Project became an arena serving a function similar to that which the NCBC had served, offering an opportunity for members of the black clergy and other radicals to be engaged in the black liberation struggle.

Because TIA had additional projects involving other minorities and liberation-oriented persons who articulated their concerns, it was not possible for blacks to limit their focus to racism. The problems of classism and sexism became special concerns; projects were undertaken to analyze these problems. It was the TIA Women's Project and the newly organized Ecumenical Association of Third World Theologians (EATWOT) that introduced the urgency of feminism and Marxism to the interpreters of black theology.[78]

The third stage of black theology is also characterized by a decisive turn to the black church, with ecumenism among black denominations as a chief concern. There is also a return to the early criticisms of the black church that the NCBC introduced but did not implement. With James Forman's *Black Manifesto* exempting black churches from reparations (at least by implication and for the purpose of strategy; see chap. 2, pp. 44f., below) and with the NCBC saying explicitly "that the black church does not stand in the same dock as the white church,"[79] many black church leaders assumed that the blackness of their skin exempted them from theological criticism. They failed to realize that their liberating heritage actually demanded of them a greater responsibility of service than that incumbent on white churches. My address, "Black Theology and the Black Church: Where Do We Go from Here?", and the statement of the 1977 Atlanta meeting, "Message to the Black Church and Community" (written by Gayraud Wilmore and Charles Spivey, an AME minister and then chairperson of the Black Theology Project), accented both a critique and an affirmation of the black church.[80]

THEOLOGY AND LIFE

I firmly believe that the issues to which theology addresses itself should be those that emerge out of life in society as persons seek to achieve meaning in a dehumanized world. This does not mean that theologians should ignore the scriptures and the traditions of the churches, or that these sources of the past should be manipulated to accommodate contemporary concerns without regard to their original historical setting and meaning. Rather it means that theologians should not do theology on the basis of scripture and tradition *as if* the existential and historical concerns of present-day humankind were nonexistent.

I believe that Christian theology achieves its distinctive identity when it takes on the issues of those who are struggling to be human in an oppressive world. Christians believe that their faith has something to say about this world and about the human beings in it—something that can make a decisive difference in the quality of life. It is therefore the task of theology to demonstrate the difference that the gospel can and does make in human lives, using the resources of the scriptures and traditions of the churches as well as other modern tools of social, historical, cultural, economic, and philosophical analysis.

Theological problems are not given by divine fiat, nor are theologians' solutions derived only from fixed divine revelation. Theological problems arise from theologians' interests, the issues that they consider important in the definition of their discipline. To *whom* theologians talk and *what* they talk about is a *choice* that they make so as to concretize what is regarded as theology. Therefore one knows what is important for theologians by whom they talk to and by what they choose to talk about. The issues that define the work of theology define theology itself.

What theologians regard as the central issues of their discipline, therefore, cannot be separated from their place in society, from what they think, believe, and are seeking to do in society. Hence, the social location and interests of theologians must be critically evaluated in order to understand why they do theology the way they do, and why they advocate certain views and not others. This may appear to some professional theologians as a minor and self-evident point; but the vast majority of white theologians are not always honest about it, for they seem to do theology as if its definition and meaning, its issues and problems, are self-evident and need no discussion with those who are not a part of their theological club. I think that the definition of theology and the issues to which it ought to address itself come up for reanalysis in every age. Whom theologians choose as their interlocutors and what they talk about are crucial, for then, and only then, do we know what they understand the gospel to be.

The issues of black theology have been defined by its engagement with a variety of interlocutors and themes: white preachers and theologians concerned about racism in the churches and in society; black power advocates and the realities of the urban ghettoes that they symbolized and articulated; conservative mainline black churches and their relationship to the black liberation struggle; the civil rights movement and Martin Luther King, Jr.'s, perspective on integration, love, and nonviolence; the emerging feminism of black women, especially among preachers and theologians; the Marxist and global perspectives of Third World theologians; the racism of white Marxists and socialists (secular and religious). The issues and problems emerging from those dialogues have shaped the content and style of black theology during its three developmental stages.

In the chapters that follow, I shall evaluate (often critically) the issues that defined the subject matter of black theology and the persons with whom black preachers and theologians have chosen to dialogue. The chapters have been determined by the issues of black theologians and the persons they chose as dialogue partners.

Because there is continuity and change in each stage, I shall discuss them in relation to the issues, without attempting to narrate an account of black theology in historical sequence. My concern is historical to the degree that history is useful in sharpening a theological definition of the issues. I wish to analyze critically what black theology has been, what it is, and what it ought to become so as to participate meaningfully in the shaping of a black future for the 1980s and beyond.

Chapter II

Black Theology as an Attack on White Religion

We are unalterably committed to the effecting of a more equitable power "by any means necessary." Means additional to negotiation are now necessary. The time has come for us to resort to the use of unusual forms of pressure upon the white church structures if we are ever to realize the legitimate goal of a literal transfer of power.

National Committee of Black Churchmen,
"A Message to the Churches from Oakland,"
November 11–14, 1969[1]

The Catholic Church in the United States, primarily a white racist institution, has addressed itself primarily to white society and is definitely a part of that society. On the contrary, we feel that her primary, though not exclusive, work should be in the area of institutional, attitudinal and societal change. Within the ghetto, the role of the church is no longer that of spokesman and leader. Apart from a more direct spiritual role, the church's part must now be that of supporter and learner.

Statement of the Black Catholic Clergy Caucus,
April 1968[2]

Although black theology emerged out of the civil rights movement, as defined by Martin Luther King, Jr., and in response to

31

the publication of Joseph Washington's *Black Religion,* neither the civil rights movement nor Washington's articulation of the uniqueness of black religion defined the rhetoric and the essential meaning of black theology. Rather the name of black theology, the passionate energy that shaped its style, and the politics that determined its organizational links were defined by the secular appearance of black power.

As black power represented the end of black-white consensus and coalition in the politics of black liberation, so black theology represented the end of black-white consensus and coalition in the churches and theology. As black power represented the assertion of a black value system in social, cultural, political, and economic institutions, so black theology meant the incorporation of a similar value system in the churches and religious life of blacks. What black power advocates were saying to the White House, Congress, City Hall, and other symbols of white political power, black clergy radicals attempted to duplicate at the Inter-Church Center, the World Council of Churches, major denominational headquarters, and other symbols of white religion.

BLACK THEOLOGY AND BLACK POWER

The relationship between black power and black theology was sharply defined in my early writings on the subject. The influence of black power can be seen in the titles of my first article, "Christianity and Black Power," and my first book, *Black Theology and Black Power*. My main concern in both was to demonstrate that the politics of black power was the gospel of Jesus to twentieth-century America, for black power was concerned with the liberation of the black poor from oppression, and Jesus had shown just such concern for the liberation of the poor during his earthly ministry. The evidence was his teachings about God's partiality toward the poor, his healing the sick and lame, and especially his prophetic claim that God "has anointed me to preach good news to the poor, to proclaim release to captives and recovery of sight to the blind, to set at liberty those who are oppressed" (Luke 4:18).

Jesus' death on the cross represented God's boundless solidarity with victims, even unto death. Jesus' resurrection is the good news that there is new life for the poor that is not determined by their poverty but overcomes it; and this new life is available to all. Jesus' resurrection is God's victory over oppression. If this biblical message has any meaning for contemporary America, it must mean that black power represents God's resurrection in Jesus becoming embodied in the consciousness and actions of black America. I wrote:

> If we can believe the New Testament witness which proclaims Jesus as resurrected and thus active even now, then he must be alive in those very people who are struggling in the midst of misery and humiliation. If the gospel is a gospel of liberation for the oppressed, then Jesus is where the oppressed are and continues his work of liberation there. Jesus is not safely confined in the first century. He is our contemporary, proclaiming release to the captives and rebelling against all who silently accept the structures of injustice. If he is not in the ghetto, if he is not where [human beings] are living at the brink of existence, but is, rather, in the easy life of the suburbs, then the gospel is a lie. The opposite, however, is the case. Christianity is not alien to black power; it *is* black power.[3]

I connected black theology so closely with black power that many of my critics contended that I had distorted the Christian faith into a "religion of black power."[4] Almost all wanted to know what was the basic norm in my perspective of black theology—black power or the biblical witness to Jesus Christ?

I did not bother to answer my critics on this point until much later, because the urgency of the time in which we lived demanded that my intellectual energies be placed elsewhere.[5] It was not the time to debate fine points of theology according to the academic rules established in white seminaries and universities. Rather, it was time for the articulation of the word of God in contemporary white and black America. I firmly believed (as I still do) that God's word was not found in white seminaries and churches or even among middle-class black preachers and their churches.

God's word is always found on the cross, in the ghettoes and poverty-stricken villages of the world, suffering with those who have no power to defend their humanity.

If that theological claim had any merit, then God is found among the black oppressed who were being destroyed by "respectable" white murderers. I did not have the time to develop my theological argument in a way that would be acceptable to the academic expectations of white biblical and systematic theologians. The ghettoes were burning and my fellow blacks were being shot dead in the streets by white law-enforcement officers. Why should I turn to those who were far removed from and unconcerned about black suffering for guidance and approval? Those who were responsible for the victimization of blacks had no right to exercise judgment over biblical exegesis. That much I knew. And it did not bother me one bit that whites questioned the logic of my hermeneutics.

What good is a theological point if it is not useful in the black struggle for freedom? What good is an intellectually respectable black theology if it is useless as a weapon against the exploitation and dehumanization of blacks? I was not about to answer any questions coming from those who obviously had no interest in dismantling white racism or in empowering poor blacks to fight against it. That was why I continued to write about black theology as if I had never read Karl Barth's strictures on ideology. Why should I acknowledge the strictures of white neoorthodox theologians when they did not acknowledge black humanity in their theology?[6]

I was not the only interpreter of black theology who connected it with black power. I have already referred to Albert Cleage's black Christian nationalism, which led to his break with the NCBC. He was a friend of Malcolm X and shared the platform with him on several occasions. The titles of his sermons are a clear indication of his nationalist views: "An Epistle to Stokely," "We Are God's Chosen People," and "Brother Malcolm."

Cleage was attempting to interpret the Christian faith in such a manner that it would be antithetical to everything Europeans had said about Jesus and his gospel. He wanted to create a church that would be truly black and Christian, and unreservedly identified with the black power message of liberation as defined by the black radicals in the Student Non-Violent Coordinating Committee (SNCC or "SNICK"). In one of his sermons, "An Epistle to Stokely," he said:

> I address my remarks this morning . . . to Stokely Carmichael, and to the young men who make up SNICK's organization throughout the country, and to other young men who work in the movement in other organizations. I address my remarks to those who believe in the Christian church because they do not understand that the movement is the Christian church in the twentieth century and that the Christian church cannot truly be the church until it also becomes the movement. So then, I would say to you, you are Christian, and the things you believe are the teachings of a black Messiah named Jesus, and the things you do are the will of a black God called Jehovah; and almost everything you have heard about Christianity is essentially a lie.[7]

Cleage realized correctly that unless the white image of Christ was changed to that of a black Christ involved in the fight for freedom, the Christian religion would remain a hindrance to the black liberation struggle:

> Until black Christians are ready to challenge this lie [a white Christ], they have not freed themselves from their spiritual bondage to the white man, nor established in their minds their right to first-class citizenship in Christ's kingdom on earth. Black people cannot build dignity on their knees worshiping a white Christ. We must put down this white Jesus which the white man gave us in slavery and which has been tearing us to pieces.[8]

No black theologians or ministers were more vehement in their condemnation of the white Christ than was Cleage, and all members of the radical black clergy supported him in spirit even though many rejected his literalism. Cleage's association with black power led him to conclusions that many of us found questionable on both theological and historical grounds:

> When I say Jesus was black, that Jesus was the black Messiah, I'm not saying "Wouldn't it be nice if Jesus was black?" or "Let's pretend that Jesus was black," or "It's necessary psychologically for us to believe that Jesus was black." I'm saying that Jesus *WAS* black. There never was a white Jesus. Now if you're white, you can accept him if you want to, and you can go through psychological gymnastics and pretend that he was white, but he was black. If you're such a white racist that you've got to believe he was white, then you're going to distort history to preserve his whiteness.[9]

Although the radical NCBC black clergy believed that Cleage was distorting history and the Christian gospel, we nonetheless enjoyed quoting him to white Christians in order to shake them up a bit. One of our favorite passages was his identification of Jesus with the Zealots, as Cleage claimed:

> [Jesus was a] revolutionary black leader, a member of the Zealots, the activist group that spurred the succession of rebellions against Rome, culminating in the destruction of the Temple in Jerusalem by Titus in A.D. 70 and the fall of Masada in 73. He sought to free Israel's black Jews from oppression and bondage, dying, not for the eternal salvation of the individual, but for the rebirth of the lost Black Nation.[10]

Although Cleage was not very successful in convincing either black power advocates or other interpreters of black theology, he defined the importance of connecting blackness and the gospel. All black theologians and preachers had to take him seriously. On the negative side, his theology illustrates what happens when black theologians reduce the Christian gospel to a *literal* identification with the ideology of black power.

The link between black power and black theology can also be

seen in the writings and actions of other black theologians and in NCBC documents, especially the "Black Power Statement" of 1966, the black clergy caucus statement at the NCC conference, "The Church and the Urban Crisis" (1968), and the "Black Theology Statement" of 1969. Some NCBC participants wrote significant texts on black power and were prominent participants in black power conferences. For example, Nathan Wright, an Episcopal priest, authored one of the early and widely read texts on black power, *Black Power and Urban Unrest* (1967). In one of its often quoted passages he connected black power with God's creation:

> A God of power, of majesty and of might, who has made [people] to be in his own image and likeness, must will that his creation reflect in the immediacies of life his power, his majesty, and his might. Black power raises, for the healing of humanity and for the renewal of a commitment to the creative religious purpose of growth, the far-too-long over-looked need for power, if life is to become in the mind of its Creator [what] it is destined to be.[11]

He made a similar point in an article, "Power and Reconciliation":

> Black power is a positive, creative concept. . . . [It] speaks to human dignity. It is a clear and uncompromising assertion of the worth of that human handiwork of God which had been systematically desecrated in the nation's culturally-conditioned life.[12]

Nathan Wright was one of the few members of the black clergy who at the same time participated in NCBC work, influencing the development of black theology, and took part also in major conferences of black power advocates. He was the chairman of the steering committee of the first National Black Power Conference, held in Newark, New Jersey, July 20–23, 1967.[13] Several NCBC members, including Gayraud Wilmore, attended that conference.

The close relationship between black power and the rise of

black theology can be easily noticed in the titles of early articles by black ministers and theologians. Representative examples are Henry H. Mitchell, "Black Power and the Christian Church"; Vincent Harding, "Black Power and the American Christ"; Preston Williams, "The Ethics of Black Power"; J. Deotis Roberts, "Black Consciousness in Theological Perspective"; and his "The Black Caucus and the Future of Christian Theology." All black ministers and theologians who were seeking to develop a new black theology were stimulated by the political movement of black power. They refused to condemn black power as the liberal white and conservative black clergy had done. Preston Williams was speaking for many when he said:

> The black church, many felt, should have turned its back upon "black power" and added its weight to those condemning the new, more militant slogans of the black community. Yet, to have done so would have been to turn against the imperative need for massive social change both in order to implement what was already legislated and to root out what grave evil remained. To have condemned black power would have involved the black church in the substitution of symptom for cause, which was and still is the strategy of so much of the nation and the church today.[14]

The extent to which the black clergy's imagination was captured by the spirit and language of black power can be seen especially in the creation of black caucuses in white churches. Reflecting upon the rapid rise of black caucuses in white denominations, Wilmore writes:

> It should not be doubted that the dynamic for this turn of events within American Christianity came from outside rather than inside the churches. It was the black folk of Watts, Newark, Detroit, and hundreds of other communities across the nation, and the young men and women of the SNCC and northern-based nationalist groups, who convinced black ministers that the church was expendable if it proved to be unwilling to immerse itself in the vortex of the

black power movement. It was not difficult to show that the movement was catching on everywhere and that its basic motif was pregnant with moral and religious meaning. Black believers could not evade its magnetic force once the people of the streets took the cause into their own hands.[15]

The black clergy in white churches saw in the rise of black power God's gift to the Christian church that would radically transform black-white relationships. The "Black Methodist's Response to Black Power" is representative:

The greatest opportunity in this century for black Methodists and the greatest gift to white Methodists is the concept of black power. Through the creative and responsible application of Black Power, both white Methodists and black Methodists will begin to see themselves and each other in an entirely new perspective. In the new relationship which the dynamics of black power could create, there hopefully may develop a new humanity in which the special uniqueness of every [person] may be joyfully given and received.[16]

The Black Methodists for Church Renewal (BMCR) was the largest and most vocal caucus in white denominations. It was organized in Cincinnati, Ohio, February 1968. Stokely Carmichael was present at the meeting, as was C. Eric Lincoln. The "Black Paper" that emerged from their meeting connected them firmly with the spirit of black power. "How then," they asked, "do we respond forcefully and responsibly to racism in the United Methodist Church? We unashamedly reply—black power!"[17] They went so far as to identify black power as "a call for us to respond to God's action in history which is to make and keep human life human."[18]

The black power rhetoric was the only language we had that was both radical and also was derived from and accountable to black history and culture.[19] It was the only tool we had that named the enemy in clear, forceful, and uncompromising language. It was an added bonus that white church persons detested our use of black power. The more they resisted its use, the more we were determined to champion it as an expression of our Christian identity and political commitment.

Although there is not much evidence that the radical black clergy significantly influenced black power advocates, the latter used black churches for their meetings, invited the radical clergy to participate in the religion workshops of their conferences, and quoted their writings to conservative black Christians and liberal whites. For example Stokely Carmichael quoted from the 1966 "Black Power Statement" in his speeches;[20] I led the religion workshop at the first major conference of the Congress of African Peoples;[21] the Black Panthers used many churches for their breakfast programs; and James Forman's *Black Manifesto* was strongly supported by the NCBC.[22] It was the close association of black theology with black power that made it level such a vehement attack on white religion.

THE ATTACK ON WHITE RELIGION
BY THE NCBC AND BLACK THEOLOGY

All creative Christian theologies come into being as persons encounter contradictions in life about which they cannot be silent. The same was true of the appearance of black theology in the 1960s. As Martin Luther could not remain silent about indulgences in the Catholic Church, and as Karl Barth could not remain silent about the inordinate confidence of liberal theology in human goodness, so black theologians could not remain silent about the ever increasing manifestations of racism in the white church and its theology. We had to speak out or there would be no way we could defend ourselves against black power advocates' claims that Christianity is a white religion. We not only had to separate ourselves from the "white religion" but also *attack* it and thus uncover its demonic and sinister nature. Just as Luther spoke of "the Babylonian captivity of the church," attacking the doctrine of seven sacraments, we saw a similar analogy with the white church, enslaved, as it was, by its own racism. Just as Luther and Barth were uncompromising in their stand against the corruption in the theologies and churches that elicited their theological rage, black theologians and preachers were also uncompromising in their confrontation with white racist churches and their theologies.

When theologians and preachers experience contradictions in life that shake the foundation of the accepted faith of the community, they are forced by faith itself to return to its source so as to interpret faith in a new light and thereby be empowered to struggle against the forces of evil that seek to destroy its credibility. Luther returned to the scriptures, especially the letters of the Apostle Paul, and encountered a gracious, loving God. Barth returned to the Reformation and then to scripture, especially the Apostle Paul, and encountered what he called "the strange new world within the Bible." Black theologians returned to the mothers and fathers of black faith and then to scripture, especially the Old Testament and the New Testament gospel portrayal of Jesus. They encountered what Cecil Cone called "the Almighty Sovereign God," and what black Christians call the "power from on high" that "picks you up when you are falling" and "props you up on every leaning side."

Both Luther's and Barth's encounter with scripture disclosed the central theme of the gospel to be justification by faith (grace) alone, and both used different aspects of this theme to attack the Roman Catholic Church and liberal theology. Both wanted to turn the religion of their day upside-down so that God's true gospel could be heard and obeyed. They wanted to "let God be God" by making God's grace—not merits or the so-called goodness of humanity—the heart of the gospel. It was their view that the gospel is of God that made Luther break with Rome and Barth with liberal theology.

Black theologians' encounter with the scriptures through lenses of black faith disclosed the central theme of the gospel to be the liberation of victims from oppression, and they used it to level a fierce attack on white religion. It was like discovering the "pearl of great price," for they took many risks in order to proclaim and to live it. They acted like children who just discovered that someone had given them an unexpected and precious gift. In moments of uncontrolled ecstasy, they bragged about it and laughed at the whites who were too blinded by their own racism to recognize the value of their new gift. Black ministers now spoke with confidence and walked as if they controlled the space that they occupied, daring whites to even act as if they wanted to move them out of it.

Like Luther and Barth, black preachers firmly believed that they were living in a revolutionary time, an era that would eventually lead to a complete transformation of black-white relationships in the U.S.A. and the world. One has only to read the NCBC documents, statements by black caucuses, and articles by black ministers and theologians to capture the spirit of the time among the black clergy. The word "revolution" was frequently used, because the effect of the biblical message of liberation upon the theological mind and the sensitivities of the black clergy was indeed revolutionary.

Some blacks even spoke of violence in positive terms, and none accepted the easy distinction that whites often made between violence and force, attributing the former to the rhetoric and actions of black militants and the latter to white policemen who killed and wounded blacks. The black clergy was especially eager to uncover the structural violence of white institutions that were characterized by the racism that dehumanized blacks and denied the dignity and worth of our history and culture. The attacks of black clergy radicals on the white church were severe and uncompromising because of the depth of the racism embedded in its structures and because blacks truly believed that the kingdom of God's liberation was at hand—if not God's eschatological kingdom, at least the "beloved community" in which blacks and whites would indeed be real brothers and sisters. Black separatism was thought of as being strategic and temporary so as to prepare both whites and blacks for a completely new world of human relationships.

The NCBC movement from militant integration to radical black separatism and a fierce attack on white religion was gradual. When members of the black clergy wrote the 1966 "Black Power Statement," they still felt that moral suasion backed up by sound theological argument could produce meaningful change in white preachers and their churches. They still supported an "honest kind of integration," but rejected a "false kind of 'integration' in which all power was in the hands of whites." That was why they still referred to themselves as "Negroes," for the term "Negro" had historically been associated with a desire for integration. By July 1967, exactly a year later, black clergy radicals were having second thoughts about integration and the possibility of building a coalition for justice with white preachers.

The first National Black Power Conference was held in Newark, New Jersey, July 20–23, 1967, immediately following a riot in the same city. Twenty-six persons died in the rioting, more than a thousand were injured, and about fourteen hundred were arrested. About twenty-six hundred national guardsmen and fourteen hundred police turned out to restore "order." Following the conference, the Detroit riot erupted during the same month; forty-three persons died. Again large numbers were injured and arrested by thousands of national guardsmen and policemen. Because black preachers' churches were in the ghettoes, they could not avoid the real issues that ignited the riots.[23] Therefore when white preachers of suburbia began to theologize about violence and nonviolence, condemning the rioters and advocating a return to "law and order," black clergy radicals moved rapidly from Martin King's theology of integration to Malcolm X's philosophy of black separatism. As related in the previous chapter, the decisive turning point in the movement to separatism came at the NCC Conference in September 1967.

Although black clergy radicals used the word "black" in their NCC conference statement, the movement toward black consciousness was not complete: when, following the NCC meeting, they formed an organization in Dallas, they named it the National Committee of *Negro* Churchmen.[24] However, by the spring of 1968 it had become the National Committee of *Black* Churchmen and the word "Negro" had become anathema.

The assassination of Martin King (April 4, 1968) had much to do with this complete turn toward militant black separatism. After King's death members of the white clergy never knew what to expect from members of the black clergy, because the latter had now become emotionally charged with a mission to "blackenize" the gospel for the purpose of liberating their people. With Martin King's murder, a murder condoned and encouraged by countless hypocrisies in American culture about the use of violence in the solution of political conflicts, the rage of black clergy radicals could no longer be contained by pious white appeals to love and reconciliation. The black clergy unleashed violent verbal attacks on the white clergy. Most whites were confused about what they had said or done to warrant such "uncivilized and unchristian behavior." Whites were caught off guard; some thought that black preachers had gone "crazy," that some unknown "black spell" had engulfed them, and they hoped that in time blacks would return to sanity.[25]

Albert Cleage's *The Black Messiah* was published in the fall of 1968 and my *Black Theology and Black Power* in the early spring of the next year. These two texts documented black rage against white religion. When white and black members of the clergy discussed issues of race and religion, blacks often quoted from these newly published texts and dared whites to dispute their arguments, unless they were ready for a *real* fight, not verbal but physical.

The climax of the attack by black clergy radicals on white religion occurred with the appearance of James Forman's *Black Manifesto*.[26] On Sunday, May 4, 1969, James Forman walked down the aisle of Riverside Church in New York City and read the *Black Manifesto*, "demanding $500,000,000 from the Christian white churches and the Jewish synagogues . . . 15 dollars per nigger."[27] That event sent shock waves throughout the white religious and theological communities. The very idea of reparations for blacks sounded preposterous to whites, especially to Christians and Jews. But then to insist that they give the money to a person with the "blasphemous" behavior of James Forman (or to persons who represented him in the Black Economic Development Conference [BEDC]) sounded even more ridiculous. Most white religious leaders did not even bother to discuss the matter with him or with persons who supported his views.[28]

With the *Black Manifesto* the NCBC was given a revolutionary tool with which to attack white religion. The failure of the white churches to respond merely intensified the attack. The NCBC strongly supported the *Manifesto* and referred to Forman as a "modern-day prophet."[29] The NCBC also agreed to serve as a conduit through which reparations could be given to the BEDC, the organization that Forman had used to launch his manifesto.

Gayraud Wilmore wrote a response to the *Black Manifesto*, interpreting its theological meaning.[30]

When white churches refused to accept the claims of the *Black Manifesto* even when advanced by the NCBC, black clergy radicals became even more militant. They could understand why whites rejected Forman's demands. He was Marxist, and his physical appearance and the language he used were not what whites would recognize as an instrument of God. But NCBC members dressed appropriately, with suits and ties, and they knew how to talk with reason and a calm spirit—traits evidently regarded as essential characteristics of faith and of Western civilization. Therefore, NCBC members became disgusted when whites refused to negotiate with honesty and integrity. Their anger and frustration were clearly stated in "A Message to the Churches from Oakland" (October 1969) and in "The Black Declaration of Independence" (July 4, 1970). In the Oakland statement, they expressed their deep disappointment with "fruitless negotiations":

> Having thus analyzed our situation . . . we have been made to recognize that it is not enough simply to call white churches to the negotiation table. Long, agonizing months of fruitless negotiations with these churches, in efforts to lead them to recognize and to fund the Black Economic Development Conference, have forced us sadly to acknowledge the harsh reality that the white churches and church structures are not capable of positive responses to the considered opinions of their black peers.[31]

Although NCBC members felt that they may have lost the battle over reparations at the negotiation table, they still believed that the war over reparations was not over, and they were still determined to win it. They decided to enhance their firepower by changing their style of fighting from the negotiation tactics of Martin King to the "by any means necessary" tactics of Malcolm X. They said:

> We are unalterably committed to the effecting of a more equitable power balance "by whatever means are neces-

sary.'' Means additional to negotiation are now necessary. The time has come for us to resort to the use of unusual forms of pressure upon the white church structures if we are ever to realize the legitimate goal of a literal transferral of power.[32]

In the Oakland statement, Nat Turner, Denmark Vesey, Martin Delany, Marcus Garvey, W.E.B. DuBois, and Malcolm X became saints alongside traditional black churchmen such as Richard Allen, James Varick, and Martin Luther King, Jr. But it is clear that the former group was much more decisive in determining the content and style of its message. Some of the group were cultural nationalists, others revolutionary nationalists, and all were unquestionably committed to black liberation. NCBC members now became openly nationalist and also revolutionary—at least in their rhetoric if not with guns. The faith commitment of black clergy radicals and their organizational link with the mainline black churches of Allen, Varick, and King and also with white denominations kept them within the bounds of Christian "decency" and thus inhibited them from acting out the revolution that they articulated.

The black clergy radicals' failure to anticipate that whites would not accede to their demands for reparations on the basis of the ethical rightness of the claim rendered their revolutionary rhetoric innocuous. Their past personal relationships with the white clergy partly blinded them to the depth of white racism in the churches. Although they knew that whites were white first and Christian second, the black clergy believed that the order could be reversed, provided that whites were presented with the radical claims of the gospel. They really believed that whites would change their racist ways after it was demonstrated theologically that racism and Christianity were completely incompatible.[33] Therefore, when whites ignored them and began to move ahead with their own white agenda for blacks, NCBC members did not know what to do. They had no plan of action in case whites rejected the idea of reparations, because they thought that whites and they *shared* the *same* faith even though it came in different colors.

Most NCBC members did not question the truth of white

Christianity. They merely insisted on the equal truth of black Christianity and attacked whites because they denied it, at least by implication. Reflecting upon the theological meaning of the *Black Manifesto* crisis, Gayraud Wilmore expressed it clearly:

> Since 1966 the new interest in "black theology" among black churchmen is evidence that the theology which has been dominant in the American churches failed black Christians. It found social prejudice and discrimination to be the denial of the sovereignty of God and the Christian doctrine of [humanity], but *it made no allowance for the black experience of faith and life in the community of poverty and oppression.*[34]

For blacks in white churches, the white denial of the theological value of black history and culture in the doing of theology meant a denial of black humanity and an establishment of white Christianity as normative for all Christians. Therefore the fight was not just for the acquisition of economic and political rights, but also for the establishment of the dignity of black humanity as defined in its cultural past and in its current fight for material freedom. But because black clergy radicals relied too much upon theology and not enough on the social sciences, they were caught off guard when they realized that whites were not about to effect significant changes in the power relationship within their churches in order to accommodate the economic empowerment of the black community.[35]

The last gasp of NCBC radicalism was expressed in its "Black Declaration of Independence." Although the language borders on treason, whites were not too worried: the battle for reparations was over, and even the NCBC knew that whites had outsmarted them by dividing their ranks. But black clergy radicals stayed together long enough to say:

> Unless we receive full redress and relief from these inhumanities, we will move to renounce all allegiance to this nation, and will refuse, in every way, to cooperate with the evil which is perpetrated upon ourselves and our communities.[36]

Although the NCBC did not win the fight for reparations, that struggle deepened the black clergy's determination to make a black theology that white churches could not ignore. They may have lost the battle over reparations, but the black clergy and an emerging group of professional theologians were determined to win the *theological* war. It was the black theologians' and preachers' new-found theological vision that kept alive their attack on white religion and moved it to an intellectual level. They were determined to differentiate true Christianity from white religion, because that was the only way they could establish a genuine solidarity with the suffering black people. Some of the black clergy soon discovered that white racism was far more deeply embedded in white Protestant churches than they had realized. Thus much more than James Forman's *Black Manifesto* was needed to eliminate it.

BLACK CATHOLICS' ATTACK
ON THE CATHOLIC CHURCH

Black Protestants were the major participants in developing a black theological attack upon white religion, but black Catholics also participated and played significant roles. They were involved in the NCBC during the early stages of its development. They also initiated battles in the Catholic Church that continue today.

Lawrence Lucas's *Black Priest/White Church* was one of the early exposés of racism in the Catholic Church.[37] Such organizations as the National Black Catholic Caucus, the National Black Sisters Conference, National Black Lay Catholic Caucus, and National Office of Black Catholics were organized in the late 1960s and early '70s in order to fight racism in the Catholic Church. With the birth of the civil rights movement and Martin King's courageous leadership, black Catholics were forced, by the urgency of the times, to ask: "Is it possible for a person to be black and a Catholic?" The blatant racism in the church seemed to demand the answer "absolutely not!" But with the appearance of black power, radical black Catholics, to the surprise of both white Catholics and non-Catholic blacks, answered "Why not?"[38]

When the Black Catholic Clergy Caucus (BCCC) was organized in Detroit (1968), it shocked the white Catholic hierarchy with the blunt statement: "The Catholic Church in the United States [is] primarily a racist institution."[39] Of course most persons knew then and also now (inside and outside the church, blacks and whites) that the statement was true. In fact, as recently as November 14, 1979, the U.S. Catholic bishops' pastoral letter on racism, entitled "Brothers and Sisters to Us," stated that "racism is an evil which endures in our society and in our church."[40] The Catholic Church had issued declarations against racism in its "Discrimination and Christian Conscience" (1958) and "National Race Crisis" (1968). What, then, was all the fuss about?

The "problem" was that black Catholic priests had had the audacity to separate themselves into a caucus and call the church racist. Whites viewed such actions as not only "un-Christian" but also "uncivilized." For whites it was as if blacks were rejecting the reconciling love of Jesus and separating themselves from the Catholic Church. That was why the BCCC statement was ignored by the Catholic hierarchy, apparently with the hope that its authors would come to their senses. But the BCCC refused to accept silence and insisted that the hierarchy respond to its demand, which focused on an autonomous central office for black Catholics.

Unlike black Protestants (most of whom run their own churches, and others who, in white denominations, have some degree of ecclesiastical space to speak their mind without risking many reprisals), black Catholics have little space for challenging the white Catholic Church. Blacks are vastly outnumbered. At present there are over 50 million U.S. Catholics, of whom only about one million are blacks, with seven bishops, fewer than four hundred priests, and a little more than six hundred sisters. During the 1960s the numbers were much lower. The white ecclesiastical machinery with which black Catholics have to do battle is so powerful and determined in its own self-righteousness that blacks who dare challenge it had better be prepared for harsh and "divinely" ordained punishment. Referring to black Catholics who dared to challenge the church, Bishop Joseph A. Francis says:

The Catholic Church in the United States had brief encounters with persons like the Rev. Lawrence Lucas, Brother Joseph Davis, the Rev. Donald Clark, the Rev. Rollings Lambert, Sister Martin de Porres Grey, and others. Each of these persons has left a legacy of courage, but they paid dearly. History will be generous to them, but their contemporaries have done little to heal the wounds. I consider their contributions invaluable, and I often envied their courage and prayed to possess their integrity.[41]

It was black Catholics' declaration that they were "black first and Catholic second" that upset the white Catholic hierarchy.[42] The bishops expected blacks to be pleased with the few opportunities available to them, even if they were "treated like children—or worse, like wards of the church."[43]

Black lay Catholics also initiated a similar attack upon the Catholic Church. They have a long history of expressing black solidarity, dating back to Daniel Rudd's initiation of the Afro-American Catholic congresses from 1889 to 1894 and Thomas Wyatt Turner's establishment of the Committee for the Advancement of Colored Catholics, which showed special concern for "the development of an indigenous Afro-American clergy."[44]

Following the organization of the BCCC in the late 1960s, the National Black Lay Catholic Caucus was organized (1970) and appeared to be as strong in their attack on the white Catholic establishment as the black clergy had been. They faced head-on the problem of being black and Catholic. They said: "The question of whether we can be black, Christian, and Catholic is such an important question that many blacks are leaving the church because they cannot reconcile the differences. Therefore we resolve that we are black first and then Catholic."[45] Then they issued their black power demand: "We insist upon parish community autonomy and self-determination with the belief the body founded on this philosophy will be the basic black power structure in the black parish community."[46]

Although black Catholics challenged the racist character of the Catholic Church in the U.S.A., they have not made a significant academic contribution in the field of black theology, and the reasons are at least partly obvious. The white power structure in the Catholic Church is so restrictive on what blacks can do or say that it is almost impossible to think creatively. Creative theological thinking is born out of conflict, the recognition that what is true *is not* true, that untruth has established itself as truth. Theology has the critical task of interpreting the truth of the gospel in such a way that it has continuity with the past but also challenges the present, thereby opening up a creative freedom for the future. It was the concern of black Protestant theologians to interpret the truth of the gospel for the present in the light of the past so as to break open a new future that necessitated the development of black theology.

But in addition to a conflictive situation, persons also need some space for the development of their own leadership if they are to create a theological perspective accountable to their struggle for freedom and not to the structures that oppress them. Black Catholics have little space for the development of their own leaders. That was why early unitive movements among them were initiated by lay persons. It was not until the 1960s that a significant number of voices began to be heard among the clergy. It will take a little more time, and the Catholic hierarchy will have to become a little more flexible in what it defines as theology and dogma, before a genuine black theology can emerge in the Catholic Church.

As a black Protestant who looks at the Catholic Church from the outside, the immensity of the task of trying to challenge the tradition of Catholic theology *and* also remain inside the church is so great that it overwhelms me.[47] But despite the extent of the task and because of the foundation laid in the 1960s, there are young black Catholics (priests, sisters, and lay persons) who are determined to develop a black theology that is accountable to their experience in both the black and Catholic communities. Jamie Phelps, Shawn Copeland, Sr. M. Martin de Porres Grey, Toinette Eugene, Joseph Nearon, Diana Hayes, Cyprian Rowe, Joseph Davis, Clarence Joseph Rivers, and Edward Braxton are prominent examples. In October 1978 they held a Black Catholic Theological Symposium in Baltimore, and published their papers under the title *Theology: A Portrait in Black*.[48]

Edward K. Braxton, their most prominent theologian, has written several articles analyzing the Protestant interpreters of black theology and also offering his critical comments.[49] There is no doubt that he has the theological imagination and discipline and thus could offer black Catholics a significant contribution in black theology. But his European training seems to have created an unresolved inner tension between black and white theologies, with the latter winning his allegiance.

Whether among black Protestants or Catholics, black theology is partly a product of the attack by black clergy radicals on racism in white churches. Indeed it was the presence of racism in white churches that forced black theologians to stand up and say, loud and clear: "The white church is not the Christian church!" The defense of this claim gave birth to black theology.

Chapter III

Black Theology
as Liberation Theology

Black theology is a theology of liberation. It seeks to plumb the black condition in the light of God's revelation in Jesus Christ, so that the black community can see that the gospel is commensurate with the achievement of black humanity. Black theology is a theology of "blackness." It is the affirmation of black humanity that emancipates black people from white racism, thus providing authentic freedom for both white and black people. It affirms the humanity of white people in that it says no to the encroachment of white oppression.

National Committee of Black Churchmen,
"Black Theology," June 13, 1969[1]

It is one thing to proclaim black theology and attack white churches as racist, but quite another to develop a systematic and comprehensive exposition of the Christian faith using the black experience of struggle as the chief source. There were no black systematic theologies that black scholars could use as models. There were only a few black theologians and scholars in ethics, biblical studies, religious education, and history. And most of them, like George Kelsey and Nathan Scott, Jr., were not interested in associating the Christian gospel with the black experience. Their views were similar to those of their white teachers and colleagues who maintained that the *universal* character of the Christian faith precluded the very idea of a black theology: it would reduce Christian theology to the *particularity* of one people.

In the absence of substantial theological texts on black theology and with most of the major established black scholars remaining cool or openly rejecting such an idea, white Christians and almost all white theologians dismissed black theology as insubstantial. Because white theologians controlled the seminaries and university departments of religion, many blacks had the impression that only Europeans and persons who think like them could define what theology is. In order to challenge the white monopoly on the definition of theology, many young black scholars realized that they had to carry the fight to the seminaries where theology was being written.

Because the term "liberation" had already emerged as the chief symbol for expressing the meaning of black freedom in politics and the churches, it was only natural that it would serve a similar function in black theology. In this chapter I shall examine the sources from which black theologians and preachers derived the theme of liberation.

BLACK POWER

Although I have discussed the impact of black power upon the creators of black theology, it may be useful to analyze the depth of their commitment to the civil rights movement and the events in it that produced such a radical change in their theological perspective.

Almost without exception (Albert Cleage being one), black preachers and theologians had been thoroughly committed to Martin King's method of nonviolent resistance as the only way for blacks to achieve justice in America, and they were proud to go to jail with him. They were strong advocates of integration and firm believers in King's dream that the U.S.A. would soon truly become the "land of the free and the home of the brave." Like

King, their hope was deeply rooted in the Declaration of Independence, the U.S. Constitution, and the Christian claim that all human beings are created to be free. They, like other blacks, including SNCC radicals, believed that they were living in the age in which freedom would be actualized and that their children would inherit a society that would be defined by justice and equality, not by oppression and slavery.

The successful "stride toward freedom" by King and the blacks of Montgomery in 1955–56 marked the beginning of their hopeful struggle, motivated by the 1954 U.S. Supreme Court decision on the unconstitutionality of segregated public schooling, reinforced by the sit-ins and freedom rides of the early 1960s. The high point of their hope came with the 1963 march on Washington and King's "I Have a Dream" speech. After that speech, they firmly believed that the arrival of justice in America, long awaited by black Americans, would soon be realized.[2]

Unfortunately we did not listen to Malcolm X and his analysis of the depth of racism in American society. After the march on Washington came Selma (1965) and then Chicago (1966). When King made his move to Chicago (1966), the first major northern urban riot had already happened—in Watts (Los Angeles), August 1965. It occurred only two weeks after Lyndon Johnson's signing of the Voting Rights Act. The Watts riot and the other eruptions like it should have told black preachers something about the inadequacy of their analysis—both in terms of the method of nonviolence and the goal of integration.

In contrast to the south, blacks "up north" had always been able to vote and use public facilities; the riots were dramatic indications that they had nothing for which to vote and they could not afford to live outside the ghetto. The riots were shocking evidence that the oppression of blacks was much more complex and deeply rooted than had been articulated by Martin King. Its elimination would take more than a moral appeal to ideas of freedom and equality in the American liberal tradition or the idea of love in the traditional white view of the Christian faith.

A much more radical analysis was needed if the depth of racism was to be understood, and a much more radical method of change was needed if it was to be eliminated. Although the 1965 Watts riot clearly pointed to the bankruptcy of the ideas of integration and nonviolence, black preachers still did not read the message. They continued along the same path of trying to achieve the "beloved community" by turning the other cheek.

However, when King took his nonviolent movement to Chicago and failed at almost every point, because he and black preachers failed to analyze the complexity and depth of northern racism, it began to dawn upon many radical black preachers that King's approach had serious limitations. Malcolm X began to make sense to them. It was while King was struggling against Richard Daly's racist political machine that James Meredith was shot in Mississippi, "marching against fear." The shooting of Meredith once again reminded black Americans of the deep roots of white racism. They had a long way to go before its elimination would be a fact.

In what became the last attempt to publicly display a symbol of unity in the black freedom struggle, King (SCLC), Stokely Carmichael (SNCC), Floyd McKissick (CORE), Whitney Young (NUL), and Roy Wilkins (NAACP) convened in Memphis in order to continue Meredith's march.[3] By the summer of 1966, SNCC and CORE members had already decided, *before* their leaders' meeting with King, Young, and Wilkins in Memphis, that a *new* day had come in the civil rights movement. Sharp conflicts between the members of the SNCC and King's SCLC had already surfaced in Albany, Washington, Selma, and other cities in the south. Differences in goals, methods, and personalities had always threatened the unity of the civil rights movement. But it was not until the Meredith-Mississippi march that everything came out in the open for the world to see.

SNCC and CORE members insisted that no whites be allowed to participate in the march and they insisted they would make no pledge of nonviolence as a response to whites' violence. Young, Wilkins, and King were truly shocked into disbelief at such a suggestion. The manifesto that defined the march stated: "This march will be a massive public indictment and protest of the failure of American society, the government of the United States, and the State of Mississippi to 'fulfill these rights' " (referring to a slogan of the Johnson administration).[4] Criticism of the Johnson administration, insistence on the exclusion of whites, and refusal to promise adherence to nonviolence were clearly viewed by mainline civil rights advocates as outside the bounds of acceptable rhetoric and behavior.

Young and Wilkins were so disturbed that anyone would make such proposals that they left, saying that they would have no part in such a march. They withdrew NAACP and NUL endorsement of it. How were they going to continue to appeal to whites for support of NAACP and NUL goals if they participated in a march from which whites were excluded, nonviolence was rejected, and the president of the United States was severely criticized? But to Martin King's credit, he refused to leave. He debated with Carmichael and McKissick nearly all night trying to get them not to use the phrase "black power" and to allow whites to participate in the march under a pledge of nonviolence.

King succeeded in eliciting their commitment. The march began. But when the marchers reached Greenwood, Mississippi, the place where Carmichael had worked, he was arrested. Upon his release, Carmichael, who had been in many southern jails and the federal government had done nothing about it, mounted a platform and protested, "This is the twenty-seventh time I have been arrested—and I ain't going to jail no more!" He continued: "The only way we gonna stop them white men from whippin' us is to take over. We been saying 'freedom' for six years, and we ain't got nothin'. What we gonna start saying now is 'black power!' " At that moment, Willie Ricks, called "the preacher" because of his persuasive sermonic style, took over and brought the crowd to ecstasy, chanting "black power!" The crowd responded enthusiastically with the same phrase. Although King tried to stem the tide of the crowd's enthusiasm for "black power," he did not succeed and many of his own disciples followed Carmichael and Ricks. From that point on, "black power" replaced "freedom now," and "we shall overcome" was replaced by "we shall overrun" as slogans of young black radicals.

The rise of black power created a radical change in the consciousness of many young radicals in the SNCC and their followers. Organized in the spring of 1960, they had adopted Martin King's nonviolent direct action as a strategy for social change, even though most did not accept it as an ideology. They had used King's method throughout the south—Mississippi, Georgia, Ala-

bama, and Arkansas. By 1966, after attending many of their comrades' funerals, after being beaten and shot as the FBI took notes
and did nothing, the complexity and depth of white racism became clearer to them. They wryly noted that northern blacks
burned the cities even though they had the "rights" that southern
blacks risked their lives to achieve.

The black power cry was the response of young blacks to white
power that had camouflaged itself in the Christian garb of love. It
was their way of saying to whites that they were "on to their
tricks" and thus would no longer allow them to use Martin King's
idea of Christian love to keep the black revolution in check. They
now sang:

> I love everybody,
> I love everybody,
> I love everybody in my heart,

but they quickly added:

> I just told a lie,
> I just told a lie,
> I just told a lie in my heart.[5]

Young black preachers were placed in an existential dilemma.
Their faith was closer to King's but their politics closer to Carmichael's. In an effort to resolve the conflict, they began to reflect
on how the gospel can be reconciled with the black power politics
of liberation, especially as articulated by young black radicals
who claimed that blacks should take their freedom "by any
means necessary." Although they respected King and admired his
commitment to justice, they could no longer embrace nonviolence as an ideology, nor could they affirm integration as the
goal of the black freedom struggle. But inasmuch as King, along
with white churches and theologians, had defined Christianity as
being identical with love, and love as being identical with nonviolence and integration, how could they retain their Christian
identity and also support the black power claim that blacks
should take their freedom "by any means necessary"? That was
their theological dilemma. How could radical black preachers retain their Christian identity and also be as committed, as black

power advocates, to black liberation, refusing to accept white brutality with a turned cheek?

Black power advocates made no claim to an identity derived from Christianity. Most were secular university students or adherents of African religions, and all tended to define Christianity as "the white man's religion." Black preachers, in their struggle to be Christian *and* support black power, had to develop a theology that was distinctly black and also accountable to our faith. It was in this context that Albert Cleage wrote the *Black Messiah* and I wrote *Black Theology and Black Power*.[6] I wanted to show that black power and the gospel were identical and that both focused on the politics of liberation.

It was not easy to connect black power with the Christian gospel. The advocates of black power were not only un-Christian; they were hostile to Christianity, viewing it as a white religion. Furthermore, most Christians, black and white, were hostile to black power, viewing it as the opposite of everything that their faith represented. When black power advocates emerged as leaders in the black movement, they de-Christianized the black struggle for justice by emphasizing black separatism and self-defense. As long as Martin King was the acknowledged symbol and standard-bearer of the movement, it remained Christian, emphasizing love, integration, and nonviolence. But emergence of Malcolm's philosophy through black power meant the introduction of a radicalization that excluded Christianity.

Black theology arose as an attempt to stem the tide of the irrelevance of Christianity by combining both Christianity and blackness, Martin and Malcolm, black church and black power, even though neither side thought it was possible. The early interpreters of black theology were theologians "on the boundary" (to use Paul Tillich's self-evaluation) between integration and separation, nonviolence and self-defense, "love our white enemies and love our black skins." They refused to sacrifice either emphasis; they insisted on the absolute necessity of both.

BLACK CHURCH HISTORY

When black preachers were confronted with the dilemma posed by black power, they began to search black church history for insights and models that would illustrate and support their claim that the gospel of Jesus is identical with blacks' liberation from political bondage. Their search focused on their radical black forebears, chiefly in the masculine line. To be sure, black preachers sometimes mentioned Harriet Tubman and Sojourner Truth, but unfortunately black women did not occupy a prominent place in their analysis.[7] Richard Allen, Daniel Payne, Andrew Bryan, George Leile, James Varick, and Christopher Rush emerged as significant advocates for an independent black church movement that began in the late eighteenth century.[8]

But these black churchmen were not radical enough for the era of black power. It was Nat Turner, Gabriel Prosser, Denmark Vesey, Henry Highland Garnet, David Walker, Henry McNeil Turner, and others like them, who helped young black radical preachers articulate a black version of the gospel. It differed from an appeal to integration, love, and nonviolence, and thus, to everyone's surprise, was quite similar to the message of black power in the 1960s.

Turner, Prosser, and Vesey were insurrectionists. They had organized slave revolts in 1800, 1822, and 1831, respectively, in the name of the gospel and black freedom.[9] Garnet's "Address to the Slaves" in 1843 and David Walker's *Appeal* in 1829 sounded like black power music to our ears. They too had urged rebellion against the evils of slavery, comparing our condition in the U.S.A. with the Hebrew slaves in ancient Egypt.[10] Henry M. Turner's claim that "God is a Negro" (1898) suggested a historical and theological depth to the claim that God is on the side of blacks for freedom.[11]

Black theologians and preachers of the 1960s began to realize that they were not the first in the attempt to find theological meaning in blackness and the gospel. Indeed, blacks have a usable heritage, a revolutionary past, that can give direction in the search for the truth of the gospel in the struggle for black freedom.

We also found out how little we knew about black history, especially a black history that correctly located the role of the black church. All we knew were a few denominational histories and as few names of nineteenth-century black preachers. Our denominational histories could hardly stand the test of critical scholarship, for they were written from the perspective of a particular ecclesiastical history and for the purpose of glorifying its leaders.

Some few other personages were hardly known beyond a few historical references: not enough to give us substantive guidance in the age of black power.

Unfortunately no serious research had been done on the history of the black church since Carter G. Woodson's *The History of the Negro Church* (1921). E. Franklin Frazier's brief volume *The Negro Church in America* (1961) was helpful but was too much of a sociological reduction as defined by the University of Chicago school of sociology. "The Negro Church" (1903) by W. E. B. DuBois, in his Atlanta University Publications, was useful, but it was even older than Woodson's work. Benjamin E. Mays's *The Negro's God* (1938) and his volume with J. W. Nicholson on *The Negro's Church* (1933), though not as old as the works by DuBois or Woodson, did not adequately meet our historical needs. What we needed was a well-written, comprehensive, and scholarly history of the black church and religion that could meet the test of both critical historical scholarship and also be useful in our attempt to develop a black theology.

Gayraud Wilmore responded to that need by writing his *Black Religion and Black Radicalism* (1972). This text is one of the most important contributions emerging out of the black theology movement. A social ethicist by academic training and an ordained minister in the Presbyterian Church, Wilmore has been the moving force behind the NCBC, serving as its historian and theologian. More than anyone else, he was deeply committed to uncovering our history, not just in the U.S.A. but all the way back to our African past. He would not let young black radicals remain content with sloganeering about black church heroes but pushed them to search for the religions of Africa before the whites came with their slave ships. He encouraged us to study African traditional religions, and he was one of the chief forces behind the NCBC creation of an African commission, which established dialogues with African church persons.

From the very beginning, Wilmore's concern was to create a black theology that was truly black—that is, *African*—and not a white version of Western Christianity colored black. He wanted the definition of black theology to be shaped by an African meaning of liberation and not simply by Western bourgeois ideas of freedom and equality, or a Marxist idea of liberation. The key to

Wilmore's new appreciation of the autonomy of the black religious tradition—or at least one important and neglected stream of it—was W. E. B. DuBois's *The Souls of Black Folk* (1903). It was DuBois who pushed him toward Africa, and Wilmore then pushed us to read John Mbiti (*African Religions and Philosophy*;[12] *New Testament Eschatology in an African Background*),[13] Bolaji Idowu (*Olódùmare: God in Yoruba Belief*;[14] *Towards an Indigenous Church*),[15] Harry Sawyerr (*Creative Evangelism*;[16] *God: Ancestor or Creator?*),[17] and Kwesi Dickson and Paul Ellingworth (editors of *Biblical Revelation and African Beliefs*).[18]

Charles H. Long, then professor of the history of religions at the University of Chicago and later at the University of North Carolina at Chapel Hill, concurred with Wilmore as to the importance of the study of African religions.[19] Jerome Long, Charles's brother, also supported the same emphasis, as did my brother Cecil Cone in his *Identity Crisis in Black Theology*.[20] We had many spirited debates about the role of African religions in black theology, with some advocating it as a source equally important as Christianity in the definition of black religion and others defending biblical Christianity as its primary source.

Two meanings of liberation emerged from our historical past. One emphasized socio-political freedom as derived from the biblical theme of the exodus and nineteenth-century black freedom fighters. The other emphasized cultural liberation as derived from the black nationalism of H. M. Turner, Marcus Garvey, Malcolm X, and especially the religions of Africa. No one wanted to exclude either emphasis entirely, but there was much debate about which should be normative for the definition of black theology.[21]

Although we debated our differences about the precise meaning of liberation, we all agreed that it had to be defined by our black past. There can be no creative theology without a tradition upon which to base it. We knew that if we were going to sustain our attempt to make a black theology of liberation, we had to find persons in our history who had laid the groundwork for us. Therefore the attempt to create a black theology of liberation meant searching for its meaning in our historical past.

THE BIBLE

In addition to black power and black church history, many black theologians and preachers turned directly to the Bible for the content of the meaning of liberation as a theological category. Realization of the usefulness of the Bible as a support for the liberation of the black poor came partly from our study of black church history. Henry Garnet, David Walker, Nat Turner, Gabriel Prosser, Harriet Tubman, Sojourner Truth, and many other black freedom fighters used the scriptures in support of their resistance to and rebellion against oppression and slavery. In addition there were the black sprituals and their emphasis on freedom—both here and hereafter. Although the black spirituals had been interpreted as being exclusively otherworldly and compensatory, our research into the testimonies of black slave narratives and other black sayings revealed that the theme of heaven in the spirituals and in black religion generally contained double meanings.[22] "Steal away" referred not only to an eschatological realm, but it was also used by Harriet Tubman as a signal of freedom for slaves who intended to run away with her to the north, or to Canada.[23] According to Frederick Douglass, the song "O Canaan" referred not only to heaven but also to Canada and the north.[24] In these slave songs were found also unambiguous demands for freedom:

> O Freedom! O Freedom!
> O Freedom! I love thee,
> And before I'll be a slave
> I be buried in my grave
> And go home to my Lord and be free.

A similar emphasis is found in "Go Down, Moses." While many black leaders from Harriet Tubman to Martin King have been identified with Moses, almost all blacks in America—past and present—have identified Egypt with America, Pharaoh and the Egyptians with white slaveholders and subsequent racists, and blacks with the Israelite slaves:

Go down, Moses,
Way down in Egyptland,
Tell old Pharaoh
To let my people go.

When Israel was in Egyptland,
Let my people go,
Oppressed so hard they could not stand,
Let my people go.

Go down, Moses,
Way down in Egyptland,
Tell old Pharaoh,
"Let my people go."

"Thus saith the Lord," bold Moses said,
"Let my people go;
If not I'll smite your first-born dead.
Let my people go."

Go down, Moses,
Way down in Egyptland,
Tell old Pharaoh,
"Let my people go!"

With the Old Testament sharply in view, the New Testament Jesus was defined as the liberator whose ministry was in solidarity with, and whose death was on behalf of, the poor. In our investigation of our own black church history, we were driven to scripture itself so as to analyze its message in the light of our struggle for freedom.

Because white theologians and preachers denied any relationship between the scriptures and our struggle for freedom, we bypassed the classic Western theological tradition and went directly to scripture for its word regarding our black struggle. Although whites looked down with a condescending intellectual arrogance at our attempt to uncover a liberation theme in the scriptures, we were not discouraged. Intuitively we knew that we were right, and they were wrong. Furthermore some of us had been trained by them, with a few doctorates to our credit, and we did not internalize everything we were taught. Besides, some things we had been taught in the seminary had far more revolutionary potential than our white teachers had envisioned.

For example, almost every biblical and theological teacher I had encountered in graduate school, as well as most of the well-known biblical scholars I read, claimed that revelation was not an abstract propositional truth but rather a historical event, God's involvement in history. Many of us had read Ernest G. Wright's *Book of the Acts of God*, Oscar Cullmann's *Christ and Time*, Gerhard von Rad's *Theology of the Old Testament*, Bernard Anderson's *Understanding the Old Testament*, and many other neoorthodox biblical scholars. We merely asked that if God is known by God's acts in history, what, then, is God doing in and through historical events? What is the meaning of salvation as an act of God? Basing ourselves on the exodus and the message of the prophets, we black theologians agreed with our neoorthodox teachers that God is known by God's acts in history and that these acts are identical with the liberation of the weak and the poor.

As long as we blacks located the liberating acts of God for the poor in ancient Hebrew history, that was acceptable biblical exegesis from the viewpoint of white scholars. But when we tried to do systematic theology on the basis of our exegesis, applying God's liberating acts to our contemporary situation in the U.S.A., focusing on the relations between blacks and whites, white scholars vehemently rejected both the procedure and the message. They tried to get around our contemporary application of the biblical message by saying that there were other themes in the Bible besides liberation (which we never denied). Our concern was to locate the dominant theme in scripture and to ask what its message was for the black struggle for freedom today.

We black theologians contended that if God sided with the poor and the weak in biblical times, then why not today? If salvation is a historical event of rescue, a deliverance of slaves from Egypt, why not a black power event today and a deliverance of blacks from white American racial oppression? When we pressed these questions on white theologians and preachers, they always turned to the white, meek, pale-faced, blue-eyed Jesus, as if we blacks were expected to embrace him as our Savior. But we vehemently rejected that Jesus.

In place of the white Jesus, we insisted that "Jesus Christ is black, baby!" That sent shock waves throughout the white seminary and church communities. Whites thought that blacks had lost their religious sanity. It was one thing to identify liberation as the central message of the Bible, but something else to introduce color into christology. They could even keep their composure as we discussed together whether the title "liberator" can be appropriately applied to Jesus or whether he was a revolutionary. But to color Jesus black, that was going too far, and they could hardly sit still during the discussion. "That is racism in reverse!" they said, "and such a claim has no biblical warrant." But we did not listen to them. We merely searched the scriptures with the resources we had, knowing that in time the truth of our claim would be demonstrated so clearly that even whites would have to take notice of it!

The vehement rejection of the black Jesus by whites merely reinforced the determination of black clergy radicals to develop a christology that took seriously Jesus' blackness—both literally and symbolically.[25] The literal significance of Jesus' blackness meant that he *was not* white! He was a Palestinian Jew whose racial ancestry may have been partly African but definitely not European. Therefore white pictures of Jesus in Christian churches and homes are nothing but an ideological distortion of the biblical portrait. By making this point, black clergy radicals wanted to show that the so-called scientific biblical exegesis of white scholars frequently was not scientific at all. For they have helped to maintain the white image of Jesus through their silence about his true color, thereby suggesting the European Jesus was the historical one.

The major importance of the claim that "Jesus is black" rested on the symbolic meaning of that affirmation. We were strongly influenced by Bishop Henry M. Turner's claim that "God is a Negro" and Countee Cullen's poetic reflections on "The Black Christ" (1929), which Sterling Brown referred to as "a narrative poem about lynching."[26] The blackness of Jesus had definite political implications that we derived from the New Testament witness. It was our way of saying that his cross and resurrection represented God's solidarity with the oppressed in their struggle for liberation. The oppressed do not have to accept their present misery as the final definition of their humanity. The good news is: God, the Holy One of Israel, has entered the human situation in Jesus and has transformed it through his cross and resurrection. The poor no longer have to remain in poverty. They are now free to fight for their freedom, because God is fighting with them. In the U.S.A. this claim meant that God was on the side of oppressed blacks in their struggle for freedom and against whites who victimized them. For black clergy radicals, the best way to describe that insight was to say that "Jesus is black."

Of course, the blackness of Jesus did not mean that he could not be described also as red, brown, yellow, or by some other characteristic that defined materially the condition of the poor in the U.S.A. and other parts of the globe. Black clergy radicals never denied the universal significance of Jesus' death and resurrection. We merely wanted to emphasize the theological significance of Jesus in the context of the black liberation struggle in the U.S.A. We wanted to expose the racism of white churches and also encourage black churches to embrace the biblical Christ who looks much more like oppressed blacks than white oppressors.

White theologians resented our refusal to listen to them, because they had taught us and they were the experts in the field. But I ask any fair observer, why should we listen to those who have done nothing to assist blacks in their liberation struggle? White biblical scholars have not even bothered to train blacks to acquire the skills that they regard as necessary for sound biblical exegesis. What right, then, do they have to say that our exegesis is unsound? We blacks merely responded to white scholars by saying that the kingdom that Jesus embodied in his life, death, and resurrection was not promised to the learned but to the meek, the humble, and the poor. If white biblical exegetes think that the God of Jesus gave them a hermeneutical privilege in biblical interpretation, then they have not only misread scripture but have substituted their scientific knowledge about the Bible for a genuine encounter with biblical faith.

Despite the prescientific approach by most blacks to the Bible, we claimed that their focus on liberation was historically accurate and theologically sound.[27] A study of black church history, therefore, led us to a study of scripture, and once again the theme of liberation became the dominant emphasis.

EUROPEAN POLITICAL THEOLOGIES

In 1967 Jürgen Moltmann's *Theology of Hope* [28] was published in the United States. It emphasized the biblical theme of God's promise as embodied in the struggles of the poor for freedom. Later the works of Johannes B. Metz also stressed a similar eschatological theme.[29] The theology of hope with a political ingredient became a dominant theme in American theology, and many conferences were held in order to explore its implications. Moltmann and Metz lectured frequently in the U.S.A.[30]

I remember well the excitement of reading Moltmann and Metz, one Protestant and the other Catholic. "Now," I said to myself, "my view of liberation in the Bible has some theological support from Germany—widely known as having the leading theological centers in the world. How will run-of-the-mill white North American theologians now be able to deny black theologians' claims about the theme of liberation in the Bible?" The feeling that Moltmann's theology supported the liberation of the poor accounted for why he was quoted so liberally in my work; he provided "respectable" theological support for my claims regarding God's solidarity with the poor.[31]

Other black theologians were also influenced by Moltmann and Metz. The title of the first book by Major J. Jones on black theology reflects this dependence—*Black Awareness: A Theology of Hope.*[32] The writings of J. Deotis Roberts refer frequently to Moltmann and Metz.[33] Black theologians quoted from European theologians because they had developed a theological language that appeared to support similar claims in black theology. White North American theologians could ignore our attempts to develop an argument for a black theology of liberation on the basis of our limited knowledge of scientific exegesis, but we knew that they would not (indeed, could not!) ignore major European theologians, for Europe is the continent of their origin and the place to which they and their students frequently return in order to deepen their theological knowledge. If a major European theologian said something, North Americans listened carefully, even if they strongly disagreed. As we black theologians expected, white Americans did pay close attention to the European theology of hope (political theology).

But European theologians did not help us as much in developing a language for black theology as we had originally expected.[34] Indeed we black theologians began to move away from the progressive theologies of Europe when we saw how easily they were adopted by white North Americans as a substitute for taking black theology seriously. How could white North American theologians devote so much attention to the hope thematized in European theology and completely ignore the hope emerging from the nearly three hundred and fifty years of black struggle in North America?[35]

The songs of hope, the "Negro spirituals," seemed to be the logical place to turn for any North American theological reflection on hope. Why were they ignored by white North American theologians who claimed to be interested in applying the ideas of hope and promise to life in the United States? Their silence baffled me, because the spirituals played such a dominant role in the civil rights movement. Furthermore, many of these same theologians were present at the march on Washington and had marched with King in Selma, singing these songs as everyone else, because of the empowerment and the courage they bestowed upon the marchers. Why, then, did they ignore them when they sat down at their seminary or university desks to reflect on hope? Were white theologians too blinded by their own racism to hear the truth of the gospel that was erupting from the struggles of the black poor?

It seemed that the silence of white theologians on black theology and religion was and is their way of saying that blacks cannot think. But as Gustavo Gutiérrez has said, "Even the poor have the right to think. The right to think is the corollary of the human right to be, and to assert the right to think is only to assert the right to exist."[36] By ignoring our hopes and dreams in their theologies of hope, white progressive theologians were saying that blacks cannot think, because they do not exist. That was why some of them could say, and still do, that there is no such thing as black theology.

The white theologians' claim that there is no such thing as black theology did not upset us; white acceptance was never our primary concern. Indeed, in one sense, I was pleased with their dismissal of black theology because it meant I was even more free to reread the Bible without having to answer the technical concerns of white theological academics. It also made me more determined to create a black theology of liberation that was not dependent upon my white theological mentors.

When whites asked me whether black theology was a "fad," I responded negatively, and with a theological confidence, and touch of arrogance that showed my disdain for anyone who asked such a question. I often said, "With over twenty million blacks in the U.S.A., most of whom are extremely poor, how can you be so insensitive as to ask whether reflection on their religious history is a passing fad?"

The black theologians' move away from the political theologies of Europe was also motivated by our uneasiness over their tendency toward theological abstractions. Progressive theologians of Europe were not concrete; they did not name enemies.[37] It was the Latin American liberation theologians' critique of the progressive theologies of Europe that really demonstrated the Achilles' heel of European progressive theologies.

Gustavo Gutiérrez's distinction between the problem of the unbeliever as created by the European Enlightenment and the problem of the nonperson as created by European colonization and exploitation of the Third World clarified our unexpressed suspicion about the political theologies of Europe. "The poor," he writes, "are not, in the first instance, questioning the religious world or its philosophical presuppositions. They are calling into question first of all the economic, social, and political order that oppresses and marginalizes them."[38] And he also observes that "one of the best ways to refute a theology is to look at its practical consequences, not its intellectual arguments."[39] When we blacks observed the practical consequences of European thought and its North American mirroring, it was quite clear that we could not base black theology upon a liberation derived from Europe.

We then decided to incorporate into black theology the challenge of Frantz Fanon, a West Indian deeply involved in the Algerian war for independence from France. Fanon helped us to realize that we must be suspicious of European intellectuals even when they use a language of liberation that appears to be supportive of the Third World. Not everything that is is what it appears to be. Underneath the European language of freedom and equality there is slavery and death. That was why Fanon said:

Come, then, comrades; it would be well to decide at once to change our ways. We must shake off the heavy darkness in which we were plunged, and leave it behind. The new day which is already at hand must find us firm, prudent and resolute. We must leave our dreams and abandon our old beliefs and friendships of the time before life began. Let us waste no time in sterile litanies and nauseating mimicry. Leave this Europe where they are never done talking of [humanity], yet murder [human beings] everywhere they find them, at the corner of their own streets, in all the corners of the globe. For centuries they have stifled almost the whole of humanity in the name of a so-called spiritual experience. Look at them swaying between atomic and spiritual disintegration.[40]

Fanon captured our imagination because his analysis rang true, and he convinced us that black thought could create no genuine future for its people by looking to Europe for support. Europeans created the problem that necessitated our need for liberation, and it was naive of us to expect that our theological salvation could come from Europe:

That same Europe where they were never done talking of [humanity], and where they never stopped proclaiming that they were only anxious for the welfare of [humanity]: today we know with what sufferings humanity has paid for every one of their triumphs of the mind.[41]

Fanon's challenge involved more than turning away from Europe; it also involved a turning to the resources found in the victimized peoples of the world:

If we want humanity to advance a step further, if we want to bring it up to a different level than that which Europe has shown it, then we must invent and we must make discoveries. . . . For Europe, for ourselves, and for humanity, comrades, we must then turn over a new leaf, we must work out new concepts, and try to set afoot a new [humanity].[42]

The application of Fanon's message to black theology affected our understanding of our theological task. We now realized it consisted in something more than simply ebonizing European concepts in theology. Gayraud Wilmore and Charles Long saw the necessity and complexity of this task much clearer than most of us. They took the lead in directing black theologians to Africa first and then to Latin America and Asia.

THIRD WORLD THEOLOGIES

When black clergy radicals began to develop a black theology of liberation, they had no knowledge of a similar theological development going on in Africa, Asia, and Latin America. To be sure, like most civil rights activists, we had been influenced by the rise of the African movement toward independent nations during the 1950s and '60s, and we had heard about a parallel movement in religion, creating a renewed interest in African traditional religions and indigenous churches. Missionary churches, implanted by European and white North American missionaries, were being critically evaluated through the newly created organization called the All Africa Conference of Churches (AACC). The AACC, founded in 1958, was similar to the NCBC in that it was ecumenical and it began to provide the context for the creation of an African theology that would question the europeanization of the gospel.[43] But despite these creative political and theological irruptions in Africa, the early interpreters of black theology did not know much about them. Most of us had never been to Africa and had spent little time studying it.

Although Frantz Fanon's *The Wretched of the Earth* was the catalyst that drew our attention away from Europe, it was Gayraud Wilmore and Charles Long who accepted the radical implications of his challenge and pushed us toward Africa as the critical source for the development of a black theology based on black religion. When we began to read African theologians, such as John Mbiti and Bolaji Idowu, their talk about "africanization" and "indigenization" reinforced the importance of cultural liberation, which many North American black nationalists had stressed.

Some of us, however, were greatly disturbed about the political conservatism of many African theologians. We knew that Fanon would not look favorably upon a cultural nationalism that did not radically transform economics and politics. But despite our reservations, we continued to listen carefully and viewed African theology as far more important to us than European political theology. When black theologians of South Africa responded theologically to their situation of oppression by using the phrase "black theology," North American black theologians became even more determined to learn from Africa in our efforts to develop a theology that was black both politically and culturally.[44]

Many black theologians were greatly surprised to discover that Latin American theologians were using the term "liberation" to define the heart of the gospel.[45] Almost none of us knew Spanish and thus were limited in our knowledge of Latin American theology. However, because U.S. white religious radicals of a socialist bent (at least in language) adopted them, as liberal and neoorthodox white theologians adopted the progressive theologies of Europe, we blacks were very skeptical of this new liberation theology from Latin America.[46] Why were white religious radicals so interested in the poor in Latin America and so indifferent to the poor black in North America? I was reminded of Sartre's comment: "The only way of helping the enslaved out there is to side with those who are here."

Furthermore, Latin American theologians' focus on classism and their silence on racism troubled many black theologians. In Brazil alone, there are more than 40 million blacks and in Latin America more than 70 million. Why, then, are there no black or Amerindian theologians among them? I have written about the early encounters of black and Latin American theologies elsewhere, and I shall, in a later chapter, comment upon our mutual support, along with African and Asian theologies, in our efforts to create a common Third World theology.[47] My concern here is to emphasize that during the early development of black theology, we blacks were much too suspicious to learn as much as we should have. An early incorporation of class analysis into black theology could have prevented some of its most obvious and excessive weaknesses, which I shall take up later.

Most of us did not know anything about Asian theology. Dialogue with Asian Christians is more recent, and it is quite promising. More will be said about it in a later chapter.

Black clergy radicals began to develop a black theology of liberation springing from the particularity of our history, the urgency of our present struggles, and our creative hope for the future. Most of our ideas about liberation came from the depth of our political and spiritual struggle as we attempted to make sense out of black existence in white America. Although black preachers' formal theological knowledge may have been limited, and most did not have the educational credentials that would have entitled them to teach in white universities and seminaries, yet they did have the prophetic vision that enabled them to discern the truth of the time! Black theology, therefore, was created out of the sermonic imagination of black preachers as they fought to establish the freedom for their people that white Americans had denied but that God had foretold and promised.

THE LITERATURE OF BLACK THEOLOGY AND RELIGION

Although black clergy radicals were the chief initiators of the idea of a black theology, a small number of black theologians in seminaries, universities, and colleges were often present during their deliberations. Near the end of the 1960s, writings of black professors began to be published.

The "dean" of black scholarship in religion is without doubt C. Eric Lincoln, who was a professor of sociology and religion at Union Theological Seminary during the late 1960s and early '70s and later took up a similar post at Duke University. He is the author of the classic study *The Black Muslims in America* (1961).[48] Additional texts include *My Face is Black* (1964),[49] *The Sounds of the Struggle* (1967),[50] *The Black Church since Frazier* (1974),[51] and (as editor) *The Black Experience in Religion* (1974).[52]

In addition to his many published books and articles on black religion, no one has done more than Lincoln in encouraging black scholars to write and to publish. His C. Eric Lincoln Series in

Black Religion made it possible for black scholars to publish their radical ideas.

Although Joseph Washington's *Black Religion* was strongly criticized by almost all black scholars and preachers, the importance of the text should not be minimized. Its importance is not simply the negative function it served in motivating black theologians to develop a black theology. It served a positive function that is not often emphasized. Washington's *Black Religion* was the first text to demonstrate the uniqueness of black religion, separating it from Protestantism, Catholicism, Judaism, and secularism. This was a major scholarly achievement, and it should be recognized as such. Black scholars (Gayraud Wilmore, Cecil Cone, Henry Mitchell) used his arguments to demonstrate the uniqueness of black religion even though they rejected his negative appraisal of it. Washington actually reconsidered his views in his next book, *The Politics of God* (1967).[53] His *Black and White Power Subreption* (1969)[54] was an important treatment of the theology of black power, and his *Black Sects and Cults* (1972)[55] represented a further investigation of the African roots of black religion.

The first texts on black theology were my *Black Theology and Black Power* (1969) and *A Black Theology of Liberation* (1970). Both used liberation as the central theme of the gospel message and thus as the organizing principle for the systematic presentation of the Christian gospel from the standpoint of the black struggle for freedom. The next volume, with a similar purpose in mind, was *God of the Oppressed* (1975).

J. Deotis Roberts is an important scholar in black theology; he has published several texts and many articles on the theme, the most important being *Liberation and Reconciliation: A Black Theology* (1971) and *Black Political Theology* (1974). Roberts is best known for an emphasis on reconciliation along with liberation in contrast to what he regarded as my one-sided stress on the latter.

A similar treatment to Roberts was Major Jones's *Black Awareness: A Theology of Hope* (1971) and his *Christian Ethics for Black Theology* (1974).[56] His ethics and theology are closer to those of Martin Luther King, Jr., with an emphasis on love and reconciliation in black-white relationships. Although I have been

critical of both Roberts's and Jones's views in black theology—
because of what I considered as overemphasis on white theological norms for black theology—they will always be regarded as
among the major interpreters of black theology, bridging the gap
between the Martin King era and the rise of black power in religion and in the churches.[57]

No one has provided a deeper challenge to black theology than
has the philosophical critique of William Jones. His book, *Is God
a White Racist?* (1973),[58] shook black theologians out of their
"liberation complacency" and forced them to deal with the problem of theodicy at a deeper level. If God is liberating the black
poor from oppression, as black theologians say, where is the liberation event that can serve as evidence of that fact? The question
has not been answered to anyone's satisfaction, and thus continues to serve as a check against the tendency of substituting liberation rhetoric for actual events of freedom.

Another text that sparked a great deal of discussion was that by
Cecil W. Cone, *The Identity Crisis in Black Theology* (1975).[59]
Along with Wilmore's *Black Religion and Black Radicalism*
(1972) and important articles by Charles H. Long, Cecil Cone's
book criticized black liberation theologians for their emphasis on
political liberation and also for their dependence on white theologians, thereby separating them from the religion of the "Almighty Sovereign God" of the black people. He claimed that an
authentic black theology must use black religion as its chief
source.

Although Wilmore agreed with Cecil Cone regarding black religion as the chief source of black theology, he disagreed with him
regarding *who* had the identity crisis. According to Wilmore,
"the crisis is not in black theology but in the contemporary black
church."[60] Wilmore's perspective on black religion and theology
is persuasively argued in his *Black Religion and Black Radicalism*.

Differing with Cecil Cone at a different point was Charles
Long, who questioned whether a black theology of liberation is
possible in any sense if one takes black religion seriously. He
claims that theology is a discipline of European conquerors and
thus alien to the experience of blacks who have been enslaved by
them.[61]

I have already discussed the significant impact of Albert Cleage's *Black Messiah* (1968); his *Black Christian Nationalism* (1972)[62] is a practical analysis of his theological program. Other early interpreters of black theology and religion included Henry Mitchell (*Black Preaching* [1970][63] and *Black Belief* [1975]);[64] Lawrence Jones, who wrote important articles in history;[65] Preston Williams, Herbert Edwards, and Carlton Lee, who made contributions in social ethics;[66] Robert Bennett in Bible studies;[67] Bishop Joseph Johnson and Warner Traynham in theology.[68] Leonard Barrett's *Soul Force* (1974)[69] is an important study of black religion in the U.S.A., Africa, and the West Indies.

No list of literature in black theology and religion of the 1960s and early '70s would be complete without mentioning the outstanding work of Vincent Harding. His essay "No Turning Back?" is required reading for anyone interested in a critical interpretation of the documents of the NCBC. His "Black Power and the American Christ" and "The Religion of Black Power" are important for an interpretation of the mood that gave birth to black power and the challenge it presented to a religion of love based on the typical American theological perspective.

Since the late 1960s and early '70s many black scholars have been writing in the area of black theology, dwelling on different aspects and variations on the theme of liberation. The Fund for Theological Education and the Society for the Study of Black Religion, both then under the direction of C. Shelby Rooks (later president of Chicago Theological Seminary), did much to support and to encourage young black scholars.[70]

Although the number of black theologians has increased since 1966, there are still significant problems to be addressed in relation to the strengths and weaknesses of black theology in terms of its origin and present state. And if we black theologians are hesitant to critically evaluate our work, then we should ask: For whom do we do theology—for ourselves or the black poor? If the latter, then we must critically evaluate our work in order to assess whether it is accomplishing what we claim.

Chapter IV

Strengths and Weaknesses
in the Early Development
of Black Theology

Black theology is not an unsophisticated, anti-intellectual reaction to whatever is happening at any moment in time—a mixture of emotion and pious propaganda. It is, rather, a hardheaded, practical, and passionate reading of the signs of the times in the white community as well as the black. It is an elucidation of what we have understood God to be about in our history, particularly in the history of our struggle against racist oppression. . . . Black theology was formulated by Christian activists in response to events—events which had the unmistakable sign that God is saying and doing something about black people in white America.

Gayraud S. Wilmore[1]

Every theology is limited by the social location of the ones who create it. This is true of black theologians and preachers who created black theology with the Bible in one hand and the newspaper in the other. Black theology, as Wilmore has put it, is "eventful theology"[2]—that is, a theology that came into being through black theologians' response to the eventful happenings of their time. They believed that God was involved in the revolu-

78

tion that was erupting in America, and their task was that of identifying God's liberating presence in the events so they could announce the coming kingdom of freedom and participate in its implementation.

Because theology is limited by the place and time of its creation, it is important for theology to evaluate itself critically, identifying its strengths and weaknesses, so that it can build upon the former and, as much as possible, avoid the latter. If theology does not become self-critical, it will definitely lose its Christian identity by becoming nothing but an academic reflection of the self-interest of those who do it.

Black theologians have been particularly critical of white theology because of its lack of self-criticism in relation to racism. That criticism will continue to have credibility only to the degree that black theologians apply to themselves what they say is lacking in white theology.

As one of the early interpreters of black theology, I cannot claim to be perfectly objective in my evaluation. Despite this limitation, I shall attempt to be self-critical regarding black theology, realizing that my own personal involvement in it necessarily prevents me from seeing what may be some of its most obvious and serious limitations.

THE STRENGTHS OF NASCENT BLACK THEOLOGY

Faith and Struggle

The most original and lasting contribution of black theology has been its ability to relate creatively the Christian faith and the black freedom struggle in American society. Although black preachers, before and after the Civil War, had already made important contributions in this area, it was the NCBC black clergy radicals who deepened the connection between the gospel and the struggle to the degree that it has acquired a permanent place in the theology and activity of the black church. Some conservative members of the black clergy tried to ignore the radical, political side of their heritage, but they found it increasingly more difficult to deny it when confronted with the persuasive historical analysis of Gayraud Wilmore's *Black Religion and Black Radicalism* and its contemporary manifestation in the writings and activities of the NCBC clergy.

The central question that gave birth to black theology was: "What has the gospel of Jesus to do with the oppressed black people's struggle for justice in American society?" The radical black NCBC clergy pursued a substantial examination of that question, which separated them from both white liberal and black conservative church persons. In the process of rereading the Bible in the light of black history, black clergy radicals concluded that both biblical and black histories revealed God's unqualified solidarity with the poor in their fight against injustice. This revelation disclosed *God's salvation* as being identical with *human liberation*. In the United States, black theologians were the first to identify liberation with salvation, and thus with the core of the Christian gospel. It was in this context that they began to refer to God as the liberator of the oppressed Hebrew slaves in Egypt and to Jesus as the new liberator whom God has anointed "to preach the good news to the poor, to proclaim release to the captives, and to set at liberty those who are oppressed" (Luke 4:18, 19, RSV).

White liberal and black conservative preachers distanced themselves from the radical NCBC interpretation of the gospel as liberation, and many openly claimed that the gospel could not be identified with the politics of the poor or the rich, black or white. White biblical and theological experts often looked with a condescending scholarly arrogance upon our biblical exegesis, saying in essence that anyone with appropriate theological training knows that the gospel cannot be identical with the black struggle for justice. But black theologians refused to retreat from their claim that the God of the Bible is the liberator of victims of oppression. If that theological claim has any merit, they concluded, then the God of Jesus must be identified with the politics of black liberation.

Subsequent to black theologians' identification of the gospel with liberation, this theme has been enlarged with their discovery of similar emphases in the writings of feminist and Third World theologians in Latin America, Africa, Asia, and the Caribbean. Even many white biblical scholars have begun to give lip service to the centrality of the liberation theme in the Bible. But it is significant that black theologians were the first in the United States to identify liberation as the heart of the gospel of Jesus.

Attack on Racism

Another contribution of black theology was its exposure of and attack on racism in the white church and its theology. Although blacks have always identified racist acts as un-Christian, they had seldom claimed that racism in white churches excluded them from the Christian community. Of course white theologians and preachers, with perhaps a few exceptions, have not defended racism (certainly not as openly and consistently as in South Africa). But it was the black NCBC clergy that exposed the existence of racism in white churches and condemned it for what it was: an un-Christian heresy. This prophetic denunciation of white racism also made members of the black clergy realize that an alternative theology was needed if they were going to develop an interpretation of the gospel that would empower blacks in their liberation struggle.

According to the NCBC, racism was not limited to the obscene acts of the Ku Klux Klan; it was also seen as being embedded in American "law and order" and was justified and perpetuated by white religion. Through the rise of black power and James Forman's *Black Manifesto*, NCBC clergy radicals were determined to challenge the institutional character of white racism in American society and its churches. Their claim was that the church cannot be Christian and racist at the same time. If a church is racist, it cannot be Christian. Black clergy radicals refused to discuss degrees of racism with whites, as if one could be somewhat racist and still be Christian. Blacks told whites to redistribute power in the church and society *or* blacks would treat them as heretics— that is, enemies of the gospel of Jesus.

Of course, NCBC black clergy radicals were not the first to attack the racist bent of white churches. Denunciation of white racism by black and white abolitionists are well known, especially since David Walker's "Appeal," Garnet's "Address," and the writings of Frederick Douglass. A similar denunciation was made by Martin King in his efforts to create the "beloved community" in America. The difference between the NCBC denunciation of white racism and that of other black clergy before them was the connection of its analysis with black power, thereby expanding the definition to place the primary emphasis on the institutional manifestations of racism—namely, the absence of black power. The NCBC claimed that black power was the only remedy to white racism. Anything less may remove its obscene public symbols but not its deadly roots embedded in northern white sociopolitical and religious structures as much as in their southern counterparts. According to the NCBC, racism was found wherever blacks did not have power commensurate with their numbers—and commensurate with the justice long denied them.

Accent on Black History and African Heritage

The black clergy radicals' rereading of black history in the context of their attack on white racism led to a deeper appreciation of their cultural past, extending back through slavery to Africa. "Black" replaced "Negro" and Africa acquired a special importance as black theologians searched for the theological meaning of their historical roots. "What has Africa to do with African-Americans?" That was the question that inspired our theological imagination and made us realize that Western Christianity could not exhaust the theological meaning of our religious past. The NCBC "Message to the Churches from Oakland" stated:

> We black people are a religious people. From the earliest recorded time we have acknowledged a Supreme Being. With the fullness of our physical bodies and emotions we have unabashedly worshiped him with shouts of joy and in the tears of pain and anguish. We neither believe that God is dead, white, nor captive to some highly nationalistic and dogmatic formulations of the Christian faith which relate him exclusively to the canons of the Old and New Testaments.[3]

It was Gayraud Wilmore who brought the theological significance of blackness and Africa into NCBC documents. His *Black Religion and Black Radicalism* analyzed black religion as defined by its African heritage. Looking back, Wilmore said that the

NCBC "launched the first attempt since Garveyism to separate mainline black Christianity from the theology of the white churches and conceived liberation in the context of the legitimate use of ethnic consciousness and power."[4]

Others who supported Wilmore and also made significant published contributions included Henry Mitchell, Leonard Barrett, Charles Long, Albert Raboteau, and Cecil Cone.[5] The investigation of the relationship between Africa and black religion in the U.S.A. had a profound effect on the interpretations of black theology. The emphasis on Africa and ethnic consciousness, along with the liberation theme, separated black theology from the religion of white churches. With the accent on Africa, the theme of *survival* was combined with that of liberation—the latter being influenced most by biblical and black church histories, and the former derived from African religions and philosophy.[6]

Due to my limited knowledge of the impact of Africa upon black religion in the U.S.A., black theologians were particularly critical of my inordinate dependence upon European theology and philosophy in my initial efforts to develop a black theology of liberation. If theology is to be black, must it not use the cultural resources in black and African history for an explication of its identity? Can theology be black if it uses European theological and philosophical concepts as the primary tools for its interpretation of human existence? Black theologians forced these questions upon me, making it impossible to do black theology apart from a serious encounter with black history and culture.

The idea of a black God and a black Christ began to acquire a deeper meaning than merely that of a reference to the political and economic liberation of blacks. It acquired a cultural meaning that was unique to blacks as defined by their slave and African past. Although black theologians need to do much more historical investigation in this area, we have called to the attention of the black Christian community the theological significance of its African heritage.

Challenge to Conservative Black Churches

Just as black theology attacked the racism in white churches, it also criticized the conservative posture of black churches that tolerated racism. Although the black church was born in slavery as a beacon of liberation for enslaved Africans, the black church of the 1960s seemed to have forgotten its liberating heritage. Many young blacks of the urban ghettoes dismissed the black church because they did not see any real distinction between its gospel and the religion of whites. Furthermore, most black church leaders seemed unconcerned about the black struggle for freedom in society and focused their emphasis on a heavenly freedom in the next world. NCBC radicals attacked the pie-in-the-sky religion of black churches as an imitation of white religion. In *Black Theology and Black Power* I wrote:

> So far, the black church has remained conspicuously silent, continuing its business as usual. The holding of conferences, the election of bishops, the fund-raising drive for a new building or air conditioner seem to be more important than the blacks who are shot because they want to be [human]. The black church, though spatially located in the community of the oppressed, has not responded to the needs of its people. It has, rather, drained the community, seeking to be more and more like the white church. Its ministers have condemned the hopeless and have mimicked the values of whites. For this reason most black power people bypass the church as irrelevant to their objectives.[7]

When NCBC and other black theologians criticized the black church for its failure to proclaim and to be an embodiment of liberation in the black struggle, it was the first time that a significant group *from within* the black church publicly questioned the integrity of its mission. Of course, other black historians and sociologists, and other blacks, have often criticized the black church for its pie-in-the-sky religion, which seems to benefit materially only the ministers who proclaim it. On several occasions, Martin King made similar criticisms for the failure of many black churches to be involved in the civil rights movement. But it was radical ministers, with a black power consciousness, who leveled a sustained critique of the black church for failing to be in the 1960s what it was in its origin in the late eighteenth and throughout most of the nineteenth century.

Unfortunately, black theologians did not continue their critique of the black churches throughout the 1970s. Part of the reason had to do with black theologians' desire to establish a link with the mainline black churches. I shall have more to say about black theology and black churches in the next chapter.

Accent on Black Ecumenism

With the rise of black theology, it became clear that the denominational identities that black churches derived from the white churches from which they separated were completely irrelevant in our struggle for freedom. As Malcolm X taught us:

> When we come together, we don't come together as Baptists or Methodists. You don't catch hell because you are a Baptist, and you don't catch hell because you are a Methodist . . . , you don't catch hell because you're a Democrat or a Republican, you don't catch hell because you are a Mason or an Elk, and you sure don't catch hell because you're an American; because if you were an American, you wouldn't catch hell. You catch hell because you're a black [person]. You catch hell, all of us catch hell for the same reason.[8]

The NCBC was created in order to transcend the denominational barriers that separated black churches. Beyond that they created an ecumenical vision that sought solidarity with the advocates of black power and other radical spokespersons in the black liberation struggle, persons "outside" the churches. NCBC members knew that the only way to make the black churches a viable vehicle of black liberation was to eliminate division among the churches through a political commitment as defined by the black consciousness movement.

A black ecumenism that was defined by a radical commitment to the black poor sounded new to most twentieth-century black church persons. Martin King's civil rights movement created a similar ecumenical spirit, but it was destroyed with the rise of black power. But NCBC radicals were determined to reestablish communications and solidarity with those radicals who had broken with King. Black clergy radicals wanted to convince secular black activists that one can be radically black and also Christian. For according to the NCBC, one's Christian identity is defined more by one's commitment to the liberation of the poor than by repeating a confession of faith in Jesus written by Europeans.

THE WEAKNESSES OF NASCENT BLACK THEOLOGY

Because theology is a human undertaking, it reflects the limitations of those who do it. I wish to point out four interrelated weaknesses in the development of black theology by black theologians and preachers.

Negative Overreaction to White Racism

We allowed our definition of black theology to be too much a *reaction* to racism in the white churches and society. A new black theological consciousness began with the publication of the "Black Power Statement" on July 31, 1966. It was written primarily as a reaction to the white church establishment that assumed that its liberal and neoorthodox theologies provided the most appropriate answer to the issues raised by black power. Instead of rejecting black power as the sin of pride among blacks (as whites asserted), black clergy radicals endorsed it as an appropriate assertion of black dignity in the context of conscienceless white power.

On November 6, 1966, black clergy radicals issued another statement, "Racism and the Elections: The American Dilemma, 1966." As Gayraud Wilmore said, "Its purpose was to speak to the issues of racism and power on the eve of a congressional election threatened by white-backlash candidates seeking to exploit the civil disorders in Chicago, Cleveland, and other northern cities that year."[9] Then came the third statement, "The Powell Affair—A Crisis of Morals and Faith," in reaction to the expulsion of Congressman Adam Clayton Powell from his seat as chairman of the powerful House Labor and Education Committee.[10] Another important statement emerged in reaction to and out of the NCC conference on "The Church and the Urban Crisis" in September 1967. This statement publicized the growing rift between black and white members of the clergy.

With the NCBC statements "Urban Mission in a Time of Crisis" (April 5, 1968), "Response to the Black Manifesto" (May 7, 1969), "Black Theology (June 13, 1969), "A Message to the Churches from Oakland" (November 11–14, 1969), and "The Black Declaration of Independence" (July 4, 1970), a black theological perspective was developing that was shaped almost entirely by its reaction to white racism in the churches and in society.[11]

A similar weakness is found in my early texts on black theology, especially *Black Theology and Black Power* and *A Black Theology of Liberation*. It was as if the sole basis for black theology were racism among whites. But if so, and if racism were eliminated, then there would be no need for a theology based on the history and culture of blacks. I said:

> The appearance of black theology on the American scene then is due exclusively to the failure of white religionists to relate the gospel of Jesus to the pain of being black in a white racist society. It arises from the need of black people to liberate themselves from white oppressors.[12]

Black theology, then, was being created out of a negative reaction to whites rather than as a positive reaction to the history and culture of blacks.

Although no one was as guilty as I of defining black theology as a reaction to white racism, it was also a prevalent theme in the works of most major black theologians, including J. Deotis Roberts, Preston Williams, Major Jones, Cecil Cone, Leon Watts, Gayraud Wilmore, and others. A measure of reaction was necessary and appropriate because racism is evil and must be attacked and destroyed. But one's theological vision must be derived from something more than merely a reaction to one's enemy.

Again it was Gayraud Wilmore who accented the need to base black theology upon a foundation that was more than just a reaction to something else. He urged us to turn to black and African history in search of our theological roots so that black theology could become something more than the mere "blackenization" of white Western Christianity. Others including Charles Long,

Henry Mitchell, and Cecil Cone joined Wilmore in this emphasis, and I was greatly instructed by them.

Lack of Social Analysis

The response of black theologians to white racism was based too much upon moral suasion and too little upon the tools of social analysis. The assumption of the black clergy radicals of the NCBC was that the racism of white members of the clergy could be eliminated through an appeal to their moral guilt and consciousness as Christians. Although the un-Christian behavior of whites caused us to question their Christian identity, we still assumed that if the contradiction between racism and Christianity were clearly pointed out to them, they would change and act in a Christian manner. We were naive, because our analysis of the problem was too superficial and did not take into consideration the links between racism, capitalism, and imperialism, on the one hand, and theology and the church on the other. The connection between theology and racism became clear to us only gradually, because we did not have the theological training that could offer a serious intellectual challenge to Euro-American theology. Though we were convinced that white theology was racist, we could not articulate this conviction conceptually. The inability to articulate the theological meaning of the relationship of Christianity to blackness created a theological ambiguity in the early NCBC documents. If we had used the tools of the social sciences and had given due recognition to the Christian doctrine of sin, then it is unlikely that we would have placed such inordinate dependence on the methodology of moral suasion.

No one has given a more creative critique of the early NCBC documents than Vincent Harding in his "No Turning Back?" It is required reading for all black church members who have a radical bent. He points out the integrationist slant of the 1966 "Black Power Statement," which speaks of "our beloved country, of basically American goals, and of the desire for participation 'at all levels of the life of our nation.' "[13] There is no creative social analysis and thus no program for radical change. It seems that we thought that change would occur through rhetoric alone. There is no analysis of the depth of racism or capitalism.

One reason for this serious limitation is related to the middle-class origins of black theologians and preachers, as well as the ecclesiastical context of the documents. The NCBC was reacting almost exclusively to white churches, and there was not much dialogue outside the context defined by our reaction to whites. As Vincent Harding expressed it:

> The churchmen were essentially reactors, not initiating concepts or programs, but answering, interpreting the initiatives of others. They had been called together by crisis—like so many black protestors—and had not developed an ideology beyond blackness, or a set of prophetic directions for black struggle. So they were forced to be vague. Indeed, there were not even any significant specific initiatives proposed for a movement to integrate into American society. Somehow, as a group, they were unprepared to provide them, and it was this lack of its own clear thrust, its own initiating point of view, which crippled the NCBC position.[14]

The appeal to the moral goodness of whites reflected the continued influence of Martin King rather than that of Malcolm X. The content of the NCBC message was still derived primarily from Martin King, but the militant spirit in which the black clergy expressed it suggested a definite movement toward Malcolm X. The emergence of black theology, then, is due to the attempt of black theologians to integrate a cleavage in black life: Martin and Malcolm, Christianity and blackness, Christian love and a militant defense of black dignity. This was the paradox that captivated us and demanded a theological resolution. It was also the paradox that revealed our most serious limitations.

When a people's response to a situation of oppression is defined exclusively by its feelings of moral outrage, an appeal to the morality of the oppressor usually follows. This method of change is found throughout black history, from Frederick Douglass to Martin Luther King, Jr. It is the typical response of integrationists, because they are firm believers in the American Dream as defined by the Declaration of Independence and the faith of American churches. The early interpreters of black theology fall within this tradition, even though we were moving toward the nationalist philosophy of Malcolm X. The assumption behind the choice of the method of moral suasion was that the oppressor was unaware of the depth of the evil of racism, and that if its demonic consequences were revealed and acknowledged, the oppressor would be morally embarrassed and stop being racist.

How wrong we were about that assumption can be seen in the responses of the white churches to the crisis created by James Forman's *Black Manifesto*. The typical white response to the demand for reparations was to "thank God for the challenge," and then proceed to ignore the issue or to set up structures of response that could be controlled. Because the NCBC did not want white churches to seize upon the "un-Christian" appearance and tactics of Forman as an excuse to avoid the legitimate demands for reparations, its board of directors issued a statement saying that NCBC was "ready to participate in whatever conference or negotiations may ensue from the demands of our brothers for the reparational relief of the suffering of black people."[15] But white church members did not care whether it was Forman or Jesus himself; they had no intention of making a response to the *Manifesto* commensurate with the depth of black suffering that they and their ancestors had created. But we were too naive to realize that, and we thus continued to articulate the moral justice of reparations, expecting white Christians to feel guilty and respond to the demands of the *Manifesto*. Inasmuch as we had already issued a similar demand about a year earlier with our statement "Urban Mission in the Time of Crisis" (April 5, 1968), we should have known that whites would ignore the *Manifesto* as they had the earlier demand. No one achieves freedom through a mere moral demand for justice, and whites knew that NCBC radicals could not force them to "divest themselves of their own great wealth" or "force the transfer of requisite countervailing power to oppressed people."[16]

The NCBC "Message to the Churches from Oakland" and the "Black Declaration of Independence" revealed the despair of black clergy radicals, because they now knew that whites were not about to "negotiate in good faith." They acknowledged "the harsh reality that white churches and church structures are not capable of positive responses to the considered opinions of their black peers."[17]

The decline of the NCBC is directly related to its failure to anticipate the nonresponse of whites and its failure to develop a program that included something more than black militant rhetoric. Referring to the NCBC "unprogramed radicalization," Vincent Harding correctly analyzed our problem:

> The documents . . . remind us of how nearly impossible it has been for the radical rhetoric to be transformed into radical action. They remind us that the men who control the systems of American oppression have consistently found ways either to cajole, co-opt, threaten, or destroy a frighteningly large portion of those black leaders who move in such radical directions. They remind us that the system itself has managed to absorb just enough changes demanded to assuage the immediate hurts. . . . Perhaps most importantly, they remind us that rhetoric has not often been turned into action, because rhetoric did not become analysis and analysis did not develop program and program did not lead to insistent, careful organizing of our people to effect radical change.[18]

If we had studied history, analyzed the reality of our situation, and developed programs for radical change through sustained teaching and organizing, then we, perhaps, could have avoided some of our mistakes. Because black clergy radicals failed to analyze comprehensively the nature of the system and the method and goals that we had set for ourselves, we allowed ourselves to become entrapped in blatant contradictions. For example, although the NCBC and black caucuses attacked white religion on the basis of black power philosophy, their organizational existence depended on money from the white churches that they attacked. Black independent churches did not involve themselves in the attack on white religion and thus did not provide much financial support for the NCBC. NCBC support came from the pressure that black executives applied to their white constituencies.

The same critique that Malcolm X made regarding the white support of Martin King and other integrationist participants in the civil rights movement is applicable here. Any movement of freedom that is dependent upon the oppressor's support for survival is doomed to failure from the start. First, white church members implemented the failure by insisting that their money be limited to the black caucuses in their own denomination. That decision meant that the NCBC, an ecumenical group, would be left with little or no funding. Secondly, white church executives chose to promote their own trusted black executives into power positions in the church organizational structure, with the result that black caucuses found themselves fighting their own black brothers and sisters rather than whites.

If black is the sole criterion for right and wrong, what is a black caucus to do when black executives say that their occupancy of high offices means that progress is taking place and racism is being eliminated? In some instances, white church officials even set up their own programs or commissions to fight racism and they chose their favorite blacks to head them. It was like letting Jesse James choose a posse to catch him. The failure of blacks to anticipate this move by whites led to a decline of black caucuses and thus to the end of the black attack on white religion by blacks in white churches.

As I reflect back over our early history, evaluating our strengths and weaknesses, Vincent Harding's question continues to haunt me:

> Shall we continue to be reactors to the thrusts of white racism, producing eloquent protest documents by the ton and alienated black [persons] by the hundreds? Or shall we create programs and organizations and institutions which capture the initiative for our people and provide alternatives to alienation, romanticism, cooptation, and despair?[19]

Lack of Economic Analysis

Related to our failure to move beyond moral suasion to the development of radical programs for change based on social analysis was our avoidance of Marxism as a tool for economic analysis. The black church in particular and the black community generally have a long history of avoiding Marxism, as I shall detail in chapter 9.[20] Avoidance is partly due to the mutual marginality of Marxists and the black community, as well as the sectarian nature of the former and the reformist attitudes of the latter.

Therefore, it is understandable, though not to their best interests, that black churches have remained aloof from Marxism, especially because it has always been difficult to separate Marxism as a tool of social analysis from Marxism as an atheistic ideology. How could one expect barely literate black church members to embrace a sectarian philosophy such as Marxism while living in the belly of the beast of capitalism?

However, when one reflects upon the 1960s and '70s, it can be argued that black clergy radicals could have deepened their radicalism by using Marxism as an instrument (not ideology) for analyzing the institutions of racism. They had tried integration while following King and later moved toward Malcolm's nationalist philosophy. Both responses have a long history in the black community and neither has achieved alone or together our desired goal—liberation! That fact alone should open us up for new ideas so that we can move beyond the rhetoric of a moral appeal.

Because of the success of Marxism in the Third World and because Soviet Russia no longer defines its essential meaning, young black radicals of the black power era began to experiment with it. The Black Panthers of Oakland are well known for their Marxist bent. Others included the League of Revolutionary Black Workers[21] and several black power advocates in the SNCC. In fact, the preamble to James Forman's *Black Manifesto* was defined by a neo-Marxist ideology. This provided an occasion for black clergy radicals to face head-on the question of Marxism as a tool for analysis. But to my knowledge, we did not even consider the issue seriously. In fact when the NCBC board of directors responded to the *Manifesto,* it did not even mention the Marxist analysis on which it was based, nor did Gayraud Wilmore deal seriously with Marxism in his theological response. The NCBC focused on the demands, not the philosophy. It was not until whites referred to the Marxist philosophy in the *Manifesto* as an excuse for rejecting the demands that the NCBC took up the issue. But even then, we did not really consider Marxism seriously. In our most radical posture (as in the "Message to the Churches From Oakland"), we avoided the issue:

> We do not shrink from the revolutionary, anticapitalistic implications of the *Manifesto*. While all of our members do

not give unqualified endorsement of every strategy and tac-
tic stated or implied in the original document issued in Detroit, the National Committee of Black Churchmen, as a
body, is committed to the essential spirit and meaning of the
analysis and proposals, and will continue to press them
upon the churches and synagogues of America.[22]

What was true of the NCBC was also true of the major interpreters of black theology during its early stages. None of my early
texts dealt with Marxism, and the same is true of other black
theologians. This was due partly to a limited educational exposure and partly to an internalization of the ideal of the American
Dream. Despite our black militant rhetoric, we wanted a piece of
the capitalistic American pie, and that was one reason why we
rejected Marxism. Furthermore, when some of us got a little piece
of that pie, we quickly lost our radicalism and became "big-time"
executives and seminary professors. In fact, the absence of a
comprehensive theological vision defined by the scientific tool of
social analysis always leaves open the door to unchecked opportunism among those who claim to be the leaders of the masses.

My first serious encounter with Marxist thought took place at a
WCC symposium on black theology and Latin American liberation theology (May 1973). Present from Latin America were
Hugo Assmann and Paulo Freire, both of whom emphasized the
importance of Marxist class analysis. Assmann felt so strongly
about it that our communication was strained, because Marxist
analysis was conspicuously absent in my perspective on black
theology, and an analysis of racism was conspicuously absent in
his theology (and he a citizen of Brazil with more than 40 million
blacks!). I remained cool toward Marxism.[23]

Black theologians also encountered Latin American liberation
theologians at the TIA conference in Detroit in 1975.[24] About
twenty of us met together because of heated public discussions
regarding the interrelatedness of racial and class oppression. The
dialogue was even more intense in our private meeting, with many
black theologians avidly promoting capitalism over socialism. It
was at that time that it became clear to me that either black
theology would incorporate class analysis into its perspective or it
would become a justification of middle-class interests at the ex-

pense of the black poor. Although claiming to speak for the poor, we actually speak for ourselves.

No one else has excoriated the opportunism in the black middle classes as sharply as E. Franklin Frazier. Although written over twenty-five years ago, much of his *Black Bourgeoisie* still rings true today:

> The lack of interest of the black bourgeoisie . . . in the broader issues facing the modern world is due to the fact that the Negro has developed no economic or social philosophy except the opportunistic philosophy that the black intelligentsia has evolved to justify its anomalous and insecure position. . . . [Therefore] when the opportunity has been present, the black bourgeoisie has exploited the Negro masses as ruthlessly as have whites. As the intellectual leaders in the Negro community, they have never dared think beyond a narrow, opportunistic philosophy that provided a rationalization for their own advantages.[25]

It is most revealing that even as I write these pages, black theologians generally still have not dealt seriously with the class problem in the black community as defined by Marxism. One significant exception is Cornel West's *Prophesy Deliverance!*, and he is a recent participant in our discussions.

Since the 1975 encounter with the Latin Americans, I have become convinced that economic analysis is not only an option but a necessity (see chap. 9, below). I am concerned about black theologians' silence on Marxism. How can we provide a genuine check against the self-interest of black theologians and preachers who merely use the language of liberation and the gospel in order to justify their professional advancement? Unless black theologians and preachers face the class issue, the integrity of our commitment to justice for the poor will remain suspect to other freedom fighters and to the poor we claim to represent. Again Frazier was right:

> Although the black bourgeoisie exercise considerable influence on the values of Negroes, they do not occupy a dignified position in the Negro community. The masses re-

gard the black bourgeoisie as simply those who have been
"lucky in getting money," which enables them to engage in
conspicuous consumption. When this class pretends to represent the best manners or morals of the Negro, the masses
regard such claims as hypocrisy.[26]

The absence of the tools of social analysis may also explain why
the black church tends to be as conservative as white churches on
other social issues besides racism: women's rights, gay rights, and
similar human concerns. We were also slow in taking a stand
against the U.S. involvement in Vietnam, not to mention other
Third World countries. Asia, Africa, and Latin America were not
referred to in NCBC documents until the end of the 1960s, when
the Third World was mentioned in a cursory manner. The same
was true of other interpreters of black theology. It was as if we
were blind to the global nature of human oppression. Martin King
was miles ahead of us on that issue; and it is ironic that many of us
thought he was too conservative! The fact is that he was in many
ways too radical, because he was moving toward an economic
analysis, and some say even Marxism.[27]

The reason why King was and still is more radical than the
clergy of the NCBC and other interpreters of black theology was
the integrity of his commitment and the depth of his analysis.
Commitment without analysis leads to romanticism and eventually to despair. Analysis without commitment leads to opportunism and eventually to a betrayal of one's people. The black
community needs black theologians who have both a commitment to their people's liberation and the intellectual expertise
needed to analyze the nature of their oppression.

Lack of Sexual Analysis

Although I will discuss sexism in black theology and the black
church in some detail later (chapter 6), it is important to identify it
as a serious weakness among the early interpreters of black
theology. Like our failure to deal with classism, sexism blinded us
to the depth of the problem of oppression in the black community, and it stifled the development of the human resources for
fighting against it. I realize that it was not likely that we could

have been progressive and prophetic enough to view sexism as a problem to be addressed in the black community and the society at large. But I believe that the gospel combined with social analysis provides Christians with insight into evil that others often overlook. That is what creates prophets: the gift of God's grace combined with critical interpretation.

I regret very much that we black theologians missed a great opportunity by failing to relate the problem of racism to sexism. We were confronted with the issue by the presence of so many women in our churches and so few in leadership positions. We were also confronted with the problems of women in the ministry and the society through the emergence of feminism in the white community. But most black males in the ministry labeled women's liberation as a "white thing." I can remember my reluctance to even consider the issue, and I am greatly embarrassed by my silence and by the sexist language of my early works on black theology.

I introduce this weakness in this chapter because if we blacks are not self-critical in regard to our historical failings, we will not be able to correct ourselves in the present so that we can create a meaningful future. As we shall see later, it is unfortunate that the black church has not moved much further today than it did in the 1960s in addressing this problem. I hope that by identifying sexism as a serious problem in the black community, ministers and laypersons will recognize the need to face this issue head-on. I know of no black theologian or minister who addressed sexism as a serious issue in the black community during the 1960s. Our failure to deal with this problem weakened our struggle for liberation. If black theologians do not acknowledge this problem with the intentions of overcoming it, I see no way that the problem of racism can be eliminated. Sexism, racism, and classism though not identical are interconnected, and thus none can be adequately dealt with without also dealing with the others.

Black theologians and ministers, men and women, have major problems to face in the church and the society. Will we be able to face them adequately and thereby create structures in our churches and the community that are liberating? Do we have the *courage* to "tell it like it is," not only in relation to white racism but also in regard to sexism and classism in our churches and our community? Telling the truth can be a risky venture in a church that defines its life on the basis of the professional self-interest of its leaders. It is always much easier to tell the truth about others, and black theologians and preachers have done this task well. But the critical test of the gospel that we preach is whether we can tell the truth about ourselves. For I believe that the gospel of Jesus demands that we tell the truth about our churches that claim to be Christian but in fact has denied that faith with devilish deeds. In the remainder of this book, I will investigate the faithfulness of the black church in relation to urgent problems in our contemporary world in hope that we will face up to our responsibility to live in solidarity with those who are struggling for freedom.

Chapter V

Black Theology
and the Black Church

*One of the continuing paradoxes of the black church as the
custodian of a great portion of black culture and black religion is that it is at once the most reactionary and the most
radical of black institutions; the most imbued with the
mythology and values of white America, and yet the most
proud, the most independent and indigenous collectivity in
the black community.*

Gayraud S. Wilmore[1]

The black church is the single most important institution in the
black community. Beginning in the late eighteenth century and
continuing to the present, it has been the oldest and most independent African-American organization. Its importance is so great
that some scholars say that the black church *is* the black community, with each having no identity apart from the other.[2] Even if
some will deny this claim, no informed person can deny the centrality of the black church in the black community. Therefore
black liberation is, at least in part, dependent upon the attitude
and role that the church assumes in relation to it.

Although African slaves were introduced to Christianity by
white preachers and missionaries who told them that it condoned
their slavery, most Africans did not accept that part of white reli-

99

gion. Despite the fact that most of them were illiterate, they adapted the "Christianity" that they received from whites to their life situation by reinterpreting the gospel as an affirmation of their identity as human beings and as an empowerment to fight for the liberation of all blacks. The outstanding achievement of the black church in service to the black community can hardly be overstated. Referring to the black church, Wilmore has appropriately said:

> Led for the most part by illiterate preachers, many of whom were slaves or recently freedmen, poverty-stricken and repressed by custom and law, [the black church] converted thousands, stabilized family life, established insurance and burial societies, founded schools and colleges, commissioned missionaries to the far corners of the world, and *at the same time* agitated for the abolition of slavery, supported illegal actions in behalf of fugitives, organized the Underground Railroad, fomented slave uprisings, promoted the Civil War, developed community political education and action in behalf of civil rights, and provided the social, economic, political, and cultural base of the entire black community in the United States.[3]

The black church has been radical, serving as the most important instrument of black liberation, but it has also been one of the most conservative institutions in the black community. This is the paradox. It has produced the Martin Luther Kings who creatively joined black religion with the struggle for justice; but it has also produced many Joseph H. Jacksons whose views on Christianity and politics were as conservative as King's were radical.[4] The reactionary, pie-in-the-sky dimension of black religion is what many critics of the church point to, and it is also something that progressive black preachers do not like to talk about in their public discourse about the church. However, because the black church is so central in the black community, and because black theology and the black church both say that they are concerned about the liberation of blacks, it is important to inquire about their past relationship to each other as they served the black community.

THE RELATIONSHIP BETWEEN BLACK THEOLOGY AND THE BLACK CHURCH: RECENT HISTORY

There has been some disagreement among black preachers and theologians regarding the relationship of black theology to the black church. There are those who would say that black theology has nothing to do with the black church, because it is an academic discipline that is taught in seminaries and universities (mostly white) and thus unrelated to the spiritual and worshiping life of the black Christian community. There are others who would say that black theology is the prophetic voice of the black church, calling it back to its liberating heritage, thereby enabling it to become a more effective instrument of black liberation. With these two sharply different versions of the importance of black theology to the black church, it is clear that some misunderstanding (if not antagonism) does exist regarding the acceptance of black theology in the black church. I hope that an investigation of their past relationship will help to create a context for a more fruitful dialogue.

In earlier chapters, black theology was described in terms of its attack on the white churches, identifying their religion as racist and thus contrary to the gospel of Jesus Christ. However, it is also important to remember that black theology also addressed the black church—both positively and negatively. On the positive side, it praised the black church for being an example of the black power that is already present in the black community. On the negative side, it criticized the otherworldly character of much of the spiritual life in the black church. For example, the 1966 "Black Power Statement" commented:

> Too often the Negro church has stirred its members away from the reign of God in *this world* to a distorted and complacent view of an otherworldly conception of God's power. We commit ourselves as churchmen to make more meaningful in the life of our institution our conviction that Jesus Christ reigns in the "here" and "now" as well as in the future he brings in upon us. We shall, therefore, use

more of the resources of our churches in working for human justice in the places of social change and upheaval where our Master is already at work.[5]

It is very important to point out that when black theology first emerged it had no existence apart from the black church. Indeed it was simply the black church criticizing itself in order to become a more effective participant in the black liberation struggle. Most of the early interpreters of black theology were members of the clergy, not seminary or university professors. They therefore viewed themselves as prophetic voices within the black church who were summoned to condemn not only racism in the white church but also the conservatism in the black church that tolerated racism. In view of the fact that the critique of the black church made by black theology is often forgotten, Wilmore has said:

> It should always be remembered that from the beginning black theology intended to speak to the black church and community about the ethnic pride, political realism, and religious radicalism hidden in the deepest recesses of the black experience but almost forgotten by black people in their rush to embrace white standards and values.[6]

Theology as prophetic self-criticism of the church is found in most of the early writings and speeches of the creators of black theology. In earlier chapters I have already discussed their statement emerging out of the NCC conference on "The Church and the Urban Crisis" (September 1967). In that document they were even more critical of black churches and of themselves as ministers for failing to be more creatively involved in the struggle for black liberation. They admitted that "as black churchmen we find ourselves in the unenviable role of the oppressor," and thus "we are in real danger of losing our existence and our reason for being, if indeed we have not already lost them."[7]

In their effort to repent of their sins they called upon black churches to reorder their priorities by making the liberation of poor blacks the central reason for the existence of the churches.

They identified five immediate concerns to which black churches should make a commitment:

1. To the establishment of freedom schools to offset the degradation and omissions of a white-dominated public school system.
2. To workshops fostering black family solidarity.
3. To training lay leadership in community organization and other relevant skills.
4. To massive efforts to give financial support to black groups working for self-determination.
5. To the removal of all images that suggest that God is white.[8]

Black clergy radicals also issued a call for the transformation of the National Committee of Negro Churchmen (NCNC) into a permanent ecumenical organization to embody their new theological vision of the black church. They called upon the NCBC:

> To establish regional offices through which every black churchman can participate in the institutional and theological renewal of black religion, enabling it to make its unique contribution to the universal church free from pernicious racism.
>
> To divest itself of internal partisan politics and ecclesiastical gamesmanship.
>
> To structure itself in such a way as to provide the kind of revolutionary impetus needed for these crucial times.
>
> To call for a conference of black theologians to consider the theological implications of black power.[9]

Thus the NCBC was emerging as the prophetic black-church voice within black churches. It represented "the remnant" within black churches, reminding them of their "original reason for being."

A similar theological critique of black churches was made by the Philadelphia Council of Black Clergy with its statement "Black Religion—Past, Present, and Future" (1968). As was true of NCBC statements, this document made a bitter attack on white religion; but its attack on the religion of contemporary black churches was equally severe. It said that "when one views the contemporary black church, it becomes abundantly clear that its main purposes . . . do not serve the needs of the people who attend these churches; but quite the contrary, they serve the needs of the larger exploitative society."[10]

With Jesus the liberator as the norm of their view of genuine Christianity, they urged the creation of religious institutions in the black community that would be a liberating force, "devoid of denominationalism, sectarianism, and any of the kind of religious traditions we are used to in America."[11] They called for honesty and frankness regarding the complete irrelevance of black churches to the urgent needs of the oppressed black community, saying that institutional patterns of those churches "are built on the very principle we are fighting against."[12]

What was needed was a new black religious force that was derived from and accountable to the black community:

> Unlike the present-day black church, it [the black religious force] will have to be authentically black and Afro-American. It is our position that there is no such entity presently existing in the black community; an entity that is authentically black. We must be cautious not to mistake thoughtless emotionalism or empty intellectualism as authentic marks of the black church; but rather we will have to use for a model our authentic prototype that existed in the slave church. When we analyze the Afro-American religious force as it was experienced in the slave community, we discover . . . that it was committed to the liberation of black people; and it embodied all of its spiritual strength toward that end. Similarly, the emerging black religious institution must also encourage and strengthen the black community toward this holy goal of liberation.[13]

In addition to the NCBC and the Philadelphia Council of Black Clergy, the black caucuses within white denominations expressed similar prophetic self-criticism. Black Methodists for Church Renewal (BMCR) is representative. Its "Black Paper" begins with a confession:

> We, a group of black Methodists in America, are deeply disturbed about the crisis of racism in America. We are

equally concerned about the failure of a number of black people, including black Methodists, to respond appropriately to the roots and forces of racism and the current black revolution.

We, as black Methodists, must first respond in a state of confession because it is only as we confront ourselves that we are able to deal with the evils and forces which seek to deny our humanity.

We confess our failure to be reconciled with ourselves as black men. We have too often denied our blackness. . . .

We confess that we have not always been relevant in service and ministry to our black brothers, and in so doing we have alienated ourselves from many of them.

We confess that we have not always been honest with ourselves and with our white brothers. We have not encountered them with truth but often with deception. We have not said in bold language and forceful action, "You have used white power in and outside the church to keep us in a subordinate position." We have failed to tell our white brothers "like it is!" Instead, we have told our white brothers what we thought they would like to hear.

We confess that we have not become significantly involved in the black revolution because, for the most part, white men have defined it as "bad"; for the other part, we have been too comfortable in our "little world," and too pleased with our lot as second-class citizens and second-class members of the Methodist Church.

We confess that we have accepted too long the philosophy of racism. This has created a relationship in which white people have always defined the "terms," and, in fact, defined when and how black people would exist.

We confess that we have accepted a "false kind of integration" in which all power remained in the hands of white men.[14]

Self-Criticism

The black church has always had outside critics from the time of its origin in slavery to contemporary black and white scholars, especially among sociologists, psychologists, and historians.[15] But seldom has the black church created the context for prophetic criticism to arise from *within*—that is, from among its own clergy and laity.[16] This fact makes these documents remarkable in the history of the black church. Never before had its ministers been as forceful and frank about the failure of their institution to serve as a liberating force in the black community. As is true of other professionals, black preachers have been critical of each other behind closed doors, but they have seldom aired the shortcomings of the black church in public. Therefore to acknowledge their own failures publicly, with the intention of making a radical change in their practice of the faith, was indeed a revolutionary step.

What was it that accounted for this radical change that created a sharp break between them and conservative black church leaders? It was their deeply felt conviction of being gripped by God's liberating Spirit and being called to follow Jesus the liberator into the ghettoes in order to liberate black humanity from unbearable suffering. The odds were against them, and they knew it. But the revolutionary Spirit that gripped them was far more powerful than the odds against which they fought. Looking back ten years later, Wilmore described it in these terms:

> Something new was happening in black Christianity between 1966 and 1969 and we knew it. Although among our members were some of the most powerful church leaders in America we knew that we were but a tiny minority of black church people with almost no support from the inner circles of the great black denominations. Even Dr. King studiously avoided us—deploring our close collaboration with the young militants of black power—and although we had penetrated some of the top leadership of the National Baptist Convention—for a brief time—we knew very well that we had no great following among millions of black people who were affiliated with that powerful citadel of black Protestantism.[17]

As black professors joined the NCBC and other radical black clergy organizations, they also advanced positive and negative critiques of the black church. Following Joseph R. Washington's interpretation of the black church before and after the Civil War, many black theologians limited their praise to the pre-Civil War black church, pointing to its involvement in the Underground Railroad, slave insurrections, and other illegal activities. They often had severe criticism for the black church after the Civil War because of its close association with the accommodation philosophy of Booker T. Washington and its failure to be at the forefront of the civil rights movement. After the Civil War, praise was limited to individuals such as Reverdy C. Ransom, Adam C. Powell, Martin Luther King, Jr., and other members of the clergy associated with the black freedom struggle.

With the creation of the NCBC, of black caucuses in white denominations, and of other religious organizations, black professors were invited to participate in the development of black theology. Preston Williams, then at the Boston University School of Theology and later at Harvard University Divinity School, became the second chairman of the NCBC theological commission, following Gayraud Wilmore. It was during his chairmanship that the "Black Theology Statement" was written and published in the *Christian Century* with his commentary. Although black professors, almost without exception, defended the black church against Joseph Washington's critique, their critique of the black church was similar to that of the black clergy in the NCBC and black caucuses.

It is difficult for me to write about the relationship of black theology to the black church without letting my own personal involvement in both of them govern my analysis. When I wrote *Black Theology and Black Power*, I was nearly as angry with the black church as I was with its white counterpart. That was why I wrote:

> It is hard to know whether to laugh or weep as the churches make bargains with the principalities and powers: prayers on public occasions, tax exemptions, shying away from vital issues, exhortation to private goodness, promotion of gutless "spirituality," institutional self-glorification—they are all knotted together in a monstrous ungodly tangle that spells death to black humanity. There is, of course, a dif-

ference between white churches and black churches. But the similarities are striking. Both have marked out their places as havens of retreat, the one to cover the guilt of the oppressors, the other to daub the wounds of the oppressed. Neither is notably identified with the tearing-healing power of Christ. Neither is a fit instrument of revolution.[18]

As one who had been an active minister and occasional pastor in the AME Church since an early age and who, as a professor of theology, had critically studied other black churches, I felt that I could make an informed evaluation regarding the possibility of renewal in the churches. But my conclusion was:

> The idea of "renewal" seems futile. Renewal suggests that there is a core of healthy, truthful substance under all the dirt and rust. But dirt can grind away a delicate mechanism, and rust can consume rather than merely cover. The white church in America, though occasionally speaking well and even more rarely acting well, generally has been and is the embodiment of what is wrong with society. It is racism in ecclesiastical robes. It lives and breathes bigotry. The black church embodies a response to racism at the level of sheer survival at the price of freedom and dignity. Both have taken the road marked "the good life," avoiding the call to discipleship, which is the call to suffering and death. For this reason, renewal in any ordinary sense seems out of the question.[19]

During the early 1970s, black clergy radicals and theologians dropped much of their negative critique of the black church and concentrated mainly on the positive, with particular emphasis on the nineteenth century. As the NCBC and black caucuses in white churches declined, the black clergy used the concept of the black church to challenge white power in their respective denominations.[20] Black professors used it in a similar manner in white seminaries.

During this period, which has been called the second stage of its development, black theology ceased to address the black church and came to be concentrated almost exclusively in seminaries and universities. Its organizational embodiment was found in the Society for the Study of Black Religion, and black professors spent most of their time writing books, training graduate students, and reading papers to each other. The black church was chiefly an object of study rather than a place to effect radical change in society.

Putting Black Theology Back in the Black Church

It was not until the mid-1970s that black theologians began to recognize the need to base black theology in the churches, as it had been during the 1960s. Several events drew special attention to the necessity of localizing black theology in the churches. Gayraud Wilmore never ceased to advocate the need to keep black theology in the churches and resist the tendency to confine it within academia. The publication of Cecil Cone's *The Identity Crisis in Black Theology* (1975) was a cogent reminder that black theology would never become a creative instrument of black liberation as long as it was primarily situated in white academia, studying white questions that had little to do with black religion.

That same year a new organization was founded, the Black Theology Project of the TIA, with a special emphasis on doing theology from the standpoint of the poor and with a mixture of grassroots persons, pastors, and theologians. It was headed by two activists, Muhammed Kenyatta, a Baptist minister, and Shawn Copeland, a Catholic sister. The Reverend Charles S. Spivey, an AME minister, chaired the board of directors.

In 1976 the NCBC issued a new statement on black theology written almost exclusively for black denominations. It was written mainly by J. Deotis Roberts, Roy Morrison, John Satterwhite, Gayraud Wilmore, and myself. It was widely distributed in a Lenten booklet under the title *Liberation and Unity*, which was sponsored by the three major black Methodist denominations, the NCBC, and the Consultation on Church Union.

During this same period, the bishops of the AME Church invited me to lead a workshop on the mission of the church in 1974 and 1975. Lawrence Jones and Bobby Joe Saucer, both of whom were teaching in New York at Union Theological Seminary at the time, also participated. However, the milestone marking the return of black theology to the black church was the Black Theology Project conference (supported by the NCBC) in Atlanta, August 1977. Pastors, theologians, and grassroots persons were all present, and it was reminiscent of the NCBC days of the 1960s.

Although the document issued by the conference was critical of the white church and society, it was addressed specifically to the black church and community. It was written by Gayraud Wilmore and Charles Spivey, who chaired the conference. The emphasis was on the "inseparability of the black church and community" and the "power of the black church."[21] This conference is seen as the beginning of the third stage of black theology, characterized by a return to the black church and community as the primary workshop of black theology, a focus on the Third World, and the identification of sexism and classism as evils along with racism.

When black theology returned to the black church, its negative critique was deemphasized and its positive side came into greater prominence. Negative critique is found in my discussions with the AME bishops, in my address at the Black Theology Project conference in Atlanta, and in the writings of Gayraud Wilmore. But it was not as sharp as in the 1960s, because we did not want to alienate black theology from its base in the black church and community.

Since the return of black theology to the setting of its origin, several black theologians have become deeply involved in serving the black church, mostly through the training of future ministers, conducting seminars and leadership training programs, participating in retreats, and writing with the black church as the primary audience. Wilmore teaches at New York Theological Seminary, a school that is especially designed to meet the needs of in-service pastors and lay leaders in the black and Hispanic communities. Lawrence Jones left Union Theological Seminary to assume the post of dean at the Howard University Divinity School in order to serve the black church and community while pastoring a major black church in Washington, D. C.

J. Deotis Roberts[22] and Major Jones, unlike most other black scholars, have always served at black seminaries, which created in them an openness to the problems in black churches that many others overlooked. The same may be said of Cecil Cone, who became the president of Edward Waters College, an AME school founded shortly after the Civil War. The late Joseph Johnson, a major interpreter of black theology, taught at the Interdenominational Theological Center for many years before his election to the episcopacy. Like Wilmore, he always advocated the necessity of keeping black theology in the churches, and for many of us he was a model for how to do it. C. Eric Lincoln has been conducting a major study of the black church with the approval and assistance of many major black churches.[23] He, along with James Forbes of Union Theological Seminary and Lawrence Jones of Howard University, has served as a consultant to the newly founded black ecumenical group called the National Congress of Black Churches, headed by Bishop John Adams of the AME Church. Partners in Ecumenism (PIE), another major black ecumenical church organization, with Donald Jacobs as executive officer and Bishop Frank Madison Reid of the AME Church as president, has used William Watley of the Consultation on Church Union and me as consultants.

With black theology moving toward and into the black church for its primary audience, a growing awareness can be observed among black Christians that we become the church only by serving those in need, especially the poor near at hand.

BLACK THEOLOGY AND THE BLACK CHURCH: STRENGTHS AND WEAKNESSES IN THEIR PAST RELATIONSHIP

The major strength of the relationship between black theology and the black church in the past was their mutual interdependence and thus common participation in the black struggle for justice. When black theology first came into being, it was the radical, prophetic voice in black churches, calling them back to their liberating nineteenth-century heritage by attacking racism and affirming black identity extending back to Africa. At this time the theologian was *in* the church, for the preacher was the theologian and the theologian was the preacher. The NCBC, the Alamo Black Clergy, the Philadelphia Council of Black Clergy, the Sons of Varick in the AMEZ Church, and other radical black clergy organizations became *the* black church within black churches, challenging them to be what they were called to be now and in the future—namely, God's liberating agency in behalf of the black poor.

The decade of the 1960s was a great moment in the history of the black church. The church was the chief support of the civil rights movement, with Martin Luther King, Jr., as its preeminent symbol, and ministers such as Wyatt T. Walker, William Jones, Jesse Jackson, Andrew Young, C. T. Vivian, and James Lawson as major leaders—to name only a few. The rise of black power and black theology took the consciousness of the black church to another level. Using black theology, the black church of the 1960s became self-critical. This was one of the healthiest periods for the black church and black theology.

Without prophetic self-criticism, churches become self-serving institutions for their ministers, officers, and members. And theology, without the Christian community as the place of its origin and its continued existence, becomes sterile academic discourse uninterested in the quality of human life in society. Fortunately black clergy radicals avoided both mistakes by creating a theology for the black church that offered negative and positive criticisms of it so that it could become a more effective instrument of liberation. If they had attacked racism without criticizing the opiate character of their own churches, their attack on the white church would have had little credibility.

The major weakness of the relationship between black theology and the black church in the past was the departure of black theology to white seminaries, universities, and churches. The NCBC, whose leadership was weighted heavily toward black clergy in white churches, began, in the late 1960s and early '70s, to direct its message almost exclusively to white Christians. Black professors did the same in white seminaries and universities. That was a grave error, as indicated by the decline of the NCBC and of black caucuses and the emergence of an identity crisis in black theology.

How could black theology retain its *black* identity by directing its message primarily to whites? Even during the earliest stage of black theology, its critique of the churches was always directed more to the white church than to the black church. This was probably due to its dependence on the black power movement, which leveled a similar attack on white society, and to the presence of a great number of black pastors and church executives in the white church as its interpreters. That was why almost all NCBC statements and early texts on black theology (especially mine) addressed their concerns to the white church and its theologians. That was also why NCBC statements were published in the *New York Times* and not the Harlem *Amsterdam News* or some other news organ in the black community.[24] We spent entirely too much of our time writing protest documents to whites, who, as we should have known, were not going to disinherit themselves of their privileges in order to relieve the suffering of the black poor. Reaction to white racism consumed too much of the mental energies that should have been directed to black churches in an effort to have them make Jesus' liberating gospel their primary concern.

White oppressors were an easy target, because their crimes against blacks, indigenous peoples, other ethnic minorities, the poor in their own community and in the Third World are so obvious and overwhelming that one hardly needs great insight to see them and denounce them. With their development of modern technology for the purpose of material profit (regardless of the human costs), they have plundered humanity, and white churches and their theologians have usually ignored this plunder by talking about other matters or justified and supported it as the will of God. What an easy target for black theology to attack!

A much more difficult and complex matter is that of speaking a liberating word to the victims so they can begin to build autonomous institutions that will bear witness to God's intention to deliver the poor from their poverty. Ignoring black churches, we ignored the presence of black power in the black community. If black theologians and clergy radicals had been more reflective about fusing black theology with black power as we said in our rhetoric, we would not have overlooked the need to place it within the worship and organizational life of independent black churches, which are the most obvious presence of black power in the black community. What was it that made us ignore black churches and instead direct our theological rage against whites?

The reasons are many and complex, and my personal involvement probably hinders me from understanding them adequately. But more than I care to admit now and could not acknowledge at the time, one reason seems obvious: we had internalized too much of the theological values of the whites whom we were attacking. Therefore even when we attacked them for their racism, we could not separate ourselves from them, because we wanted to become like them, teaching at their schools and writing books to prove that we could think as well as they. In the meantime, we were separating black theology from the only source that could give it theological credibility—the black church and the black community.

By the beginning of the 1970s, black theology had become too much of an academic discipline, competing with other white interpretations of the faith. That may have been flattering for the intellectual morale of black seminary students and professors, but I do not see that it contributed much to the survival and liberation of black humanity in the 1970s. Black theologians should have expended more effort in associating black theology with the churches that were open to its presence.

I still am not convinced that the major black denominational churches are ready for renewal, but I do believe that there were and still are many genuinely committed black pastors and lay persons who transcend the limitations of their dominational identity by becoming identified with Christ through a commitment to the poor. They are found in all denominations (black as well as white) and they seemed determined to build more humane church structures that serve the community. They are feeding the hungry, holding workshops on economics and politics as well as black church history and theology, building alternative schools for black children, and working at many other creative projects of freedom. These pastors and members refuse to withdraw from the world by engaging in internal church politics. They are concrete examples that the black church is not an opiate of the people, but rather a liberating force in behalf of the victims of the land. And as theologians of the black church, we should have spent more of our time with them.

When black theology sought to return to the church of its origin in the late 1970s, it found that its absence had created an alienation and that black church leaders were not open to criticisms coming from professional theologians teaching in white institutions. In order to cement their renewed connection with the churches, theologians neglected the prophetic criticism of the 1960s. The NCBC statement "Black Theology in 1976" and the "Message to the Black Church and Community" of the Atlanta conference (1977) omitted a serious critique of black churches. Few, if any, noticed that Cecil Cone's *Identity Crisis in Black Theology* failed to point to a similar crisis of identity in black churches due to their theological and sometimes spiritual dependence upon white evangelical and fundamentalist churches.

If black theologians were having identity problems because of their location in white seminaries, answering white questions and thereby separating themselves from the authentic religion of our mothers and fathers, many black pastors and their churches were having a similar problem as they mimicked the religion of Billy Graham and even the blatant racist Christianity of the Moral Majority. According to James S. Tinney, a reliable black interpreter of the movement, such prominent black clergy as Dr. E. V. Hill, a Los Angeles pastor, Dr. Joseph H. Jackson, previous head of the influential National Baptist Convention, and the Most Rev. J. O. Patterson of the Church of God in Christ have been associated with the Moral Majority, giving the appearance of supporting it.[25] "The Rev. J. Herbert Hinkle, pastor of the Cathedral of Faith in Inkster, Michigan, has gone so far as to organize a black 'wing' of the Moral Majority on a national scale, known as 'Minorities for Morality.' "[26] It is because black pastors have lost contact with the religion of their black and African heritages that they can say (as does Emmanuel L. McCall) that black theologians "speak mostly for themselves" and do not "represent the thinking and attitudes of the 'rank and file.' "[27] Responding to McCall's judgment, Gayraud Wilmore said that of the separation of black theology from the black churches:

> [It] is not because black theology is obscure, unbiblical, or has no doctrine of the church, but because the majority of black preachers confuse themselves with Billy Graham and the most unenlightened versions of white evangelicalism. Because they do not know the rock from which they were hewn, they and their people do not know who they are and

the inheritance that was passed on to them by men like Benjamin Tucker Tanner, William W. Colley, and Alexander W. Waters. Because their sense of sin is personal and individualistic, they have an understanding of redemption that cannot admit the sanctification of secular conflict and struggle. Because they are willing to accept . . . "Americanity" as normative Christianity, they are unable to see how their own ethnic experience in the United States authenticates the truth of God's revelation in scripture and how the gospel then illuminates and gives meaning to the most profound symbol of that experience—the symbol of blackness.[28]

Not many black theologians were as direct and sharp in their criticisms of black churches as was Wilmore. They tried to correct the error of neglecting the black churches by restraining the prophetic voice of black theology, an error perhaps more serious than the other. There can be no genuine Christian theology without prophetic self-criticism of the Christian community that gives birth to it. A prophet is always a member of the community to which the words of judgment and grace are given. Although black theology returned to black churches with a word of grace, one could hardly hear God's judgment upon us for having made our churches and theology into self-serving instruments of our professional advancement.

I think that the time has come for the black church and black theology to build on their past strengths, avoid past errors, and move together in our participation of God's future kingdom of freedom that is coming through the liberation of the poor.

PROSPECTS FOR THE FUTURE

As black churches and black theology prepare for the future, it would be wise for them to move beyond their mutual ignorance and antagonism and begin to recognize their need of each other. We must ask not what is best for the survival of black churches or black theology, but rather what is best for the liberation of the black poor in particular and the poor of the whole world in general. Unless we black preachers, theologians, and lay persons are prepared to measure our commitment to the gospel in terms of our participation in the liberation of the poor, then our gospel is not good news to the poor but instead an instrument of their oppression. We must be willing to submerge our personal ambitions, transcend denominational differences, and overcome personality conflicts in order to bear witness together that God's liberation of the oppressed is at hand in the words and actions of black Christians.

In order to pursue this essential commitment, certain attitudes must be adopted and consistently applied. The first thing that needs to be said is that black theologians must never speak and write black theology as if they are not a part of black churches and are not involved in the criticisms that are made against them. When we speak and criticize black churches we are criticizing our own community and thus ourselves. It is our solidarity with and participation in black churches that give us the right to speak prophetically. To think that we can do black theology apart from black churches is sheer theological nonsense. And if we do not return to black churches with the intellectual humility and openness to be taught as well as to teach, then black churches should not listen to anything we say.

Our task is not to tell others what the gospel is, as if we know and they do not. Our task rather is to take as the content for black theology the prereflective understanding of the gosepl had by black Christians, in order to make their voices heard throughout the churches and society. We do not create the gospel; we interpret it as it is celebrated in worship and as it is practiced in society. Deeply embedded in black church history are the sermons, songs, and prayers of our grandparents waiting to be put into a theological language that can serve as a guide for our contemporary efforts to be faithful. We must uncover their words about God and make them the foundation of black theology.

Black theology is not academic theology; it is not a theology of the dominant classes and racial majorities. It is a theology of the black poor, reconstructing their hopes and dreams of God's coming liberated world. The sources for this theology are not found in Barth, Tillich, and Pannenberg. They are found in the spirituals, blues, and sayings of our people. We must go back to black churches so as to authenticate our vocation by helping them to move closer to their calling to be God's instrument of liberation in the world.

However, it is clear that the discord between black theology and black church is not the result only of theologians' errors. There has been a vast reluctance in the church to recognize "varieties of gifts." God calls not only preachers for the ministry but teachers as well. Unfortunately black churches have not given due recognition to the importance of teachers of the word, and thus their preachers have not always been clear about the content of their proclamation. Preachers have often substituted sound and style for content, and thus we have created black churches that do not know the gospel that they claim to celebrate.

We have heard a great deal about the black church being a *praying* church, and one of its most prominent pastors, Harold Carter, has written an important book on that theme, *The Prayer Tradition of Black People.*[29] I have nothing against prayer, because it does "change things" and is thus an indispensable element in Christian life and worship. But so is critical theological reflection. Black churches ought also to be *thinking* churches— that is, churches that are so concerned about the authenticity of their faith that they are willing to subject it to the most rigorous intellectual questioning. Only in that way can we black Christians not fail to remember the need to continually test and correct our faith by the biblical witness and the faith of our forebears.

It is important to point out here that the growth of anti-intellectualism and a disdain of serious theological reflection in black churches are a recent development. All historians of the black experience give special tribute to black churches for their emphasis on education during and following slavery. They founded many schools, including colleges and seminaries for the education of their ministers.

At the 1880 general conference of the AME Church, Bishop T.M.D. Ward stressed the importance of education for ministers: "Brain power will be supreme. Encourage learning and you will live; despise it and you will die. An enlightened ministry, whose talents and calling have been consecrated to God, will make an intelligent, large-hearted church."[30] Bishop L. J. Coppin of the same church used even stronger language in 1916: "It would be no less than a crime, not to say sacrilege, for him who has the care of souls to be content to remain ignorant as it relates to the prevalent learning of the day."[31] Many black church leaders seconded what Bishop J. A. Handy said: "The first duty of church is to educate its ministry."[32] Some went even further and accented the need for a theology: "The time has come," said Bishop B. T. Tanner in 1888, "for the Negro, and even all the colored races of the earth, to construct a theology for themselves."[33]

What happened to the creative intellectual dimension of black faith? Why do so many black preachers today reject education and their ethnic identity as irrelevant to the gospel? A good index of the attitudes of black churches toward an educated leadership is their attitude toward seminary training and their support of their own seminaries. Few churches insist on the necessity of serious intellectual study of the Bible and black history as a requirement of their leaders. Their seminaries are almost totally neglected and few promising ministers would attend or accept a teaching position in one of them. Churches that do not invest time, money, and intellectual resources in the training of their ministers do not take the gospel seriously. Black churches leave most of the training of their ministers to *white* seminaries.[34]

How strange, because such a procedure contradicts what black churches claim about themselves. And how sad, because it is an indication of apostasy. Black churches have taken the responsibility that God gave to them and have given it away to enemies of the gospel. Those who are most responsible for the oppression of blacks and the distortion of the gospel are the ones whom black churches have given the major responsibility for the training of their ministers. With black preachers being trained by white seminaries, it is no wonder that black churches do not understand the gospel as being identical with the liberation of their people from oppression.

There are still some black preachers who argue that they do not need any training in theology in order to preach the gospel. That may have been an acceptable position in days past when there was little or no opportunity for formal study. But not today! Black preachers who think so have confused the gospel of Jesus with their own distorted piety or personal interests. Why would God call persons for ministry who were uninterested in training their minds to their highest potential? Why did God give us minds if intelligence is not needed for ministry? I do not think that education alone is sufficient for God's ministers, but it is an essential preparation for interpreting God's liberating word in our times.

Without a clearly articulated theological position in creeds and theological textbooks, black preachers and their members have nowhere else to turn for theological knowledge and spiritual renewal except conservative, white, evangelical churches. Of course, some black preachers and lay persons can and do transcend white theology and spirituality, but unfortunately, most do not know how to distinguish between black faith and white religion. And with the appearance of the electronic church (on radio and television), black Christians are being lured from their spiritual heritage in black churches to the false gods of the Jerry Falwells of this world. Without a critical black theology that can distinguish good religion from bad religion, black preachers are left with the option of simply imitating the false gods of the electronic church in order to keep their congregations from deserting the 11:00 A.M. service and other activities of their churches.[35]

The doing of theology, then, is not an option that black churches can accept or reject and still remain faithful to the gospel. It is a demand, an absolute necessity, because the very life of the church is dependent upon it. To preach the gospel without asking about its precise meaning for our time and situation is to distort the gospel. Good intentions are not enough. Being sincere is not enough. Praying daily for divine guidance is not enough.

A religion of liberation demands more than preaching, praying, and singing about the coming eschatological kingdom of God. It demands a critical theology based on the Bible and using the tools of the social sciences so that we can participate more effectively in establishing the kingdom in this world that we believe will be fully consummated in the next. As Gustavo Gutiérrez has put it: "Poverty of the poor is not a call to generous relief action, but a demand that we go and build a different social order."[36]

There are many issues that the church must face now and in the future. In the remainder of this book, I want to raise some of the issues that black theology and the black church need to place on the top of their agenda. They are: women in the church and in society; Third World problems in Africa, Asia, and Latin America; the relationship of blacks to other ethnic and indigenous peoples in the U.S.A.; and the role of Marxism as a tool of social analysis.

Chapter VI

Black Theology, Black Churches, and Black Women

O how careful ought we to be, lest through our bylaws of church government and discipline we bring into disrepute even the word of life. For as unseemly as it may appear nowadays for a woman to preach, it should be remembered that nothing is impossible with God. And why should it be thought impossible, heterodox, or improper for a woman to preach, seeing the Savior died for the woman as well as the man?   Reverend Jarena Lee, 1836[1]

We'll have our rights. See if we don't. And you can't stop us from them. See if you can.   Sojourner Truth, 1853[2]

To be a woman, black, and active in religious institutions in the American scene is to labor under triple jeopardy.
                               Theressa Hoover[3]

If theology, like the church, has no word for Black women, its conception of liberation is inauthentic.
                               Jacquelyn Grant[4]

Although black male theologians and church leaders have progressive and often revolutionary ideas regarding the equality of blacks in American society, they do not have similar ideas regarding the equality of women in the black church and community. Why is it that many black men cannot see the analogy between racism and sexism, especially in view of the fact that so many black women in the church and in society have expressed clearly their experience of oppression? What is it that blinds black men to the truth regarding the suffering of their sisters? What is it that makes black churchmen insensitive to the pain of women ministers, and why do we laugh when they tell the story of their suffering that we have inflicted on them?

Of course many black men, like whites in relation to racism, would deny that they are sexist. But an emphatic denial of being prejudiced against black women is no proof that black men are free of sexism: those who are not the victims of a particular form of oppression are seldom capable of developing criteria to test whether it has been eliminated. The persons best capable of evaluating sexism in the black community and church are black women who are feminists and thus engaged in the struggle to eliminate it from our community. Black churchmen today need not be surprised by militant female voices: black church women have been speaking out for a long time.

NINETEENTH-CENTURY FEMINISM IN THE BLACK CHURCH

Black feminism was developed in the context of the abolitionist movement and the rise of white feminism in the second half of the nineteenth century. It is especially important for black men to note that Frederick Douglass, the great abolitionist, was also an outspoken advocate of women's rights.[5] He was one of the first to see the connection between the freedom of African slaves and the liberation of women. That was why he attended the first women's rights convention, in Seneca Falls, New York, in 1848. Without his unqualified support, the controversial resolution of that convention on women's suffrage would not have been approved.

Nineteenth-century black women did not remain silent on the issue of women's rights. Like white women who became acutely aware of sexism during their involvement in the abolitionist movement, black women also developed a similar consciousness. Sojourner Truth was one of their most outstanding advocates. A former slave, she attended several women's rights conventions, giving her support to the cause. She is best known for her famous "Ain't I a Woman?" speech, delivered at the women's convention in 1851 in Akron, Ohio. One clergyman, who spoke at the convention, told women "to beware of selling their birthright of consideration and deference for a mess of equality pottage. What man," he asked, "would help a political or business rival into a carriage, or lift her over a ditch?"[6] To which Sojourner replied:

That man over there says that women needs to be helped into carriages, and lifted over ditches, and to have the best place everywhere. Nobody ever helps me into carriages, or over mudpuddles, or gives me any best place! And ain't I a woman? Look at me! Look at my arm! I have ploughed, and planted, and gathered into barns, and no man could head me! And ain't I a woman? I could work as much and eat as much as a man—when I could get it—and bear the lash as well! And ain't I a woman? I have borne thirteen children and seen them most all sold off to slavery, and when I cried out with my mother's grief, none but Jesus heard me! And ain't I a woman?[7]

Another preacher at the same convention had claimed superior rights and privileges for men on the grounds of the manhood of Christ. "If God had desired the equality of women," he said, "he would have given some token of his will through the birth, life, and death of the Savior."[8] To which Sojourner responded:

"That little man in black there, he says women can't have as much rights as men, because Christ wasn't a woman!" Then she paused, with her burning eyes focused on the minister who had made the comment: "Where did your Christ come from?" She repeated her question: "Where did your Christ come from?" Then she answered her own question, her voice ringing like an organ with all the stops pulled: "From God and a woman! Man had nothing to do with him."[9]

Sojourner concluded her speech with the observation that "if the first woman God ever made was strong enough to turn the world upside down all alone, these women together ought to be able to turn it back, and get it right side up again! And now they are asking to do it, the men better let them.''[10]

When there was debate about black men receiving the right to vote but not women, Sojourner shared the sentiment of other women's rights activists who strongly objected, seeing it as a bonding of white and black men against women of both colors:

> There is a great stir about colored men getting their rights, but not a word about colored women; and if colored men get theirs, and not colored women theirs, you see the colored men will be the masters over the women, and it will be just as bad as before. So I am for keeping the thing going while the things are stirring; because if we wait til it is still, it will take a great while to get it going again.[11]

Sojourner Truth was not the only nineteenth-century black woman to stand up for women's rights. Harriet Tubman was called the "Moses" of her people because of her leading more than three hundred slaves to freedom. She also attended several women's suffrage conventions and became involved in the National Federation of Afro-American Women. Ida B. Wells-Barnett, a journalist and graduate of Rust College, is best known for her solitary campaign against lynching and her involvement in the work of black club women. Mary Church Terrell, a leading club woman, organized the National Association of Colored Women (1897) and was elected its first president. She was also a charter member of the NAACP (1909), a suffragist and close friend of Susan B. Anthony and Jane Addams. Francis Ellen Watkins Harper, also a club woman and feminist, was a founder and vice president of the National Association of Colored Women.

It is important to note that black women, unlike black men and white women, could not choose between the issues of sexism and racism: they were victims of both. Black feminists today call it double jeopardy. White feminists and abolitionists parted ways at the 1869 meeting of the Equal Rights Association, because of the latters' support of the Fourteenth and Fifteenth Amendments, which excluded franchise for women. White feminists could afford to ignore racism, just as black men could sexism. But black women fought for both rights.[12]

Black women *in the church* had an additional burden, which

led Theressa Hoover to call it triple jeopardy.[13] Although black churches agreed with Sojourner Truth, Harriett Tubman, Ida Wells, and other black women regarding the abolition of slavery, lynching, and other forms of white racism, they rejected their views on women's rights.

Black church attitudes toward women ministers were similar to those of white denominations. In the AME Church, a progressive denomination in comparison with some other independent black churches, women were not permitted ordination in the nineteenth century. They were permitted only to exhort and preach without a license. Largely because of their insistence that they were called by God to preach the gospel, the offices of stewardess and deaconess were created in 1868 and 1900, respectively. Although some AME ministers licensed women to preach, the denomination did not make it official until 1884 and limited their preaching to the subordinate office of "evangelist."

Bishop Henry McNeal Turner was publicly reprimanded for ordaining a woman to preach. Later the 1888 General Conference made its position clear:

> Whereas Bishop H. M. Turner has seen fit to ordain a woman to the order of a deacon; and whereas said act is contrary to the usage of our church, and without precedent in any other body of Christians in the known world; and as it cannot be proved by the scriptures that a woman has ever been ordained to the order of the ministry; therefore be it enacted, that the bishops of the African Methodist Episcopal Church be and hereby [are] forbidden to ordain a woman to the order of deacon or elder in our church.[14]

Despite the limitations placed on black women ministers, several distinguished themselves. Jarena Lee, the first female preacher in the AME Church, was one of the most prominent. Born in 1783, she recorded the story of her conversion and call to preach in *The Life and Religious Experience of Jarena Lee*. When she told Richard Allen about her call to preach, his reply was: "As to women preaching, . . . our discipline knew nothing at all about it—that it did not call for women preachers."[15] But Jarena Lee asked: "If the man may preach, because the Savior died for him, why not the woman, seeing he died for her also? Is he not a whole Savior, instead of a half one, as those who hold it wrong for a woman to preach would seem to make it appear?''[16] Because of her persistence, Allen accepted her as a woman preacher even though he did not ordain her. In one year she traveled over two thousand miles and delivered 178 sermons.

There were other black women of the nineteenth century whose call to the ministry outweighed the rules defined by the black male clergy. When asked ''by what authority'' she ''spoke against slavery'' and whether she had been ordained, a woman named Elizabeth replied that although she had not been ''commissioned of men's hands, if the Lord had ordained me, I needed nothing better.''[17] As black male ministers continued to reject them outright or forced upon them ''the extra burden of proving their call,'' black women found ways to respond to God's call to preach the gospel.

It can be concluded that black churches were similar to white churches in their attitudes toward women during the nineteenth century. The same was true of the black community as a whole at that time.

BLACK FEMINISM IN THE CIVIL RIGHTS AND BLACK POWER ERA

The recent struggle of black women in the churches has drawn not only upon nineteenth-century sources but upon the feminist outcry of the 1960s and '70s. The language used to name women's oppression, as suggested in such terms as ''patriarchy,'' ''misogyny,'' and ''sexism,'' was developed first by women in the white community. White women initially created the language of contemporary radical feminism in response to women's subordination in the SNCC and later in reaction to a much more oppressive subordination in radical left white male groups, such as the Students for a Democratic Society (SDS).[18]

For black women, however, white feminism was not always adequate or appropriate, partly because feminism was sometimes racist and partly because patriarchy had distinctive characteristics in the struggle for racial freedom. Women seldom received the credit they deserved for contributions to the freedom movement of the late 1950s and '60s. They sometimes served as symbols for a brief time, as in the case of Rosa Parks, but seldom did men acknowledge their role in any substantive decision-making process.

Most persons do not know that Ella Baker served as the first executive director of the SCLC and that she was responsible for the founding of the SNCC in the spring of 1960.[19] Many do not know of Anna A. Hedgeman and the role she played in putting race on the agenda of the NCC.[20] Seldom mentioned are the contributions of Fannie Lou Hamer in Mississippi,[21] Daisy Bates in the 1957 crisis at Little Rock Central High School,[22] Ruby Doris Robinson and Diana Nash Bevel in the SNCC.[23] Only men—Martin Luther King, Jr., Malcolm X, Andrew Young, Stokely Carmichael, James Forman, and others like them—are given major recognition for their achievements in the black freedom struggle. The invisibility of black women in the freedom movement and the hostility of black men toward women's equality helped drive black women to form their own feminist organizations.

A more blatant display of black patriarchy in the struggle for black power was the inordinate emphasis on violence and masculine assertiveness, the stress on black women's passivity and weakness, and the glorification of the pimp and the black male's sexual exploits in such movies as Melvin Van Peebles's *Sweet Sweetback's Baadasssss Song* (1971) and his Broadway play *Ain't Supposed to Die a Natural Death* (1973). In his book *Soul on Ice* (1968), Eldridge Cleaver thematized rape as a political act, and other black male so-called revolutionaries followed suit. Most of the plays, novels, and movies that were created by black men during the civil rights and black power revolution of the 1960s accented patriarchal values similar to those in white society.

For many black men, freedom meant the assertion of their manhood, which they identified as violence against the white man with guns, rape of the white woman, and unlimited physical and mental brutality against the black woman. Inasmuch as black women were the most accessible and least capable of defending themselves, black men often made black women victims of displaced anger, doing to their sisters what they really wanted to do to white society.

No one was more influential in defining the black consciousness movement than Amiri Baraka, formerly called LeRoi Jones, by his writings and speeches, and in the organizations he headed. But, as in the case of many other radical black men, Baraka's sexism created contradictions in his nationalist philosophy. On one occasion he was asked whether a militant black man could have a white woman companion, and he replied:

Jim Brown put it pretty straight and this is really quite true. He says that there are black men and white men, then there are women. So you can indeed be going through a black militant thing and have yourself a woman. The fact that she happens to be black or white is no longer impressive to anybody, but a man who gets himself a woman is what's impressive. The battle is really between white men and black men. Whether we like to admit it, that is the battlefield at this time.[24]

Sexism, like racism, encourages violence as a way to subjugate the other. Baraka dramatized his nationalist view in his play *Madheart*. In one scene, the black male protagonist of the play demonstrates his power to use force to subdue the black woman who is urging him to leave the white woman and come to her:

BLACK MAN: I'll get you back. If I need to.
WOMAN *(laughs):* You need to, baby . . . just look around you. You better get me back, if you know what's good for you . . . you better.
BLACK MAN *(looking around at her squarely, he advances):* I better? . . . *(a soft laugh)* Yes. Now is where we always are . . . that now. . . . *(He wheels and suddenly slaps her crosswise, back and forth across the face.)*
WOMAN: Wha??? What . . . oh love . . . please . . . don't hit me. *(He hits her, slaps her again.)*
BLACK MAN: I want you woman, as a woman. Go down. *(He slaps her again.)* Go down, submit, submit . . . to love . . . and to man, now, forever.
WOMAN *(weeping, turning her head from side to side):* Please don't hit me . . . please. . . . *(She bends.)* The years are so long, without you, man, I've waited . . . waited for you. . . .

BLACK MAN: And I've waited.

WOMAN: I've seen you humbled, black man, seen you crawl for dogs and devils.

BLACK MAN: And I've seen you raped by savages and beasts, and bear bleach-shit children of apes.

WOMAN: You permitted it . . . you could . . . do nothing.

BLACK MAN: But now I can. *(He slaps her . . . drags her to him, kissing her deeply on the lips.)* That shit is ended, woman, you with me, and the world is mine.[25]

At first black women were reluctant to speak the language of feminism, because they did not want to detract from the importance of the struggle of the black community against white racism. Furthermore, they wanted to give black men a chance to "stand up like men" in the presence of white men in order to protect and to provide for the black family. This was also partly due to reaction to the myth of black female matriarchy and partly as a response to black male proclamations of assumed and justified leadership.

In an *Ebony* article, "The Black Woman and Women's Lib," Helen H. King suggested that many black women in the civil rights and black power movements accepted their place behind black men and were proud to see them stand up and demand liberation for the black community.

"We should stand behind our men, not against them," said a black woman opponent of the women's liberation movement.[26] Another is quoted as saying: "This movement won't be any different from the woman suffrage thing. White women won the right to vote way back then, but black people, including black women, didn't win this right until more than a hundred years later!"[27] Still another black woman opponent characterized the women's movement as "just a bunch of bored white women with nothing to do—they're just trying to attract attention away from the black liberation movement."[28]

Prominent black women joined the chorus denouncing the women's movement as a white and middle-class phenomenon, and thus unrelated to the black struggle for freedom. Nikki Giovanni said:

I think that it's a moot issue. Just another attempt of white people to find out what black people are doing or to control what we are doing. . . . They [white women] want "equality" to deal with black women because they've certainly dealt with black men. They're so upset about black women not coming in because they're ultimately trying to control us. There aren't any other reasons why they could be upset. Black people consider their first reality to be black, and given that reality we know from birth that we are going to be oppressed—man, woman, or eunuch![29]

The well-known poet Gwendolyn Brooks echoed the same theme:

Black women, like all women, certainly want, and are entitled to, equal pay and privileges. But black women have a second "twoness." Today's black men, at last flamingly assertive and proud, need their black women beside them, not organizing against them.[30]

Although there were a few exceptions,[31] most black women of the early 1970s remained apart from and critical of the women's movement. But when black revolutionaries began "to talk black and sleep white," black women began to question the nature of black men's commitment to the black freedom struggle and to reevaluate their place *behind* the black man. Black women started to realize that to be liberated, from both white racism and male domination, they would have to do the job themselves.

Of course, just as many blacks submitted to racism, many black women accepted the sexist role defined by so-called revolutionary black men. Some black women were willing to walk two steps behind their men and remain silent and passive. Black women wanted to be taken care of by "strong" black men, as white men had supposedly done for white women. Therefore black women were slow to complain about black male brutality.

Because black men knew that black women were deeply committed to the racial struggle, they did not even take seriously black women's concern for sexual oppression. They merely laughed, treating the hurt and pain of our sisters as a joke. When asked about the role of women in the movement, Stokely Carmichael is reported to have said: "The only position for women in SNCC is prone."[32]

Because we were so insensitive, we left black women with no choice but to declare publicly that sexism does exist in the black community and, like racism, it must be eliminated. One of the earliest texts on black feminism is entitled *The Black Woman* (1970), an anthology edited by Toni Cade.[33] But it was not until Ntozake Shange's play *For Colored Girls . . .* (1976)[34] and Michele Wallace's book *Black Macho and the Myth of the Super-woman* (1979)[35] that the idea of a black feminism became widely discussed in the black community.[36]

Although the black church has seldom been willing to accept new ideas that were not directly related to the elimination of white racism, the enormous impact of Shange's play and Wallace's book made it impossible for many black women in the church and seminary to avoid the issue of black patriarchy. One does not have to agree with the perspectives of Shange or Wallace in order to know that black women are oppressed by black men, and especially in the church by male ministers.

BLACK THEOLOGY AND BLACK WOMEN

Just as the struggles of the 1960s and '70s reinforced sexism in the black community generally, sexism in the church particularly seemed more blatant in those years. Black clergymen became bold advocates of women's inferiority, emphasizing their supposed lack of intelligence, natural weakness, and passivity. As some white male ministers began to retreat in the face of the emerging power of the women's movement in the seminary and church, black clergymen laughed at white men's inability to keep women in their place. At the same time they mimicked white antifeminist conservatives by preaching about the value of the American family in which wives are subordinate to their husbands. This was the sanctimonious—supposedly biblical—version of the male revolutionary's demand that black women stand behind their men.

Such attitudes limit women's roles in the church. Women are expected to sing in the choir, serve on the usher and stewardess boards, participate in the missionary society, cook in the kitchen, teach children in the Sunday School, and serve in all those positions that men regard as "women's work." But unlike men, women are not encouraged to enter the ministry. Women are tolerated when they insist that God has called them to preach the word. Indeed a woman's calling is often questioned until her talent and faith remove skeptics' doubts. A man's call is never questioned until a lack of faith or talent or moral integrity create skepticism among the community of believers. A man may live the most immoral life imaginable, be "converted," and still be accepted by the church for service in God's ministry. But an immoral woman who "gets" religion and then receives the call would hardly be given a similar opportunity for service in the church.

In some black churches women are still excluded entirely from the ordained ministry.[37] But even in churches that do ordain women, female ministers do not have the same opportunities as men for the exercise of their ministry. For instance, there is, to my knowledge, only one woman presiding elder, but no bishops, general officers, college presidents, or pastors of major churches in the AME Church.[38] When women push through the male-oriented pattern of expectations and *insist* that God has called them to preach, men often tell them to become evangelists, a ministry with no institutional authority. If women should insist on being pastors, they are usually urged to become assistants to male pastors. If they insist on being the head pastor, the bishop usually appoints them to small churches that men do not want. In other black denominations, the offices may have different names but the results are the same: men say to women, "This far and no farther."

Turning to theology, it is clear from earlier chapters that black theology arose out of the black church and in response to the black power movement. It is shameful but scarcely surprising that black theology learned the patriarchal bad habits of its progenitors. Only one woman, Dr. Anna Hedgeman, author and staff member of the NCC commission on religion and race, was asked to sign the NCBC "Black Power Statement" of 1966.[39] The NCBC has not been a public advocate of equality for women in the ministry. During my involvement in most of its early history, the issue of women in the ministry was seldom discussed, because the NCBC was controlled by black male theologians and ministers. When the issue was raised most men either laughed or assigned it a low priority in the struggle for black freedom. A woman has served in the position of secretary to the executive director and the board of directors. A few women have even served on the board.

The very name NCBC, with the last letter representing Church-*men,* indicated clearly the reactionary perspective of black male ministers regarding women's equality in church and society. According to the reports of some black women, the NCBC male leadership, despite repeated appeals, remained adamant in its refusal to replace the word "Churchmen" with "Christians," insisting that the word "men" is generic and not sexist. Only in late 1982 did the NCBC soften its views on the matter and change its name to National Conference of Black Christians.[40]

At first, there were only a few black women theologians who began to criticize black male theology. They included Pauli Murray,[41] an Episcopal priest and lawyer, and Theressa Hoover, an executive of the Board of Global Ministries of the United Methodist Church.[42] But they were the exceptions, and black male theologians and ministers either ignored them or laughed at their arguments. The situation changed, however, in the mid-1970s.

I remember the first time that black men and women at Union Theological Seminary came together to discuss women in the ministry. Because I had been "converted" to women's equality in society, church, and the doing of theology, and because I had just read a paper addressing that theme at Garrett Evangelical Seminary in Evanston (October 1976), Jacquelyn Grant, then a graduate student at Union and now a professor of theology at the Interdenominational Theological Center, asked me to present the same paper to black men and women at Union.

When I now read that October 1976 paper, I am embarrassed by how mildly and carefully I approached the theme of women's equality in the church. It was anything but radical, somewhat analagous to a southern white liberal reflecting on racism. But black male seminarians, almost without exception, were greatly disturbed by my paper. If my paper can be compared to that of a southern white liberal, the reactions of many black male seminarians were similar to those of most reactionary southern white racists. They quoted the Bible to justify that women should not be ordained, and some even insisted that they should not even be in the pulpit. I was shocked, as were my black colleagues, Professors James Forbes and James Washington. But black women seminarians were not surprised. They were aware of the attitudes that kept them subordinate in the church, as well as invisible in black theology.

From like encounters, repeated and multiplied countless times, black women saw the need for a black feminist theology. In this project they have had the ambiguous models of black male theology and white feminist theology. Beginning with Mary Daly's *The Church and the Second Sex* (1968),[43] feminist theology was further developed in the prolific writings of Rosemary Ruether, Letty Russell, Beverly Harrison, Sheila Collins, Judith Plaskow, Carol Christ, and many others.[44] Most black women either ignored these writings or criticized them as irrelevant to black women and the black church. However, as black feminist theology emerges, black women are affirming in varying degrees the value of their white sisters' work.

The invisibility of black women in both black and feminist theologies is striking. The most that both theologies do is to mention in passing the names of Sojourner Truth, Harriet Tubman, and perhaps Rosa Parks. But for neither is black women's experience a part of the structure and substance of the theology itself. Black women's experience is merely added to theologies whose style and content are determined by other experiences. That is why Jarena Lee, Maria Stewart, Frances Ellen Watkins Harper, Ida Wells-Barnett, and Anna Julia Cooper are seldom mentioned in either black male or white feminist theology.

Only black women can do black feminist theology: their experience is truly theirs. Therefore, even if white feminists were not so racist and black males were not so sexist, there would still be a need for black feminist theology. The need arises from the uniqueness of black women's experience. If theology arises out of the attempt to reconcile faith with life, and if black women have an experience of faith in God that is not exhausted by white women or black men, then there is a need to articulate the faith of black women so that the universal church can learn from their experience with God. Black women, by giving an account of their faith in worship and living out their faith in the world, create the context for authentic theological reflection.

Among the black women seminarians and professors who have begun to develop a black feminist theology are Jacquelyn Grant, Pauli Murray, Katie Cannon, Delores Williams, Kelly Brown, and Cherl Gilkes. Although black women's experience is related to some aspects of both women and blacks generally, their experience is not exhausted by either group. Black women have begun to feel the need to articulate the uniqueness of their experience *theologically*.

Black feminist theologians in the U.S.A. have been aided by theological reflection arising from the struggles of other minority women in the U.S.A. and women in Africa, Asia, and Latin America. When black women theologians and ministers encountered Third World women in the WCC and other ecumenical settings, they realized that they were not the only women in an oppressed community concerned about women's equality.[45] Meeting Third World women and reading their writings on women's liberation helped black women to recognize the need for the development of a black feminist theology.[46]

Black women may have been reluctant to join in a coalition with white women, but they are less reluctant to express their solidarity with African and other non-European women. The WCC, EATWOT, and other ecumenical organizations have provided many an occasion for dialogues between African-American and Third World women in the church.

A WORD TO BLACK MALE MINISTERS AND THEOLOGIANS

As a male theologian, I am in no position to say what the content and form of a black feminist theology should be. I can only support its development and be instructed by the black women who assume the responsibility to create it. However, I should like to offer some thoughts to black male theologians and ministers whose attitudes range from indifference to mild support of the development of women's fullest potential as human beings in the church and community. There are responsibilities that we have in the church that affect how women are received and what opportunities are made available to them for the fullest development of their potential for service to God in the church and in society.

It is important for black men to realize that women's liberation is a viable issue.[47] We must recognize it and help others in the church to treat it seriously. It is not a joke. To get others to accept it as an issue that deserves serious consideration and discussion is the first step. As ministers in the church, how we treat the issue will affect the attitudes of others in our pastoral care. I realize that many women give the appearance of accepting the place set aside for them by men as is still true of many blacks in relation to whites. But just as whites were responsible for creating the societal structures that aided black self-hate, so black men are responsible for creating a similar situation among black women in the church. Saying that women like their place is no different from saying that blacks like theirs.

It is also important that we learn how to listen to women tell their stories of pain and struggle. The art of listening is not easy, especially for oppressors whose very position of power inhibits them from hearing and understanding anything that contradicts their values.

When we try to understand something of the depth of sexism and how it functions in black churches and community, it is helpful to think of racism in American society and white churches. Although racism and sexism are different in many respects, they share many similarities. If black men deny this connection between sexism and racism, it is unlikely that they will recognize the depth of the problem of sexism.

To aid our comprehension of the complexity of the issue, it is necessary to read as much as possible about the history of sexism and women's struggles, especially in the Third World and particularly in the black community and its churches in the U.S.A. Just as blacks become impatient with whites who do not take the time and discipline to inform themselves about the history of their brutality against them and their struggle against that brutality, black women will have a similar feeling regarding our failure to study their history.

Black women are beginning to develop their own leadership

styles. Black men should support them. But it is already clear that the leadership roles and styles of black women will be quite different from those that have been defined for them by black male ministers and theologians. Just as blacks and other oppressed groups develop styles in ministry that are different from those of oppressor whites, so the experience of women provides ways of doing ministry that will be quite different from the patriarchal and authoritarian leadership of men. It is our responsibility as men to be open to new styles of ministry and to help our congregations to be open to them. This will involve the necessity of being critical of our brothers who are opposed to women's taking leadership positions in the church and in society. We should be prepared to lose some "friends" as we work for change in the patriarchal structures in black churches and seek to create ones that are humane and just.

Black male ministers should also insist on affirmative action for black women in churches and in the community. The goal should be to have at least as many black women in positions of responsibility in churches and in community organizations as will reflect their percentage of the overall population. We can never achieve this goal without a plan of action for its accomplishment. Blacks have used this approach vis-à-vis racism; it seems logical to apply it to the situation of black women in our churches and communities. The principle of affirmative action should be applied to all positions, including those of bishop, pastor, general officer, steward, and deacon.

Finally, it is very important for black male ministers to support black women in their attempt to discover role models of the past. In my reading and discussions with black women, they often speak of the lack of role models—both past and present. What is needed therefore is for black women (and also black men) to discover their sisters of the past and to find community with those of the present so they can share experiences with each other and thereby be encouraged to keep fighting for recognition and justice in the church. Through a discovery of their sisters and mothers of the past and the creation of community in the present, self-confidence can be enhanced and the struggle for liberation strengthened.

In addition to the suggestions mentioned above, there are many other things that black men and women can do—both together and separately. My suggestions are intended only to engender serious discussion on the role of black women in the church and in society. I firmly believe that the black church cannot regain its Christian integrity unless it is willing to face head-on the evil of patriarchy and seek to eliminate it.

Chapter VII

Black Theology, Black Churches, and the Third World

What black theology affirms is the opposite of the ideology that distorts the Christian faith to make God identical with the culture of white domination. It is, rather, that God has identified himself with the oppressed of every race and nation, and is present in their suffering, humiliation, and death. The violence perpetuated upon the oppressed is violence against God. Their death is God's assassination. But God raised Jesus from death and because we see in him the faces of the poor, oppressed peoples of the world . . . black theologians speak unabashedly of the black Messiah, this oppressed and assassinated God who is risen to give life and hope to all who are oppressed. This black Messiah who is the oppressed Man of God, who is seen in the faces of the poor, oppressed black people, and whose death and resurrection is their rising to new life and power, is the meaning of the gospel of liberation that stands opposite to the ideology of domination by which the God of the Christian culture of Europe and America was fabricated before and after the Enlightenment. Gayraud S. Wilmore[1]

It is unfortunate that African-American churches and their preachers and theologians do not know much about the churches

140

and theologies of the Third World. African-American churches have been in "mission" work in Africa and the Caribbean for more than a century, but our behavior has been less than exemplary, often sharing a missionary outlook similar to that of white colonizers and seldom linking black churches with progressive political and theological ideas in those areas.

It is sad that African-American churches still treat Africans and West Indians somewhat as whites treat us, at best as children and at worst as pagans in need of Christianity and the values of Western civilization. Instead of creating church structures that would develop quality indigenous leadership, African-American churches still send uninformed black Americans to those areas to help with charitable projects and then to decide how the charity can best be used.

The reasons for this sad situation are many and complex, but we must acknowledge where we are if we expect to overcome ignorance and negative programing. White American and European colonists give similar racist rationalizations for their oppression of African-Americans and Africans, and we must be careful not to allow their brainwashing to influence us when we encounter other black and Third World peoples, becoming ourselves neocolonialists—set in our privileged ways, blaming our victims for their oppression, and remaining closed to the truth of liberation. If African-American churches do not wake up and seriously take note of the signs of the times in the world, they will find themselves oppressors of their brothers and sisters in the Third World.

In regard to Asia and Latin America, African-American churches know almost nothing. Although there are over 40 million blacks in Brazil (second only to Nigeria, the country with the largest black population in the world) and over 30 million elsewhere in Latin America, North American black denominations are virtually unknown there. In Asia African-American churches are, if possible, even less known, and almost nothing is being done to remove this ignorance.

My concern is not to spread black Christianity to other countries and continents as whites implanted European Christianity. But I do feel that there is an urgent need to exchange information, analyses, and strategies of liberation so that we can all learn from each other's problems and methods.

As white Americans, Europeans, South Africans, and other oppressors band together in order to continue their rule over us, oppressed peoples throughout the world, across continents and nations, must band together for the liberation of all. African-Americans cannot gain their freedom in the U.S.A. until Africans, Asians, Latin Americans, West Indians, and oppressed peoples throughout the world are set free. It is a common struggle; there will be no freedom for any one of us until all of us are set free. Oppressors know that, and that is why white South Africans and Americans are such good friends, à la Ronald Reagan and Margaret Thatcher.

Oppressors also know that the most effective way to keep the oppressed under control is to divide them, keep them apart, have them fight each other or at least share views that make them suspicious of each other. As long as oppressed peoples remain ignorant and suspicious of each other, they will remain open to believing what oppressors say about the others and thus will not build a coalition movement designed for the liberation of all. Why is this allowed to continue? In part, because divisions that feed the opportunism of leaders are not resisted—both within isolated oppressed groups and in their relationships with other oppressed groups.

My concern in this chapter is to urge us to interact, in spite of our differences, with other oppressed groups in the Third World so that we can begin to build bridges of communication and cooperation in a common struggle for freedom and self-determination. We dialogue with white Americans and Europeans, although they enslaved and colonized us and continue today to brutalize us. Why, then, do we not dialogue with other oppressed peoples who have not done anything to us and who share a condition of oppression similar to our own? Why should we allow white oppressors to continue to separate us, especially when we have everything to gain and nothing to lose?

The first thing black churches need to recognize is the necessity for dialogue and cooperation with Third World Christians *in independence from* the organizations and economic support of white North American and European churches. We must create our own structures for dialogue and cooperation so that black and Third World Christians will have exclusive control of the agenda and places for our meetings together.

Black churches should assume the major economic responsibility for such meetings because of our advantaged financial status when compared with Third World Christians. We have rich churches in comparison with the churches among the poor of Africa, Asia, and Latin America. Because we have more, more is to be expected of us. And if we are serious about the message and mission of Jesus Christ's church, then we will reorder our priorities so that we can more effectively bear witness to the gospel. Indeed the test of the authenticity of our faith in Jesus Christ is whether his will is at the top of the priority list of our black churches.

After recognizing the necessity for dialogue and cooperation and after taking steps to reorder our priorities, black churches should then begin the process of creating an ecumenical organization that will facilitate their initial contacts with similar organizations in the Third World. It is possible that one of the already existent ecumenical bodies among black churches could assume the responsibility for this important task. Or it may be necessary to create an entirely new one that complements existing ones but does not conflict with their purposes. What is clear, however, is the absolute necessity for a style of ecumenism that really transcends the politics of black churches so that a genuine, creative encounter with progressive elements in the Third World is possible.

When black churches have created an ecumenical organization, a small group should be chosen to make the initial contacts with similar organizations in the Third World. The All-Africa Conference of Churches, the Caribbean Conference of Churches, and the Christian Conference of Asia may be the best organizations in those continents and regions. Similar organizations can be found or created in Latin America.

Black and Third World churches should be clear from the start regarding their purposes for coming together—namely, to find ways to share our history and culture so that we can more effec-

tively proclaim and practice together the liberating message of
Jesus Christ. With evangelization of the gospel for the liberation
of humanity as our chief goal, we can then accent both our differences and our similarities; every aspect of our reality is important for the enlargement of our vision of God's universal gospel.

BLACK AND THIRD WORLD
THEOLOGICAL DIALOGUE

As black churches reflect on the possibility of conversations
with Third World churches, it may be helpful to point out that a
model of unity and cooperation has already been developing
among black and Third World theologians in an organization
called the Ecumenical Association of Third World Theologians
(EATWOT). It held its foundational conference in Dar es Sa-
laam, Tanzania (1976), and since then has held five major inter-
continental conferences in Ghana (1977), Sri Lanka (1979), Brazil
(1980), India (1981), and Switzerland (1983).

It was not easy for Third World theologians to get together,
because our history of separation created mutual distrust, implanted and encouraged by white Americans and Europeans. The
only times we had been together were at meetings called and
planned by Euro-Americans under the auspices of the Faith and
Order Commission of the WCC and other similar organizations.
We always found ourselves responding to European and white
American theological questions, not issues arising from our own
contexts. Even when problems of the Third World were placed on
the agenda, Euro-America decided how our problems should be
analyzed and presented. Whenever Third Worlders attempted to
set the theological agenda, Euro-Americans either voted us down
or they cut off the financial resources that they had stolen from
Third World countries through military conquest and economic
imperialism.

It was because many of us realized the urgent need to overcome
the stifling and oppressive effects of the dominant theologies of
Europe and North America that we decided to try to come
together on our own in order to discuss our differences and similarities in the hope that we could begin the process of creating a
common theological vision that would emerge out of the diverse

struggles of the poor for freedom throughout the world.

During the early stages of our dialogues, our differences seemed to dominate our discussions, with each group stressing the importance of the reality most visible on its continent. Latin Americans stressed socio-political liberation with an accent on class struggle as defined by Marxism. Advocates of an African theology countered with an emphasis on the importance of cultural liberation as defined by africanization and indigenization. Asians added the importance of dialogue between the major religions of the world, cautioning against the Western tendency to absolutize Christ and stressing the need for mutual support in the elimination of poverty. Of course black Americans stressed the importance of the elimination of racism and were strongly supported by South Africans. West Indians emphasized the need to overcome racism, classism, and imperialism. Hispanic-Americans found themselves sharing concerns of Latin Americans and blacks but with their own distinctive approach to theological issues as defined by their history.

The differences were so great that they almost destroyed our nascent unity. There was much debate about what to call ourselves, especially in regard to the appropriateness of the term "Third World."[2] When we finally decided to accept it, despite its limitations, there was some discussion regarding whether black Americans and other minorities in the U.S.A. were really part of the Third World.[3] There were some who said that the acceptance by the black community of U.S. capitalism with our attempt to integrate into its society deprived our values of a Third World identity. It was finally agreed by all that "Third World" referred to a condition of poverty *and* the struggle to overcome it, and thus was not primarily or exclusively a geographical concept.

Indeed there are First World enclaves in Third World countries in that they share the capitalistic values of white Americans and Europeans. The same is true among those blacks in the U.S.A. who define freedom in terms of their equal share in the American capitalist pie with no thought whatsoever of changing the economic system so that the true causes of poverty could be eliminated not only in the U.S.A. but throughout the world. Therefore the chief characteristic that defined our concern was the commitment to do theology from the standpoint of our solidarity with the poor struggling for freedom. The title of the book that came out of our foundational meeting reflects this emphasis—*The Emergent Gospel: Theology from the Underside of History*.[4]

At the first meeting, in Tanzania, it was decided to hold four additional conferences with three focusing on the theologies of Africa, Asia, and Latin America, and one attempting to identify the elements of a Third World theology common to all. *African Theology en Route*,[5] *Asia's Search for Full Humanity*,[6] and *The Challenge of Basic Christian Communities*[7] are the published accounts of the conferences on each continent. *Irruption of the Third World: Challenge to Theology*[8] represents our attempt to define the essential elements of a Third World theology.[9]

In our dialogue with Third World theologians,[10] the striking difference between the theologies of the poor and the theologies of the rich became very clear to us. As long as our dialogue was confined to North American whites who oppressed blacks and to European theologians whom our oppressors venerated, our understanding of the theological task was determined too much by our reactions to white racism in the United States. African, Asian, and Latin American theologians enlarged our vision by challenging us to do theology from a global perspective of oppression. Third World theologians urged us to analyze racism in relation to international capitalism, imperialism, colonialism, world poverty, classism, and sexism. For the first time, black theologians began to seriously consider socialism as an alternative to capitalism.

We began to see the connections between the black ghettoes in the United States and poverty in Asia, Africa, and Latin America; between the rising unemployment among blacks and other poor minorities in the U.S.A. and the exploitation of the labor of Third World peoples; and between the racist practices of white churches of North America and Europe and the activities of their missionaries in the Third World. These discoveries deeply affected our political and theological vision, and we began to see clearly that we could not do theology in isolation from our struggling brothers and sisters in the Third World. As oppressors band themselves together in order to keep the poor of the world in poverty, the oppressed must enter into political and theological solidarity if they expect to create a movement of liberation capable of breaking the chains of oppression.

Early in our dialogue, black and Third World theologians realized the importance of building a common theological movement of liberation. Although we discovered differences in each other (especially with Latin Americans during the early stages of our dialogue, in race and class analysis), our mutual commitment to do theology in solidarity with the poor held us together. We had too much in common to allow our differences to separate us. Furthermore, it became increasingly clear that our differences were largely due to contextual diversity and our mutual internalization of the lies that our oppressors had told us about each other.

After nearly seven years of dialogue between black and Third World theologians under the auspices of EATWOT, our differences have diminished considerably. And our similarities have increased to the extent that we are now engaged in the exciting task of creating a Third World theology of liberation that we all can support.[11]

A NEW METHOD OF DOING THEOLOGY

When the question is asked, "How do we do theology?" black and Third World theologians agree that theology is not the first act but rather the second. Although our Latin American brothers and sisters, with the use of Marxist class analysis, were the first to explicate this methodological point,[12] it was already present and now reaffirmed in all our theologies.[13] The first act is both a religio-cultural affirmation and a political commitment in behalf of the liberation of the poor and voiceless of our continents. Our cultural identity and political commitment are worth more than a thousand textbooks of theology. That is why we do not talk about theology as the first order of business in EATWOT. Rather our first concern is with the quality of commitments that each of us has made and will make for those about whom and with whom we claim to do theology. We contend that we know what persons believe by what they do, and not by what they say in their creeds, conference statements, or theological treatises.

Praxis—that is, a reflective political action that incorporates cultural identity—comes before theology in any formal sense. Therefore, the initial motivation that compels us to do theology is not our desire to place books in university and seminary libraries for professors and their graduate students. On the contrary, our reason for making theology arises from our experience in the ghettoes, villages, and churches of the poor in our countries. We do not believe that it is necessary for them to remain poor. Something must be done about their misery.

Doing and saying are therefore bound together so that the meaning of what one says can be validated only by what one does. Theology for us is critical reflection upon a prior religio-cultural affirmation and political commitment to be in solidarity with the victims of our continents.

Because the starting point of black and Third World theologies is defined by a prior cultural affirmation and political commitment to be in solidarity with the poor, our theologies bear the names that reflect our affirmations and commitments. We call our theologies black, African, Hispanic-American, Asian, red, Latin American, minjung, black feminist, and a host of other names that still sound strange to persons whose theological knowledge has been confined to European and white North American theologies. The identities of our theologies are determined by the human and divine dimensions of reality to which we are attempting to bear witness.

We do not begin our theology with a reflection on divine revelation as if the God of our faith is separate from the suffering of our people. We do not believe that revelation is a deposit of fixed doctrines or an objective word of God that is then applied to the human situation. On the contrary, we contend that there is no truth outside or beyond the concrete historical events in which persons are engaged as agents. Truth is found in the histories, cultures, and religions of our peoples. Our focus on social and religio-cultural analyses separates our theological enterprise from the progressive and abstract theologies of Europe and North America. It also illuminates the reasons why *orthopraxis* in contrast to orthodoxy has become for many of us the criterion of theology.[14]

Although black and Third World theologians have been accused of reducing theology to ideology by many European and North American critics, that criticism is misplaced: it camouflages the human character of all theologies and particularly the ideological option for the rich that our critics have made. Unlike our critics, we do not claim to be neutral in our theology, because the enormity of the suffering of our people demands that we choose *for* its liberation and *against* structures of oppression. We cannot let those who support the structures of oppression define what theology is. On this point, black theologians identify with the way Malcolm X expressed it: "Don't let anybody who is oppressing us ever lay the ground rules. Don't go by their game, don't play the game by their rules. Let them know that this is a new game, and we've got some new rules."[15]

The dominant theologians of Europe and North America want the old theological rules because they made them, and their rules will help to keep the world as it is—with whites controlling blacks, men dominating women, and rich nations keeping poor nations dependent. But what most European and North American whites as well as too many African-Americans find difficult to understand is that we are living in a new world situation, and this requires a new way of making theology. Again, I like the way Malcolm put it:

> The time that we're living in . . . and . . . are facing now is not an era where one who is oppressed is looking toward the oppressor to give him some system or form of logic or reason. What is logical to the oppressor isn't logical to the oppressed. And what is reason to the oppressor isn't reason to the oppressed. The black people in this country are beginning to realize that what sounds reasonable to those who exploit us doesn't sound reasonable to us. There just has to be a new system of reason and logic devised by us who are at the bottom, if we want to get some results in this struggle that is called "the Negro revolution."[16]

In EATWOT, black and Third World theologians have been attempting to develop together a new way of making theology. In contrast to the dominant theologies of Europe and North America, largely defined by their responses to the European Enlightenment and the problems of the unbeliever that arose from it, our theological enterprise focuses on the European and North American invasion of the continents of Africa, Asia, and Latin America, an invasion that inaugurated the slave trade, colonization, and neocolonialism. Our primary theological question is not how can we believe in God in view of the modern, Western confidence in reason, science, and technology that seem to exclude the necessity for faith in God. Rather our theological problem arises from our encounter of God in the experience of the misery of the poor. How can we speak about Jesus' death on the cross without first speaking about the death of the poor? How can the poor of our countries achieve worth as human beings in a world that has attempted to destroy our cultures and religions?

The chief contradiction out of which our theologies achieve their distinctiveness is the problem of the nonperson. That is why our most important dialogue partners are not philosophers of metaphysics and other socially disinterested intellectuals in the universities; we are primarily interested in talking with social scientists and political activists who are engaged in the liberation of the poor.

Black and Third World theologians' concern for the oppressed forced us to establish links with communities of the poor, and we experienced in their ecclesial life something more than a routine gathering of like-minded persons. In their worship life is revealed a knowledge of themselves that cannot be destroyed by the structures that oppress them. The liberating character of their spirituality can be seen in the way that their faith in God evolves out of their cultural and political aspirations. It can be observed in the basic Christian communities of Latin America, the black and Hispanic churches of North America, the indigenous churches and traditional religions of Africa, and in the religious life of Asia. In their worship, the God of grace and judgment meets the poor, transforms their personhood from nobody to somebody, and bestows upon them the power and courage to struggle for justice.

Worship, therefore, is not primarily an expression of the individual's private relationship with God. It is rather a community happening, an eschatological invasion of God into the gathered community of victims, empowering them with "the divine Spirit from on high," "to keep on keeping on" even though the odds might appear to be against them. In the collective presence of the poor at worship, God re-creates them as a liberated community that must bring freedom to the oppressed of the land. Black and Third World theologies are being created out of the ecclesial and

religious life of the poor, and they seek to interpret the God encountered in religio-cultural and political struggles to overcome
Euro-American domination.

It has been within the context of the churches and the religions
of the poor that black and Third World theologies have begun to
reread the Bible. In this rereading many of us began to speak of
the "hermeneutical privilege of the poor" and of "God's bias
toward the poor." Although Latin American theologians have
done more exegetical work to demonstrate the biblical option for
the poor than have others,[17] a similar concern is shared by most
Third World theologians. Suh Nam-Dong, an interpreter of the
minjung theology of South Korea, may be quoted as an example:

> Theological activities do not end with the exposition of
> biblical texts on salvation or liberation of people by God. In
> the Bible, the exodus, the activities of the prophets, and the
> event of the cross offer new insights, but these texts ought to
> be rediscovered and reinterpreted in the context of the hu-
> man struggle for historical and political liberation today.[18]

While acknowledging that the distinctiveness of black and
Third World theologies is primarily defined by their particular
contexts, their method of making theology may be summarized
with the following emphases:

1. Black and Third World theologians make theology in complex religio-cultural contexts and with the political commitment
to liberate the poor from oppression. Theology, then, is reflection
upon the meaning of God in solidarity with the poor who are
struggling to overcome cultural and political domination. The
acid test of any theological truth is found in whether it aids victims in their struggle to overcome their victimization. There are
no abstract, objective truths that are applicable for all times and
situations. Truth is concrete, and it is inseparable from the oppressed who are struggling for freedom.

2. Because the liberation of our people is the central motivation
for us to engage in the theological enterprise, the second element
of our method is social analysis. Social analysis brings to light
that which is hidden. It unmasks untruth so that truth can be seen

in a clear light. Black and Third World theologians do not believe that the work of theology can be done unless the truth is known about systems of domination. Racism, sexism, colonialism, capitalism, and militarism must be comprehensively analyzed so that these demons can be destroyed.

We agree with Karl Marx's eleventh thesis on Feuerbach: "The philosophers have only *interpreted* the world, in various ways; the point, however, is to *change* it." In our use of the critical tools of the social sciences, as well as religio-cultural analyses, black and Third World theologians have been attempting to make theologies of liberation rather than theologies of domestication.

3. Through a political commitment informed by social and cultural analyses, a new hermeneutical situation is created. The Bible is no longer merely an ancient document whose meaning can be uncovered only by the historical criticism of biblical experts. Political commitment, informed by social analysis, provides an angle of vision that enables us to reinterpret the scriptures and thus bring to light the message that European and North American biblical exegetes had covered up.

When the Bible is read in the community of the poor, it is not understood by them as a deposit of doctrines or of revealed truths about God. Rather it becomes a living book that tells the story of God's dealings with God's people. Its importance as a source for creating theology cannot be overstated for black and Third World theologians. Even feminist and South African theologians, who question its authority (largely because of its sexist and racist misuses), do not ignore the Bible.[19] They wrestle with it, refusing to allow an abstract biblical authority, written, interpreted, and defended by white males, to negate the authority of their own experience. God, they insist, cannot be less than the human experience of liberation from oppression. We must not allow an abstract word of God to usurp God's word as Spirit who empowers persons to be who they are—fully human in search of the highest beauty, love, and joy.

4. The meaning of the gospel that is derived from our rereading of the Bible cannot be communicated by old European and white North American theological concepts. The truth derived from our people's struggles must be communicated by the histories and

cultures of our peoples. Truth is embedded in the stories, songs, dances, sermons, paintings, and sayings of our peoples. Because many of us learned how to do theology in European and North American universities and seminaries, we have had to be converted to a radically new way of doing theology. How does one make theology by using the history and culture of one's people? What method is appropriate for these sources? The answer to this question is not clear to many of us, and that is why several EATWOT members wish to spend the next three to five years working on this methodological problem.

Because black and Third World theologians have been doing theology for a short time, and doing it together for an even shorter time, we do not have a fully developed method for making theology.

These points represent our attempt to listen to what we have been saying to each other in our search to build a Third World theology derived from the religio-cultural and political struggles of our people to overcome Euro-American domination.

AFRICAN-AMERICAN CHURCHES AND THE EATWOT DIALOGUE

What has the EATWOT dialogue to do with African-American churches? I would suggest the following:

1. African-American theological dialogue with Third World Christians can serve as a model for conversations between the churches on each continent. Through a study of EATWOT literature, African-American churches can gain information regarding the best ways to initiate contact with Third World churches. It also is possible to avoid the mistakes that EATWOT made and to build upon its strengths. Indeed it is possible for African-Americans to become participants in the association. This link will not only help EATWOT but also strengthen the Third World involvement of our churches.

2. It is unfortunate that African-American churches have borrowed their theology from white fundamentalist and other denominations from which they often also derive their names. Black

churches often claim that their theologies are not different from those of white denominations. Black Methodists claim the theology of white Methodists and black Baptists follow suit. Black Christians often say that they differ from whites with regard to their ethical behavior and not with regard to their religious beliefs. As a historiographer of the AME Church put it: "The origin of the AME Church was over social treatment" and not over "religious beliefs."[20]

I, however, would argue, as would other Third World Christians, that what one believes can be explicated only by what one does. To suggest that one can believe one thing and do another is to drive an unbiblical wedge between faith and obedience. Jesus said, "Not every one who says to me, 'Lord, Lord,' shall enter the kingdom of heaven, but he who does the will of my Father who is in heaven" (Matt. 7:21, RSV). A similar point is made in 1 John: "If any one says, 'I love God,' and hates his brother, he is a liar; for he who does not love his brother whom he has seen, cannot love God whom he has not seen" (4:20, RSV).

The idea that faith and obedience belong together and cannot be separated is deeply embedded in the black church tradition. That was what our slave forebears had in mind when they sang: "Everybody talking about heaven ain't going there." That is also why black radicalism and black churches have been interrelated in African-American history. Therefore, it is indeed unfortunate for contemporary African-American Christians to say that their religious beliefs are the same as those of white racists. How can that be when they enslaved us, lynched us, and segregated us—and all in the name of God and country? African-American churches need to break off their theological link with white fundamentalist churches and begin to develop their own theology in dialogue with their own past and with oppressed Christians of the Third World.

Through an establishment of their link with progressive Third World Christians, black churches can begin to develop a theology that is both particular and universal. It will need to be particular in relation to its own ethnic history and universal by being accountable to the experiences of other Christians in the Third World. Presently, the theology of black churches is particular in the worst sense (and not universal at all!), because it is *white—*

that is, derived from the history of white Methodists, Baptists, Catholics, Presbyterians, and other white denominations. It is sad that for many black Christians "universal" means advocating the religious beliefs of the whites who enslaved them. A serious dialogue with the theology of the black poor and with the theologies of the marginalized peoples of the Third World can help to liberate our churches from enslavement to white theology.

3. African-American churches should conduct workshops on Third World churches and their theologies so as to introduce the theological literature and other information about Asia, Africa, the Caribbean, and Latin America to their pastors and laity. We can invite representative theologians and ministers of the Third World to be resource persons to help us to gain a deeper understanding of the complexity of the reality of the Third World. A reading knowledge of the reality of the Third World and of the theological reflections derived from it should receive top priority in the teaching ministry of our churches.

Reading the liberation theologies of the Third World will encourage our people to be open to the theology emerging from their own history and contemporary struggle for justice. Black theology will not sound so strange if it is seen in relation to other Third World theologies that also take seriously God's bias for the poor. Our people should know the names of Gustavo Gutiérrez and Elsa Tamez of Latin America, Allan Boesak and Amba Oduyoye of Africa, Preman Niles and Virginia Fabella of Asia, and Idris Hamid of the Caribbean. Reading these theologians can help us to appreciate our own history as we search for a theology that is both particular and universal.

4. Dialogue with Third World Christians will enlarge our perspective on the meaning of the Christian faith and its relationship to the poor of the world who are struggling to defend their humanity. It is so easy for blacks to think that racism is the chief, if not the only, instance of oppression in the world. It is also easy to think that we can liberate ourselves from racial oppression through integration into the American capitalist system or through our separation from it. What we seldom do is look at the problems of racism, sexism, classism, imperialism, poverty, militarism, and the like, in relation to each other.

There is no way for us to achieve liberation from white racism without a simultaneous liberation in the Third World. Dialogue with the progressive theologies on the Third World will reveal these connections and help us to develop strategies of liberation that will support our Third World brothers and sisters.

5. Dialogue with Third World Christians will also help us to become more acutely aware of the Third World presence in our midst, that of Asian-Americans, Hispanic-Americans, and Amerindians. With this emphasis, we enter into the subject of the next chapter.

Chapter VIII

Black Theology, Black Churches, and Other Minorities in the United States

We express our solidarity and support with all oppressed peoples of the world. We, the people of color in this conference, expect and demand recognition of our existence and contributions in the area of liberation theology. We expect and demand an expression of the concrete reality of what was put forward as the goals of this conference.

Statement by the Coalition
of U.S. Nonwhite Racial and National Minorities
at the TIA 1975 conference, Detroit[1]

If it is important for African-American churches to begin dialogues with the churches in the Third World, it also follows that conversations among African-American Christians and Hispanic, Asian, and Amerindians are also important. In fact, some will argue that a dialogue with the peoples of Africa, Asia, and Latin America independent of a similar dialogue with their racial and ethnic counterparts in the U.S.A. is doomed to failure from the start.

However, my reasons for urging dialogues between African-Americans and other North American minorities are the same as the ones advanced in the previous chapter in relation to African-Americans and Third World Christians. If the poor in any country or continent remain divided and suspicious of each other, they can be sure that they will remain powerless before oppressors who are always in complete agreement as to who shall rule and who shall be ruled.

No groups have been more divided and suspicious of each other and yet have the most to gain by mutual support and solidarity than have U.S. minorities. There have been few occasions of working together, but many occasions of indifference and hostility. Although initial dialogue will be difficult, the interdependence of our struggles requires that we begin this process.

It is strange that each racial and ethnic minority has always found reasons to overcome horrendous barriers in order to enter into dialogue with white Americans. Yet in relation to each other, across racial and ethnic groupings, the smallest and most insignificant reasons have been advanced for our lack of dialogue and mutual support. Until we begin to seek strategies to overcome our separation, whites will always exercise an inordinate power over us in our religious beliefs, as in all other aspects of our existence.

Dialogue should begin with the mutual sharing of stories in regard to our pilgrimages in the faith and our theological reflections upon it. Each group has a story to tell about its history of struggle to survive in this land and how the God of their faith empowered them to endure suffering and then to overcome it. Whites have treated us all in different ways, and each group is entitled to accent its particularity in this regard with the expectation of receiving appropriate respect from the others. But we should not fail to emphasize the *similarities* in the ways we have been treated, and that fact should encourage us to initiate and sustain our dialogue.

Mutual cultural exchanges in worship and other contexts is a place to begin. An exploration of the ways in which we can support each other politically is also important. In some community contexts, dialogue has begun at the local level. But I believe that it should be extended to the national level and eventually connected with the Third World. If we could initiate a way of sharing our hopes and dreams independent of the dominating influence of

North American and European whites, then our liberation will have taken a great leap forward.

In preparing for dialogue, all participants should recognize that whites will not look with favor upon this enterprise from which they are excluded. They will seek to "divide and conquer" us before our conversations get started. In fact whites will probably resent African-American dialogue with other U.S. minorities more than our dialogue with Third World Christians. The reasons are obvious. A coalition among minority religious leaders could lead to a radical change in political and economic configurations.

It is important for the oppressed to realize that there are forces of destruction from *within* ourselves, as well as from without, that are responsible for our continued oppression. We can easily identify many of the outside forces that oppress us—racism, corporate capitalism, police brutality, unjust laws, prisons, drugs, and so forth. The list could go on and on, and that is why it is convenient to sum them all up in one word—*whites!* But we need to look deeper than this. We have been fighting these outside forces for many years and their power over us is often magnified to unrealistic levels, because we seldom analyze critically and identify and fight the forces of destruction from within.

We are often our own worst enemy because we seldom examine analytically those factors that prevent our unity in the struggle for freedom. There are factors within each individual, within each group, and also in multiracial and ethnic groupings, that militate against our solidarity. And unless African-Americans, Hispanic-Americans, Asian-Americans, and Amerindian peoples face the problems within their group that would destroy our solidarity with each other, then we will not be very successful in our attempts to dialogue.

The greatest problem that all oppressed groups have is self-hatred. There is no way that whites could hold us in bondage so long, with minimal effective resistance and almost no coalition among us, without an effective use of negative and self-destructive programing within each group. As Malcolm X told African-Americans unceasingly, the worst crime the white man has committed has been to teach us to hate ourselves.

I have observed this most notably among minority professionals who have partly succeeded in the white system. It is not easy to detect, because professionals know how to cover it up with the language of freedom, which actually means slavery for the masses. Furthermore they are the acknowledged leaders of their people and they therefore decide how freedom is talked about and what methods are acceptable for its implementation. But these so-called leaders are often more accountable to the whites who control their people than to the people in whose behalf they claim to speak.

I realize that these problems will have to be handled with great care and sensitivity in order to prevent our conversations—within each group and across racial and ethnic barriers—from deteriorating into name-calling and personality conflicts. But we *must* face them; if not, our dialogue will get nowhere.

The *class* interests of many minority leaders and professionals often outweigh their racial and ethnic commitments, leading them to use the language of their culture and history to cover up their real solidarity with the white ruling class. That is why both groups promote cultural nationalism and integration in sociopolitical structures without offering a proposal for radical change. Marxism is a tool of analysis that could demonstrate the class collaboration of many minority leaders with the white corporate elite, but it has been effectively discredited as an atheistic ideology of Soviet Russia.

Every oppressed group must ask of each other (especially their leaders), *Who* stands to benefit from the status quo? It seems clear that those who benefit from the present unjust economic and political structures are not only the white corporate elite but also many civil rights leaders among the minorities whose organizations and personal income are dependent upon the consent of those whom we are fighting against. In our dialogue, we must face the hard problems in our communities and seek to create a method for overcoming them.

It seems that the churches provide an excellent place to start because of our common faith and religious commitment, with an emphasis on the reconciliation of all things in God. In our experience of transcendence, we are made one, and now is the time to bear witness to our oneness by meeting and doing things together that publicly demonstrate it.

AFRICAN-AMERICANS
AND OTHER U.S. MINORITIES IN TIA

African-American churches can learn from attempts to create dialogue in the past and present efforts among other U.S. minorities. One such attempt in this area is that of TIA, Theology in the Americas. The plans for TIA began in 1974 under the inspiration of Sergio Torres, a Chilean priest who had gone into exile following the military coup in Chile in 1973. In advance of its foundational conference, information regarding its purpose was sent out and individuals were contacted. According to a TIA brochure:

> The intention of the planners of the "Theology in the Americas: 1975" conference was to invite a group of Latin American theologians, representing the theology of liberation, to dialogue with North American theologians concerning the content and methodology of this new theological current. It was hoped that such a dialogue would help both groups: the Latin Americans to understand the complex reality of the U.S.A.; the North American theologians to initiate a process of evaluation of the American reality from the viewpoint of the poor and the oppressed.[2]

When this plan was presented to African-Americans before the conference, many of us objected, as did several feminists and representatives of other oppressed minorities.[3] The statement of intention implied that no theologies of liberation existed in North America. We told the organizers about black and feminist theologies, with the former using the term "liberation" to define its method of doing theology about the same time as Latin Americans, if not actually prior to them. But the organizers ignored our concerns and went ahead as planned, because they were mainly interested in dialogue between white North Americans and Latin Americans.

Initially several African-Americans decided to boycott the conference, but we changed our minds because we wanted to meet the representatives of the Latin American theology of liberation and also because we wanted to address head-on the errors implicit in the purpose of the conference. "Theology in the Americas: 1975" (often called "Detroit I") was held at Sacred Heart Seminary, in one of the black areas of Detroit. That locale provided a learning experience for most of the two hundred or so participants, most of whom were white. About thirty Hispanic, Amerindian, and African-Americans were present. To my knowledge no Asians were present.

It was clear from the beginning that the organizers of the conference did not intend for the theological reflections of U.S. minorities to receive much visibility. Black and feminist theologies were given a short time for the presentation of their perspectives in a plenary session, but other oppressed minorities were not. They were given the opportunity only to form workshops on their histories and theologies, and interested persons could choose to attend if they wished.

The main attraction of the conference was the fifteen or more liberation theologians from Latin America and white North American religious leftists. It seemed to most of us nonwhites that the latter wanted to use the Latin American reality in order to avoid the reality of oppression, especially racism, in the U.S.A.

The attraction of Latin American liberation theologians to white North American religious radicals involved several factors:

1. Both used Marxist and socialist ideology as a central element in their theological and political discourse. That meant that class analysis dominated the discussion; analysis of racism and sexism was either ignored or openly regarded as secondary and peripheral to any discussion in theology and politics. Therefore the concerns of black, feminist, and other theologies of the oppressed in the U.S.A. were minimized. The Latin Americans and the North American white religious radicals were either ignoring minorities or trying to convert them to the scientific analysis provided by Marxism.

I was then and still am too much of a race person to allow white Marxists to lure me from the importance of African-American history and culture in the doing of theology and politics. It was not that I was against class analysis. I was open to it, though at that time its importance had not made a decisive impact on my perspective of black theology. What I questioned was not class analysis or Marxism but rather the white radicals who promoted it and the way it was used to exclude questions dealing with racism.[4] Of all those who minimized racism, white U.S. leftists had shakier grounds than others, especially in view of their history of the *racial* oppression of non-Europeans.[5] What was the basis of their claim that racism is something secondary? I did not trust them; I felt that they were using Marxism as a smoke screen to cover up their own racism. I remembered Malcolm X's comment: "The criminal who has committed the crime is never the one to whom you look for a solution."

2. Another reason for the coherence of Latin American and U.S. white radicals was their common racial origin in Europe. U.S. minorities represented different cultures and histories and thus a radically different way of seeing the world. As long as minorities used the language of European culture, quoting Marx and affirming socialism at the appropriate junctures and never using the language of their ethnicity, whites had no difficulty dialoguing with them. Conflicts arose between whites and ethnic minorities when the latter began to insist that European culture did not have all the answers regarding human liberation. Inasmuch as Latin Americans and North American whites used an exclusively European language of liberation, almost totally defined by Marxism, they found it easy to talk with each other but quite difficult to comprehend why U.S. minorities refused to speak of liberation apart from their own history and culture.

3. The fact that U.S. whites controlled the money that financed the conference must have had some impact on the desire of Latin Americans to talk to them. It certainly allowed whites to control the proceedings, choose participants, and decide which issues would be discussed.

A Minority Caucus

Because white religious radicals dominated the conference in such a way as to exclude the problem of racism, U.S. minorities decided to form a caucus to challenge their theological and political arrogance. We insisted that there could be no genuine theology of liberation in the U.S.A. apart from the struggles of peoples of color for justice. U.S. minorities issued a joint statement expressing our appreciation for the conference and the opportunity to meet our brothers and sisters from Latin America. But we seriously questioned the programing of the conference because it "prevented us from sharing our similar experiences with our Latin American brothers and sisters."[6] After noting the concrete problems that excluded our particular issues, the statement said:

> We express our solidarity and support with all oppressed peoples of the world. We, the people of color of this conference, expect and demand recognition of our existence and contributions in the area of liberation theology. We expect and demand an expression of the concrete reality of what was put forward as the goals of this conference.
>
> In the spirit of solidarity and being able to correct these very shortcomings of the conference, we submit that the following are indispensable:
>
> 1. For future planning, representation of North American minority peoples on planning committees.
>
> 2. Participation of a significant and substantial representation of minority peoples in the conference, or any process.
>
> 3. A serious examination in the process of the conference of oppressive structures and situations of the Black people, the Asian people, the Hispanics, and Native Americans in North America.[7]

Because of that statement and the actions taken by the minorities at the conference, TIA was completely reorganized to include, with appropriate emphasis, the theological reflections of U.S. minorities. TIA became partly defined by a variety of minority theological projects: Black Theology Project, Hispanic Project, Asian-American Project, Indigenous Peoples' Project, Women's Project, Church and Labor Dialogue, Theologians' Task Force, and Alternative Theology Project. It has been within the context of TIA that African-Americans and other minorities have been in dialogue with each other regarding our histories and cultures in relation to our religious faith.

Although TIA has encouraged the development of theological

reflection among U.S. minorities, its primary aim has been to transcend the particularities of oppressed peoples' histories and cultures in the U.S.A. so as to move toward a "universal" approach to doing theology as defined by Latin American liberation theology, class analysis, and the socialist alternative. This was the emphasis of its founder, Sergio Torres, of the white religious left in the Labor and Church Dialogue, and of Christians for Socialism. But the Asian, indigenous, Hispanic, and black emphases on their own histories and cultures have not been received by whites with the respect and recognition expected by their representatives.

In order to insure that the Detroit II conference (1980) would not be a repeat of Detroit I, Asian, Hispanic, indigenous, and black members of the planning committee insisted that their delegates should represent the largest number of persons in attendance—that is, 500 of the 750 to be invited. Although that many minority persons could not attend, because of their financial limitations, about half of the total of 600 in attendance were persons of color.

At Detroit II, U.S. minorities began to build upon their experience at Detroit I and the intervening five years by thinking more deeply about liberation theology. What does it mean to make theology by using the experience and struggle of victims of oppression as one of its primary sources? It is one thing to say that Christian theology must come from the experiences and struggles of the oppressed, but something else again to spell out in words and practice the concrete, practical meaning of that affirmation.

No one at Detroit I or II denied that Christian theology must come from the struggles of the oppressed for justice. But how do we know whose theology is a genuine theology of liberation and at the expense of whom? That was the question that U.S. minorities were forced to deal with in view of the fact that white radicals claimed to be liberation theologians (or at least their supporters) but excluded the history and culture of U.S. minorities from the center of their concern. As we reflected on this issue, two criteria became clear to us.

First, every Christian theology of liberation must be derived from scripture and its claim that God has come in Jesus Christ for the liberation of all. There can be no Christian theology of liberation that does not receive its essential identity from Jesus Christ as witnessed in the scriptures. Without this essential witness as the source of grace and judgment, we are left merely with the particularity of our own experience. Our experience of struggle, though valuable, is not enough, for inherent in it is the encounter of the divine reality that drives us to look beyond our present suffering and struggle to the coming creation of a new humanity and a new world. It is the encounter of God in the sufferings of the poor that forces liberation theology to reread the scriptures with a special emphasis on the "hermeneutical privilege of the poor."

Secondly, every Christian theology of liberation must incorporate, as an essential characteristic of its discourse, the history and culture of the oppressed in whose name it claims to speak. If the God of the poor is liberating them from bondage, how can we speak correctly about this God if our language does not arise out of the community where God's presence is found?

My difficulty with white religious radicals is that, although they say that theology must come from the poor, they seldom bother to learn anything about the culture and history of the poor. Can one really love the poor *and* ignore their history and culture *and* minimize the racial aspect of their oppression? I do not think so! It was this issue that created conflicts between U.S. minorities and some of the white radicals at Detroit II vis-à-vis the understanding of liberation.

As the Detroit II conference progressed, minorities began to realize that they had much in common with each other, and they needed more time and space for dialogue with each other regarding their experience of suffering and struggle in the U.S.A. In my presentation in the plenary session, I decided to address the problem of the lack of dialogue among U.S. minorities:

> If we are going to make any revolutionary changes in the international structures of oppression, poor people in the First World must make a coalition with each other and also with the poor in the Third World. It is not difficult for many in the minority communities of the U.S.A. to recognize this truth, but it is difficult for us to implement it. It seems that we cannot even build structures for dialogue among our-

selves, except through the church structures controlled by white America. How, then, is it possible for us to build structures for dialogue with our brothers and sisters in the Third World? How do we build mutual structures of support for our struggles of liberation? We do not know how to make that coalition. If we could find an answer to that question, we will have made a giant step toward our collective freedom. It is unfortunate that oppressed minorities in the U.S.A. seem not to be able to talk with each other or with Third World peoples *except* through structures controlled and financed by whites. What does that tell us about our liberation struggles?[8]

When I pointed to the lack of a coalition among oppressed minorities (Hispanic, Amerindian, African-American and Asian), I had no idea that it would be received enthusiastically by so many persons. At the close of the sessions, several representatives from each group began to caucus, each emphasizing the need for minorities to have conversations around issues that are vital to us.

But the TIA conference had not been designed for meetings of various minority groups with each other. Dialogue was supposed to transcend the particularities and concerns of minorities by focusing on the "universal" issues of theology and politics as defined by Latin American liberation theology and Marxist class analysis. U.S. minorities had to find time for dialogue with each other by meeting in the early morning and late at night. Many of us insisted that whites must be excluded from our conversations until we got ourselves together. Some whites strongly resented their exclusion, and a few minorities in our coalition also objected.

Our coalition was fragile and was very difficult to hold together. We African-Americans had to be careful about our tendency to dominate, and everyone had to be careful not to make their particularity the exclusive focus. Because we had very little experience of being together, we hardly knew where or how to start a dialogue. We felt strongly the pressures from many whites who questioned our coalition and did much to try to destroy it. It was suggested that we decide only on the importance of our dialogue for the future and to propose to the TIA assembly that the organization be used as an instrument for creating a context for conversations.

We did not say that we did not want to talk with whites anymore. On the contrary, many of us strongly felt the need to be in dialogue with whites who are genuinely concerned about human liberation. U.S. minorities merely wanted to talk among each other, without a white presence, so that we could share our mutual suffering and hope in the fight for justice. When whites are present, they dominate the dialogue and often take offense when we tell our history of suffering and struggle. We did not want to spend our time arguing about what type of analysis to pursue, trying to convince whites that racism is as important as classism. How could we offer an analysis of oppression on the basis of our culture and history that could be as persuasive to them as their many versions of Marxism? U.S. minorities felt that we had no chance of making whites take seriously our historical and cultural analyses, and it was more important to meet alone so that we could think at our own pace and about our own problems in ways that were meaningful to each other.

My own ideas about interethnic/indigenous dialogue had been influenced by my participation in EATWOT. I had seen how conversations on theology and politics among Africans, Asians, Latin Americans, and U.S. minorities had enhanced the openness of all to each other, creating mutual support of each other across continents. I wanted U.S. minorities to create a similar dialogue in TIA.

Some whites strongly resented the use of TIA for creating conversation in theology among Hispanics, Asian-Americans, Amerindians and African-Americans, and they used their influence with a few minorities to keep us apart. The groups most strongly opposed to our dialogue were the white socialists of the Labor and Church Dialogue and the Christians for Socialism. Their position was that TIA had to be socialist and that the minorities there were not socialist enough. What with the tensions and suspicions among the minorities and the opposition of white radicals, we were almost defeated. But with the help of many white feminists and other concerned whites, we succeeded in maintaining our unity throughout the conference, a feat that was surprising even for most minority members and our white supporters, not to mention our opponents. As Sydney Brown said: "Blacks, Hispanics, Asian-Americans, and Native Americans came together in a single caucus. I had long been aware of the widely divergent worldviews of these groups, and marveled at their ability to unite."[9]

It was my first experience with U.S. minority groups willing to transcend their differences for a moment in order to affirm the greater truth of their unity and thereby offer an effective challenge to a common enemy, in this case dogmatic white Marxists who acted as if truth begins and ends with their analysis of the world.

Dogmatic, Undemocratic Socialism

Our experience of unity in the midst of a tense and hostile situation revealed that not all whites are our enemies. At Detroit II it was only a small, insensitive, and arrogant group of white leftists who cared more about the correctness of their analysis than they did about the victims of oppression. Their performance at Detroit II revealed some of the reasons why socialism has such a weak following in the U.S.A., and why Marxism is often associated with dogmatism and thus viewed as being antidemocratic.

It is important to point out that there were many whites who supported the interethnic/indigenous coalition and understood the reasons for our refusal to allow Marxism to suppress the significance of our own particularity. The most insightful analysis of the conference in this regard was that contained in Gregory Baum's essay, "Theology in the Americas: Detroit II." Speaking of the conflict between minority groups and white leftists, Baum said:

> The socialist language offered them by the ardent socialists at Detroit II was too "white." Why white? Because it was presented as a theory that is basically finished, in total reliance on a certain kind of rational analysis, with only the

briefest reference to the part which the various minorities of color, and women, may play in defining the society of tomorrow. There was an excessive trust in a purely economic analysis of oppression and liberation; far too little importance was attached, the minorities argued, to cultural and spiritual factors—that is, to those factors that determine their own identities. An analysis that is almost exclusively economic makes the minorities invisible.[10]

It was because our existence (our history and culture) did not count in the white leftists' analysis that they pushed so hard for their perspective on socialism. When they spoke they sounded excessively sectarian. As Baum said:

There were at the conference certain socialist voices that exhibited the confident tone of sectarians: they possessed the truth, they had the key to correct analysis, they were ahead of the crowd and hence had to manage and maneuver it. A few of these voices were in the steering committee. It was precisely the narrowness of the economic analysis that contributed to the failure of their plan. It was a useful lesson for all participants: it was a warning against political sectarianism.[11]

Baum correctly recognized that we were just as concerned to explore the socialist alternative as were the whites who talked as if they owned the label. But we were not going to allow the language of white socialists to separate us from our own people. Again Baum identified the real issue of our concern:

The people of color, in their criticism of the steering committee, were particularly aware that the ardent white socialists were on the whole leaders without a following, an intellectual elite without roots in the people, while they, the blacks, the Hispanics, the native peoples and the Asian-Americans, were identified with their people, with the great crowd. They were quite eager to explore the socialist alternative to capitalism, but they wanted to do this in a language and a style that would not separate them from their own base. They did not want to become strangers to their own people. The white socialists, they thought, tended to be alienated from their people, from their parishes and congregations.[12]

The arrogant attitude of white socialists is one of the reasons why socialism is a "foreign" word in the black community. One should like to think that by now socialists would have learned from their history, but they have learned very little about their own racism. And the continued presence of racism among socialists is evidence enough that socialism alone will not solve the racial problems in the world.

It is refreshing to know that some whites are beginning to recognize that vital fact. Indeed because of the support of many whites in TIA and because of the determination of minorities to stay together and create a new future together, we have succeeded in creating a new vision for TIA that is now aiding dialogues of minorities among themselves.

The first interethnic/indigenous dialogue of TIA was held at the Haudenosaunne Native Self-Sufficiency Center in Gray (Oneida County), New York, July 2–5, 1981.[13] Meetings have also been held in Puerto Rico (May 4–7, 1982) and in the New York City Chinatown (May 4–7, 1983).[14] The fourth dialogue is scheduled to be held in Chicago, July 1984. These dialogues have been enormously useful in sharing and receiving information about the history, culture, and theology of others so as to increase communication among us and to begin laying a foundation for our common struggle. They have helped minority peoples to recognize the value of their own particularity as well as that of others and thereby urge them to search for a universality in the gospel that includes the wisdom of all peoples.

Another significant development was the establishment of a racial-ethnic women's coalition and the designation of a liaison between this group and the white women of the Women's Project. The goal of these actions, which were initiated by the racial-ethnic women, was dialogue between the two groups. The existence of this dialogue shows that the intention of the interethnic/

indigenous struggle for unity was not to exclude our dialogue with whites but rather to deepen our unity with each other so as to create a more meaningful dialogue with whites. It is to the credit of the Women's Project that it accepted the challenge issued by racial-ethnic women.

LIBERATION THEOLOGIES IN DIALOGUE: CONCLUSIONS

1. Every theology is a product of its social environment and thus in part a reflection of it. No one has expressed this point more clearly than has Gustavo Gutiérrez:

> Theology is done by persons who, whether they know it or not, are caught up in particular social processes. Consequently, all theology is in part a reflection of this or that concrete process. Theology is not something disembodied or atemporal. On the contrary, theology is the attempt to express the word of the Lord in the language of today—in the categories of a particular time and place. Of course, I am speaking of authentic, relevant theology. No meaningful theology can be elucubrated in disconnection from concrete history, by stringing together a set of abstract ideas enjoying some manner of interior logical connection. No meaningful theology springs forth fully arrayed from dusty tomes of yesterday. No, a meaningful theological reflection consists in an expression, and a calling into question, of broad historical processes. Only as such will theology fulfill its role as a reading of the faith from within a specific social practice.[15]

To acknowledge that all theology is situated in history means that theology is done by human beings, not by God. As human discourse, it must begin with the human situation as perceived from a particular standpoint of a given people. Black theology rightly begins with the history and culture of African-Americans as they seek to interpret the meaning of God's liberating presence in their struggle for freedom. The same is true of Asian-

American, Hispanic, or Amerindian efforts to work out a theology for themselves. No one can do theology creatively by using primarily the history and culture of others, especially those of oppressors.

Unfortunately whites have controlled the language of theology and think that their view of the gospel or of Marxism is the only acceptable one. When they urged minorities to transcend their particularities and embrace Marxism, they mean *European* Marxism—as interpreted by *them*. When we are asked to embrace a radicalism in religion that includes their participation, they mean to exclude the particularities of peoples of color and use white experiences and concepts as the common language of all. Authentic liberation theology rejects this and insists that Christian theological reflection begins with the concrete experiences of the oppressed who are fighting for freedom.

2. Every theology ought to move beyond its particularity to the concrete experiences of others. No theology should remain enclosed in its own narrow culture and history. That has been the awful mistake of the dominant theologies of Europe and North America. They talk about God as if Europeans are the only ones who can think, and that is why they still have difficulty taking seriously liberation theologies in Asia, Africa, and Latin America, or that of minorities in the U.S.A. More than half of the Christians of the world are persons of color; how, then, can European and North American white theologians continue to do theology without any serious wrestling with the issues of the Third World?

Whatever else we may say about the gospel, it is not an expression of truth enclosed within, and thus limited to, one culture. Indeed to think of the gospel as if any one people had a monopoly on its truth and meaning would be to distort it. God is more than what any one people can elaborate and express; no set of concepts or experiences can exhaust the significance of God. This is true of the experiences of *all* peoples, of course—including Hispanic, Asian-American, Amerindian, and African-American.

In our efforts to accent our particularities, we must be careful not to limit God to them or to remain enclosed in them ourselves. The encountering of the God of biblical faith draws us beyond ourselves to the poor of the world. God is always to be found in the sufferings of victims. That is the meaning of Jesus' cross. The resurrection of Christ kindles the hope that our ultimate future will leave human suffering behind. We must, then, bear witness to God's creation of a new humanity by moving beyond ourselves to our neighbors for the building of community defined by love, justice, and peace.

3. Every theology needs instruments of social analysis that will help theologians define the causes of injustice. How can we participate in the liberation of the poor from poverty if its causes are not clearly understood through social analysis? Social analysis is nothing but a way of uncovering the causes of evil and exploitation. It helps us to see more clearly and thus to know the nature of the evil we are fighting against. As long as theology remains ignorant of the causes of exploitation, it will not be able to effectively fight it.

One of the most efficient tools for analyzing problems in the modern world is Marxism. It is unfortunate that the black church has ignored it. Marxism is more than an ideology that comports atheism. It incorporates a form of social analysis that can help blacks understand capitalist political economy. That is why Marxism is the subject of the next chapter.

Chapter IX

Black Christians and Marxism

Socialism places its chief value upon [humanity]. Socialism, like the inspired Carpenter of Nazareth, places more value upon [humanity] than it does upon riches. It believes that the rights of [humanity] are more sacred than the rights of property, believes indeed, that the only sacred thing on earth is a human being. Socialism would bring all the people to participate in the rivalry of life upon a footing of equality, allowing to each individual the widest possible range for the development of his powers and personality, with freedom to follow wherever his abilities may lead him.

That the Negro will enthusiastically espouse the cause of socialism we cannot doubt. Social and industrial oppression have been his portion for centuries. When he comes to realize that socialism offers him freedom of opportunity to co-operate with all [persons] upon terms of equality in every avenue of life, he will not be slow to accept his social emancipation. Rev. Reverdy C. Ransom, 1896[1]

Anyone familiar with the origin and development of black theology knows that Marxism has not been a major item on its theological agenda. With few exceptions, the chief political concern of black churches has been focused on the problem of racism with almost no reference to Marxist class analysis.

The failure of black preachers and theologians to incorporate Marxist class analysis into their theological discourse and church projects is due partly to their assumption that the problem of racism can be solved in the United States without a socialist transformation in the political economy. Apart from the racist practices of social, economic, and political institutions, most blacks have assumed that American society is essentially just and consequently has the best of all possible political systems.

The black struggle for freedom, which has been largely defined within the church and led primarily by its preachers, has been conspicuous for its promotion of two seemingly contradictory but often complementary ideologies: integration and nationalism. Apart from the emergence of revolutionary black nationalism during the late 1960s and early '70s, the philosophies of black nationalism and integration rarely included in their analysis the possibility of a radical change in the American political economy, replacing capitalism with socialism.[2] Although no group has been more critical of and resistant to injustice in U.S. society than blacks, black criticism has been almost exclusively limited to racism, with little or no reference to class oppression. Not only has the black community failed to take Marxism seriously, but there are some black preachers and theologians who unfortunately regard it as the antithesis of everything Christian and American.

The negative attitude toward Marxism in the black community and church is doubtless linked with the anticommunist attitude of the white church and the marginal status of Marxism in American society. White Americans (especially Evangelical Christians) are well known for their irrational anticommunism, and for most whites Marxism is identical with the communism of Soviet Russia. Agreeing with President Ronald Reagan, many white Evangelical Christians describe Soviet communism as "the focus of evil in the modern world," which must be opposed with all our might, including nuclear warfare.[3] Conservative white Christians associate capitalism with Christian freedom and political democracy, and they identify Marxism with Russian communism, atheism, and political totalitarianism.

White conservative Evangelical Christianity has given, for the most part, a reactionary response to Marxism, but many liberal white Christians, especially theologians, have often ignored Marxism. However, during the height of the influence of the Social Gospel movement and the Socialist Party in the early twentieth century, there were many Christians who began to read Karl Marx and also began to consider the possibility of replacing capitalism with socialism. But Christian openness to Marxism was seriously damaged with the negative reaction of the American government to the Bolshevik revolution of 1917.

With the strong influence of Soviet Russia upon the American Communist Party and its public advocacy of atheism, American Christians began to define Marxism as a godless philosophy that has nothing in common with the religion of Jesus Christ. The hostility between Christians and communists was lessened during the United Front period of the 1930s and after Russia entered World War II, but was restored and carried to extreme limits during the cold war and the McCarthy era of the 1950s. To talk with Marxists was often viewed as being equivalent to talking with the incarnation of evil.

Although conservative white Christians were much less restrained in their rhetoric against the evils of Marxism than were liberals, both groups seemed to assume that there was really nothing in common between the teachings of Jesus Christ and the philosophy of Karl Marx. Christians stated the differences in radical terms: they believed in God and political freedom; Marxists did not. Accordingly they rejected Marxism without a serious encounter with the writings of Karl Marx. Such a procedure is analogous to that of Marxists who reject Christianity without reading the Bible or its progressive interpreters.

After Nikita Khrushchev made his "revelations" at the twentieth congress of the Soviet Communist Party in February 1956 and with the end of the McCarthy era and the lessening of East-West cold war tensions, some liberal American theologians began to participate more actively, together with their European counterparts, in conversations with Marxists during the early 1960s. That was the beginning of Marxist-Christian dialogue. The Soviet invasion of Czechoslovakia in 1968 seriously damaged those discussions. White liberal theologians once again returned to the problems of theological methodology with scant attention paid to the Christian demand for the establishment of political and economic justice.

With the rise of Latin American liberation theology and its affirmation of Marxist class analysis and its vehement rejection of U.S. capitalism, white and black theologians were challenged by a Marxist perspective that was not defined by Soviet Russia or its satellites. The Marxist challenge of progressive Latin American theologians was so great that white and black theologians were forced to deal with the question of class oppression both domestically and globally. In addition to the challenge of Latin American theology, the rapid appearance of Marxist governments among the emerging nations of the Third World made it increasingly difficult for North American Christians to ignore U.S. imperialist exploitation of Third World peoples in the name of God and freedom. The embarrassing defeat of the U.S.A. in Vietnam, the dismal failure of Lyndon Johnson's war on poverty, the CIA involvement in the overthrow of the Allende government in Chile (1973), the WCC emphasis on a "just, participatory, and sustainable society," the ever widening economic gap between rich and poor nations, and the rise of an independent revolutionary Third World Christianity—these and other factors encouraged liberal white and black theologians to take another look at Marxism.

Although some theologians have begun to accept the challenge posed by Marxism, it would be grossly misleading to suggest that American churches have begun to take Karl Marx seriously. For the average American Christian and for most theologians, Karl Marx's philosophy remains atheistic and antidemocratic and thus has nothing to do with the gospel of Jesus Christ or American freedom.

The exclusive focus of the black church on racism, the reactionary anticommunism of the white church, and the narrow sectarian focus and internal conflicts of American Marxist parties continue to prevent genuine dialogue between Christians and Marxists in the United States. American Christians have ignored not only Marxists, they have also rejected Karl Marx—without even taking the time to read him. I think the time has come for American Christians, white and black, to dispel their ignorance regarding Marx and his followers. In this chapter, I shall explore the challenge and necessity of Marxism for American churches and their theologians.[4]

THE CHALLENGE OF MARXISM

The heart of Karl Marx's challenge to the Christian church is his theoretical and practical critique of religion. The theoretical side of his critique is derived from Ludwig Feuerbach. In *The Essence of Christianity* Feuerbach locates the core of religion in

human subjective states and insists that it has "no material exclusively of its own."⁵ Marx accepts Feuerbach's judgment, using
similar language in a letter to Arnold Ruge: "Religion has no
content of its own and lives not from heaven but from earth, and
falls of itself with the dissolution of the inverted reality whose
theory it is."⁶ For Feuerbach and Marx, God is nothing but an
illusion, a fantasy, a human projection that has no meaning separate from the hopes and aspirations of human beings. As Marx
puts it: "*Man makes religion*; religion does not make man."⁷ It
was on the basis of his acceptance of the cogency of Feuerbach's
reduction of religion to anthropology that Marx could claim that
"for Germany, the *criticism of religion* has been largely com-
pleted."⁸

Marx agreed with Feuerbach's analysis of religion as human
self-consciousness, but he was not content that Feuerbach's critique remain on a theoretical level and not be applied to social
reality:

> Man is not an abstract being, squatting outside the world.
> Man is the human world, the state, society. This state, this
> society, produce religion which is an inverted world con-
> sciousness, because they are an inverted world. Religion
> is the general theory of the world, its encyclopedic com-
> pendium, its logic in popular form, its spiritual *point
> d'honneur*, its enthusiasm, its moral sanction, its solemn
> complement, its general basis of consolation and justifica-
> tion. It is *the fantastic realization* of the *human being* inas-
> much as the human being possesses no true reality. The
> struggle against religion is, therefore, indirectly a struggle
> against *that world* whose spiritual *aroma* is religion.⁹

This quotation introduces the practical side of Marx's critique
of religion and sharply separates his view from Feuerbach's.
Marx accented that difference in the much-quoted eleven theses
against Feuerbach. Feuerbach's interpretation remained at the
level of theory in that he failed to connect alienation in religion
with injustice in society. For Marx, this failure was critical. It is
not enough to show the theoretical limitations of religion: that is
merely the first step. The second step is a practical critique
wherein religious alienation is shown to be nothing but a reflec-

tion of alienation in society. "Feuerbach," writes Marx in the seventh thesis, ". . . does not see that the 'religious sentiment' is itself a social product, and that the abstract individual whom he analyzes belongs in reality to a particular form of society."[10] Because Feuerbach "directs too much attention to nature and too little to politics,"[11] the concept "humanity" remained an abstraction in his analysis, thereby obscuring the significance of his critique.

For Marx, truth is concrete; it is practical activity. The question of truth, therefore, is not primarily "a question of theory but is a practical question. [Human beings] must prove the truth" through a practical transformation of the unjust structures of this world.[12] The connecting of theory with practice and the identification of truth with the revolutionary transformation of society is the heart of Marx's difference with Feuerbach and other left-wing Hegelians. Nowhere does Marx express this difference more pointedly than in his celebrated eleventh thesis: "The philosophers have only *interpreted* the world, in various ways; the point, however, is to *change* it."[13]

Marx's denial of the objective content of religion is not his most serious challenge to the church, because there is no way that believers can demonstrate to the satisfaction of an atheist that their faith affirmation is not simply a reflection of human desires and aspirations. Marx's most serious challenge is located on the concrete level of the practice of the church. It is the practice of the church that grants so much credibility to Marx's critique of religion.

Marx's famous description of religion as the opium of the people appears in his *Contribution to the Critique of Hegel's Philosophy of Right: Introduction.* His concern is not so much to show the theoretical emptiness of religion but rather its practical use by the ruling class as a camouflage for unjust socio-economic structures. As long as the victims of injustice seek their salvation in a heavenly world, they will not develop a revolutionary practice for the transformation of unjust conditions in this world. Following Marx's lead, Lenin expressed this point sharply: "Religion is an opium for the people. Religion is a sort of spiritual booze, in which the slaves of capital drown their human image, their demand for life more or less worthy of [human nature]."[14]

There can be no doubt that white American churches have presented the gospel of Jesus as an opium for the oppressed so that they would not challenge unjust conditions in society. For example, African slaves were taught about a white God and a white Christ, both of whom condoned slavery. Initially slaveholders did not permit their slaves to be christianized, because baptism implied manumission, according to some. But white missionaries and preachers convinced slaveholders that Christianity actually made blacks better slaves—that is, obedient and docile. White American churches strongly and consistently supported the slave system in particular and the subordination of blacks in church and society generally. It was the unqualified support of the slave system given by the white church that motivated a slaveholder to claim: "The deeper the piety of the slave, the more valuable he is in every respect."[15]

A similar attitude of the white church was taken regarding the worker in relation to the emerging system of capitalist production, in the early nineteenth century and afterward.

As Henry May has written:

> Support for the moral, political, and economic status quo was ingrained in American Protestantism by habit and history. When religion, the family, sound government, and property rights seemed to be menaced by radical forces, Protestant conservatism became explicit and militant.[16]

Arthur L. Perry, an influential American economist, identified " 'the fundamental laws of society with the footsteps of providential intelligence.' These laws made it particularly plain that concerted action to raise wages was immoral and useless."[17] A. H. Strong, president of Rochester Theological Seminary, claimed: "I know of no better proof of the divine origin of Christianity than this, that her laws are little by little found to be the laws of nature. . . . This I believe to be already true of political economy."[18] Another claimed that "God has need of rich Christians, and he makes them, and he assigns particular duties to them."[19] Therefore "the preacher may not, then, indiscriminately inveigh against luxuries, for the sum of wealth cannot be too great, if well used, and luxuries are the only foundation of large wealth in any community."[20] To be sure some early nineteenth-century Christians emphasized charity, but not as much as they emphasized the accumulation of wealth and the unalterable depravity of the poor. Poverty, like riches, was generally deserved.

As the churches sided with the slaveholders and against African slaves, with capital and against labor, a similar attitude was taken in regard to women's rights and other social and political problems related to the liberation of victims. Of course there were significant exceptions, such as certain abolitionists, women's rights activists, and social gospelers. But these exceptions in no way refute the Marxist claim that oppressors have used religion as a sedative in order to keep the poor passive and docile. Indeed the church has a privileged status in American society, with tax exemption benefits and persuasive moral power, because it serves as the religious sanction of the existing capitalistic system.

Almost without exception, white American churches have interpreted religion as something exclusively spiritual with no political content useful in the struggles of the poor for freedom. By identifying the gospel of Jesus with a spirituality estranged from the struggle for justice, the church becomes an agent of injustice. We can observe this in the history of Lutheran churches with their emphasis on the two kingdoms, and also in their apparent failure to extend Luther's theology of the cross to society. Unfortunately all institutional white churches in America have sided with capitalist, rich, white, male elites, and against socialists, the poor, blacks, and women.

Oppressors intend for religion to serve as an opium, but the oppressed often do not accept the religion of the dominant classes without making radical changes in it. Perhaps that was what Marx had in mind when he said that "religious suffering is at the same time an expression of real suffering and a *protest* against real suffering."[21] Inasmuch as Marx had no firsthand knowledge of the religions of the oppressed outside Europe, he was severely limited in his analysis of the meaning of religion. The word "opium" is too narrow to cover the complexity of the negative and creative elements in the history of religious victimization. Inherent in the religions of the oppressed is a revolutionary protest against unjust social, economic, and political conditions.

The absence in the white churches of a holistic view of the gospel that embraces the political demand for the liberation of the victims was one reason why blacks, women, and Third World peoples were forced to develop theological perspectives that did not encourage passivity and docility in their struggles for liberation. That was why women and blacks began to speak of feminist and black theologies. Other U.S. racial minorities, encouraged by their own religious heritage and by their struggles for political justice, also began to use similar theological language as defined by their history and culture. A Third World theology, encouraged by EATWOT, with liberation as its major emphasis, is found among churches in Asia, Africa, and Latin America. When North American blacks and Third World peoples evaluate Marxism in the light of the behavior of white American churches, they usually side with Marx and against white Christianity. Marxism is viewed as an internal critique of Euro-American churches, whose "gospel" has served as an opium of the people in its support of the status quo.

It is revealing that white American churches tend either to ignore Marx or reject him as an atheist. They seldom inquire about the truth of Marx's practical critique of their use of religion as an opium. Most seminaries offer no courses on Marx, most American theologians seldom mention him, and local churches would panic if a pastor dared to take Karl Marx seriously. Why do American churches and theologians find it so easy to dismiss or to ignore Marx? Is it because the practice and theology of American churches serve as a religious justification of the existing structures of oppression? If the churches and their theologians do not speak out against systems of oppression and seem uninterested in developing a practice to overcome them, must we not conclude that they are supporters of the ruling elites? For I contend that the only credible refutation that the churches can offer to Marx's critique of religion as an opium is a practical response that expresses their solidarity with the liberating practice of the victims of oppression.

As Nicholas Lash has said in another connection:

> [Questions concerning the "truth" of the Christian gospel] cannot be adequately responded to merely in theory—in theological reflection. They are questions whose adequate response calls for the transformation, not only of theologi-

cal description (of what Christians conceive themselves to be) but also of structures, activities, and relationships (what they, as a social fact, really are).[22]

The issue is not only "the possibility of appropriate speech about God but also the uses to which such speech is put, the function it is made to serve."[23] As Christian theologians we are challenged to ask: "Can the reality of God appear in our language in a way that does not, in fact, ineluctably lead to just that depreciation of the reality and significance of concrete particulars against which Marx protested?"[24]

Christian theologians often get carried away with our "ready-made" theoretical "solution!" Therefore "our positive religious assertions are in need of continual corrective negation or critical purification."[25] We need to "discipline our religious exuberance" by submitting our religious assertions to "appropriately rigorous 'procedures and controls.' "[26]

THE NECESSITY OF MARXISM

The challenge of Marxism emerges out of Marx's critique of religion, but the necessity of Marxism arises out of his critique of capitalism. North Americans live in a society that is defined by capitalistic values. The values of capitalism are so ingrained into American culture that many church persons assume that they are the same as Christian values. Capitalism and Christianity are viewed as partners in defending God, freedom, and democracy. Socialism and Marxism are viewed as demonic and totalitarian. Therefore they must be opposed at all costs, as the United States opposes Soviet Russia. The belief that capitalism is Christian and Marxism is godless is one of the major reasons why the church has been a consistent supporter of capital against labor, large corporations against small businesses, the rich against the poor. Any person or group offering a revolutionary challenge to ruling elites is likely to be viewed as communist—an American label for the embodiment of evil.

That socialism, Marxism, and communism are viewed as the enemy of God and country can be seen in the consistent and strong support by the church of the governmental repression of socialists during the Palmer raids at the end of the second decade of this century and the repression of communists during the McCarthy era of the 1950s. The inability of any form of socialism to take root in the U.S.A. is partly due to the pervasive and irrational anticommunism of the churches. Even civil rights activists have been forced to separate their ideas and actions from any connection with communism in order to receive support from American churches.

Martin Luther King, Jr., was so concerned about keeping the SCLC protected from association with Marxism that he dismissed Bayard Rustin, his close friend and co-worker, from his staff when Adam Clayton Powell, Jr., threatened to expose Rustin's socialist connections. The NAACP and the NUL have a long history of an even more reactionary stance in their attitude to Marxist ideas.

The Black Panther Party and black power advocates were marginalized in the black community and its churches largely because of their openness to Marxist ideology and their adamant rejection of Christianity as the white man's religion. James Forman's *Black Manifesto* had a similar fate for the same reasons. Although the NCBC supported Forman's demands for reparations, radical black preachers, influenced by an emerging black theology, ignored the Marxist basis on which Forman grounded his views.

The spirit of anticommunism and the support of capitalism are so deeply embedded in American society and its churches that one would find it difficult to hold an open and informative dialogue about these issues in almost any given local church. In the eyes of many church persons, nothing is worse than being associated with Marxism, because it is viewed as a godless philosophy that supports any violent means to achieve its ends. The depth of this anticommunist spirit in American churches can be seen in their public acceptance of crude anticommunist remarks by Reagan and the Moral Majority, the popularity of the sophisticated anticommunism of the Institute of Religion and Democracy in Washington, D.C., and in the criticism leveled at the NCC and WCC for their support of antiracial programs—for example, in

South Africa and Namibia. Because the anticommunist ethos is so deeply rooted in American churches, few of them would support any movement that used a Marxist or socialist label.

Nevertheless Marxism is too important to be allowed to be buried in its misrepresentations. Christians must undertake to clarify and reinterpret Marxism, so that it can serve as a useful tool for discovering how capitalism functions. The ruling elites of any society are able to stay in power and keep a measure of order and stability in situations of extreme injustice only so long as they can keep their victims persuaded of their right to rule. Unfortunately, the churches have allowed themselves to serve as a religious justification of the injustices that God called them into existence to resist.

Of course, the church has been known to offer its prophetic denunciation of many forms of injustice. That has been true especially for the churches of the poor among minorities. No persons symbolize this spirit of resistance more visibly in American society than black preachers in relation to white racism. In the spirit of Old Testament prophecy and the eschatological prophet from Nazareth, black preachers are well known for their courageous stands against the evils of slavery, lynching, and segregation.

But one needs more than prophetic denunciation in order to eliminate injustice in American society. One needs to know how the political economy functions and who benefits from it. Marxism as a method of social analysis can serve as an instrument for uncovering what rulers try to hide. Because "things are not what they seem to be," there is need to uncover what is hidden so that appearance and reality may coincide. As Marx expressed it:

> A distinction is made in private life between what a man thinks and says about himself and what he really is and does. In historical struggles one must make a still sharper distinction between the phrases and fantasies of the parties and their real organization and real interests, between their conception of themselves and what they really are.[27]

Christians need to apply Marx's method of analysis not only to the doctrines and practices of their churches but also and especially to the public pronouncements and practices of their government. Capitalism does not function as the ruling elites in business and government claim it does. The Christian faith does not possess in its nature the means for analyzing the structures of capitalism. Marxism as a tool of social analysis can disclose the gap between appearance and reality, and thereby help Christians to see how things really are. As with Marx, the Christian quest for truth should be a "quest for the coincidence of appearance and reality, of how things seem to be and how they in fact are."[28]

There are some—both Marxists and non-Marxists—who claim that one cannot separate the tool of social analysis from the atheism in Marxism. The claim has some validity if one considers only European expressions of Marxism. But for Third World peoples, the separation of Marx's method of analyzing social structures from his atheism is an indispensable necessity. Just as Third World peoples of Asia, Africa, Latin America, and the U.S.A. had to remake the Christianity they received from white oppressors, they are now remaking Marxism in the light of their own history and culture. Both Christianity and Marxism have identities that are difficult to distinguish from their European interpretations. In their European expressions, they are white and thus must be radically reinterpreted in the light of the struggles of oppressed peoples for freedom.

Europeans and white Americans have fixed definitions of things, because they have made them be what they are. For them history is in the past, that which has already happened. Black and Third World peoples are more fluid in their definition of the world, because they are in the process of making history. Things are in a state of flux. Nothing is nailed down. Christianity and Marxism must be redefined in the light of their origins and of the history and culture of oppressed peoples and in their current liberation struggles.

Marxism provides a creative challenge to the church and is a necessary tool for analyzing capitalism, but it certainly cannot serve as a substitute for the faith of the church. To be sure, the concern for justice is the starting point of Christian obedience. No one can be a follower of Jesus Christ without a political commitment that expresses one's solidarity with victims. But the struggle for justice in this world is not the ultimate goal of faith.

The hope engendered by faith is grounded in an eschatological affirmation that reaches beyond this world. Indeed the struggle for justice (of which Marxism is an important instrument) is a witness to God's eschatological righteousness as defined by Jesus' cross and resurrection.

The cross of Jesus expresses God's suffering presence with the victims of oppression. Jesus' resurrection is God's victory over oppression, sin, and death. However, the Christian affirmation of God's overcoming of evil in Jesus' cross and resurrection is not a substitute for making a political commitment on behalf of the liberation of the poor. Rather Jesus' cross and resurrection demand that we make an option for the poor, because God is encountered in their struggles for liberation. God's presence with the poor eliminates their despair and thereby empowers them to keep on struggling because they have a "home over yonder." The eschatological theme of the "home over yonder" is not an opium but a stimulant. It is the good news of the gospel, assuring us that our ultimate future is in the hands of the One who made us all.

Chapter X

Where Do We Go from Here?

It's impossible for a chicken to produce a duck egg—even though they both belong to the same family of fowl. A chicken just doesn't have it within its system to produce a duck egg. It can't do it. It can only produce according to what that particular system was constructed to produce. The system in this country cannot produce freedom for an Afro-American. It is impossible for this system, this economic system, this political system, this social system, this system period. It's impossible for this system, as it stands, to produce freedom right now for the black [person] in this country. And if ever a chicken did produce a duck egg, I'm quite sure you would say it was certainly a revolutionary chicken!   Malcolm X[1]

I want to say to you . . . as we talk about "Where do we go from here," that we must honestly face the fact that the Movement must address itself to the question of restructuring the whole of American society. There are 40 million poor people here. And one day we must ask the question, "Why are there 40 million poor people in America?" And when you begin to ask that question, you are raising questions about the economic system, about a broader distribution of wealth. When you ask that question, you begin to question the capitalistic economy. And I'm simply saying

*that more and more, we've got to begin to ask questions
about the whole society. We are called upon to help the discouraged beggars in life's marketplace. But one day we
must come to see that an edifice which produces beggars
needs restructuring. It means that questions must be raised.
You see, my friends, when you deal with this, you begin to
ask the question, "Who owns the oil?" You begin to ask the
question, "Who owns the iron ore?" You begin to ask the
question, "Why is it that people have to pay water bills in a
world that is two-thirds water?"*

Martin Luther King, Jr.[2]

The year is 1984:

—twenty-nine years since Rosa Park's refusal to give up her
seat to a white man on a city bus in Montgomery, Alabama, and
the subsequent birth of the contemporary civil rights movement
with Martin Luther King, Jr., as its most prominent leader;

—twenty-four years since the beginning of the sit-ins in Greens-
boro, North Carolina, and the creation of the SNCC with radical
students prepared to give their lives in Mississippi, Alabama, and
the rest of the South, because they believed in freedom;

—twenty-three years since the rebirth of CORE and the start of
the freedom rides that left many permanently injured as the federal government did little to enforce its own laws;

—twenty-one years since the Birmingham demonstrations, the
march on Washington, and Martin King's dream about American
society "transformed into a situation where little black boys and
black girls will be able to join hands with little white boys and
white girls and walk together as sisters and brothers";

—twenty years since the Civil Rights Bill, granting African-
Americans the right to eat and sleep at most places open to public
accommodation;

—nineteen years since Malcolm X's assassination, the Selma
march, the passage of the Voting Rights Act, and the beginning of
the urban riots in Watts (Los Angeles) that took many black lives
and left an even greater number permanently damaged—physi-
cally and mentally;

—eighteen years since the rise of black power, the NCBC endorsement of it, and the beginning of a black consciousness in religion that created a black theology that white churches—and many blacks—would condemn;

—sixteen years since Martin King's assassination and the beginning of the decline of the civil rights movement as a creative moral and political force in American society;

—fifteen years since James Forman walked down the aisle of Riverside Church and issued his *Black Manifesto,* demanding reparations from white churches for their involvement in the long history of the oppression of African-Americans in the U.S.A.

Between 1955 and 1984, much has happened in the relationships between blacks and whites in the U.S.A. and the world, between the East (Soviet Russia and its satellites) and West (U.S.A. and its European supporters), between the North (First and Second Worlds) and South (Third World), and between the rich and the poor who are struggling for freedom and self-determination throughout the world. The black struggle in the U.S.A. has been an important symbol of freedom in the struggles of other peoples, as their struggles have been a symbol for us. Martin Luther King, Jr., and Malcolm X are household names among oppressed peoples in many parts of the world. Frederick Douglass, W.E.B. DuBois, Marcus Garvey, A. Philip Randolph, and Paul Robeson are known to all serious students of history. The spirituals and the blues, gospel music and jazz, have revealed to many the depth of our spiritual and cultural will to survive amid situations of extreme oppression, thereby encouraging them not to lose hope but to keep on fighting until freedom comes. The spirituality of black churches, creatively expressed in worship, and the black theology emerging from it have also been taken to many parts of the globe, strengthening the determination of the oppressed "to keep their faith in the God of justice," whose righteousness is always found in the liberation of the oppressed.

The black struggle and the faith that has nourished it have been important symbols not only for other oppressed peoples; our faith has also sustained us and it has empowered us to struggle— from Montgomery to Memphis, from Richard Nixon to Ronald Reagan. In black religion, faith in the God of justice and the human struggle to implement it belong together and cannot be separated without both of them losing their authenticity. The faith of African-Americans is deeply embedded in our African and slave past. It has sustained our identity amid wretched circumstances, extending our spiritual and political vision far beyond the alternatives provided by the whites who enslaved us.

Our spirituality and the theology derived from it are unique when compared with the religion of Euro-American churches and their theology. We have developed a spirituality that plants our feet firmly on this earth, because the God of our faith demands that we bear witness to the humanity of all by refusing to adapt ourselves to the exploitation that the few inflict on the many. We have hammered out a black theology that has helped black churches to recover the authenticity of their faith so that they will not go woolgathering in a nebulous kingdom on high and forget their practical responsibility to live obediently in this world, liberating the poor from the misery of poverty.

However, as we look back over the black struggle in the United States, recounting its accomplishments and feeling proud of how far we have come, let us not forget that we are living in the year of George Orwell's 1984. The world of 1984 is a world moving toward its own destruction. Obsessed with its own power, it tries to make right wrong, and wrong right. Although the oppressed have been struggling for freedom throughout the globe, oppressors have become much more powerful than they were in 1955. In control of the mass media, they now can make lies sound factual and disseminate them further and faster than ever before. The enormous military power of the ruling elites in the U.S.A. and the U.S.S.R. is staggering, and it keeps on escalating. Multinational corporations have become giants bigger than many nations and accountable to none. The rich are getting richer and the poor poorer, dying of hunger and malnutrition in a world that seems not to care.

Since 1955 the misery of the poor has increased to massive proportions in a world of plenty for a few. Whether in terms of the gap between First and Third World nations or between the ruling elites and the poor within individual nations, the gap between the haves and the have-nots is an outrage to human decency. In addition, we are on the verge of nuclear annihilation, with no apparent means to stop it. It is insanity unchecked, sheer madness!

Do not the widening gap between the rich and the poor and the real possibility of nuclear annihilation mean that we need to reevaluate our definition of freedom and the methods we have used to attain it? Is not a deeper analysis of our struggle required if we expect to achieve liberation for the poor and survival for all?

When I evaluate the historical development of black churches and the civil rights movement, as well as the theological and political reflection connected with them, I think we blacks have a right to say that they have brought us "a mighty long way." But I am not sure that they will be able to take us much further if they do not lead to radical changes in our analysis of black freedom and the methods we have used in our attempts to implement it. No one can deny the important roles that the NAACP, NUL, CORE, SCLC, SNCC, and PUSH have played in the black struggle for freedom in the U.S.A. But neither the civil rights organizations nor black churches and their theology, in their present form, will be enough to take us into the twenty-first century with sufficient political power and spiritual health to cope with the problems of injustice and poverty that are rampant in the black community.

The ideals of integration and nationalism are insufficient for the problems we now face and for the issues with which we will have to deal in the future. We need to do more than try to be assimilated into white American society or to separate ourselves from it. Neither alternative is possible or even desirable. We need a broader perspective, one that includes the creative values of both but also moves beyond them to an entirely new vision of the future. It should be a perspective on freedom that incorporates the best in the long history of the African-American struggle—the best in Henry Highland Garnet and Frederick Douglass, W.E.B. DuBois and Marcus Garvey, Ida B. Wells-Barnett and Mary McLeod Bethune, Martin Luther King, Jr., and Malcolm X, Ella Baker and Queen Mother Moore.

Building on the strengths of black leaders of the past, we must also look beyond them and learn from the struggles of the oppressed throughout the world, as our leaders did in their lifetime. We need a vision of freedom that includes the whole of the inhabited earth and not just black North America, a vision enabling us to analyze the causes of world poverty and sickness, monopoly capitalism and antidemocratic socialism, opium in Christianity and other religions among the oppressed, racism and sexism, and the irresolute will to eliminate these evils. We must analyze these complex and deeply rooted evils in such a manner that the black struggle and faith can be seen expressing solidarity with the struggles and faiths of others who are fighting for the liberation of the wretched of the earth.

There are some African-Americans who will resist the idea of attempting to create a new vision and will insist that either nationalism or integration will suffice as the goal of our freedom struggle. They will appeal to either Malcolm or Martin, or both, as if we were still living in the 1960s. But history does not wait for those who are spellbound by romantic visions of past heroes. If we study our history critically, we shall know that a true understanding of Martin and Malcolm pushes us beyond them both to the creation of a future for which they died but which they saw only imperfectly. It is our responsibility not to romanticize them but to build upon their wisdom through a critical examination of them. It is our responsibility to promote their ideas by refusing to be imprisoned by them but allowing them to propel us toward the new black future that is linked with the future of all humankind.

There will be others who will say that the current drive for black voter registration, spearheaded by black civil rights leaders such as presidential candidate Jesse Jackson, means that African-Americans can achieve freedom through the American political process. They point to black mayors in Los Angeles, Atlanta, Chicago, Detroit, and the increasing number of black elected public officials at all levels as evidence of the black movement toward freedom. Jesse Jackson's bid for the presidential nomination of the Democratic Party aroused the interest of many African-Americans as he said: "There's a freedom train acoming. But you got to be registered to ride. Get on board! Get on board!" And many blacks did, because he touched the nerve of freedom deep within their being. Some blacks really believed him when he said that "we can move from the slave ship to the championship! From the guttermost to the uppermost! From the outhouse to the courthouse! From the statehouse to the White House!" His mission to Syria that resulted in the freedom of Lt. Robert Goodman and his showing in the 1984 presidential primaries have established the fact that the Country Preacher is no joke and thus is a viable candidate for the office he seeks. However, I wish to emphasize that though in some ways we have moved, in many fundamental ways we have stood still or indeed lost power, property, resources and, most of all, our capacity for independent thought and action!

Although I do not believe that blacks will achieve full freedom through the electoral process, I do want to emphasize that political action is a necessary step toward freedom, because it encourages us to take responsibility for our future. No people will achieve freedom if it remains passive, either in complacency or despair, while others make laws that shape the world. It is absolutely necessary for all blacks to realize that they must not leave their future in the hands of others. We must take charge of it, and that involves at least the act of voting.

But we blacks must not be so naive as to think that merely electing black public officials is going to affect significantly the lives of the black poor. We must find ways to make our leaders accountable, because there are black as well as white frauds, and we need sophisticated criteria to discern them. Not everyone who speaks the truth does the truth, and false prophets come in all colors.

In addition to the problem of the lack of integrity among politicians is the fact that politics itself is the art of the possible, which inevitably involves compromises and coalitions with questionable allies. Our politicians need to know when a compromise or a coalition is acceptable and when it is not. Unless the masses assume responsibility by voting, they will not be able to affect the political process.

Although I strongly support voter registration, I do not believe that the electoral process alone is the best method for achieving black freedom. The goal of black freedom must mean more than a share or parity in the current American capitalist system. That would mean only a few jobs and privileges for black professionals and continued misery for the masses of blacks in the U.S.A. and the poor throughout the globe. What difference does it make whether there is a black mayor in Detroit or Los Angeles or even a black president of the U.S.A. if the capitalist system of maximum profit for a few at the expense of the many remains intact?

A ruling elite of 1 percent controls over 30 percent of the wealth in the U.S.A. Western Europe and the U.S.A. comprise about 17 percent of the world population, but they control more than 70 percent of the world's wealth. More than fifty thousand persons die each day of hunger and malnutrition. All of this must be radically changed so that the right to life under decent, human conditions is protected by churches, governments, and other organizations.

Unfortunately, there will be some black Christians who will be content to let whites run the world and to solve the problems they created. They will say: "You can have the world, just give me Jesus." That is the most serious mistake that African-Americans could make politically and theologically. Politically, because nearly four centuries on this continent as slaves and second-class citizens should be enough to convince us that our freedom will never be realized by sitting back watching whites run the world. Theologically, because as the writer of the Gospel of John says: "God loved the world so much that [God] gave [God's] only Son, so that everyone who believes in him may not be lost but may have eternal life" (3:16, JB). How can Christians withdraw from the world when Jesus died for its redemption? The freedom of our children and of others in the world is dependent upon our political engagement in the struggles for justice. We cannot ignore the world and still retain the ethical credibility of the Christian faith. To be a Christian is to love one's neighbor, and that means making a political commitment to make the world a habitable place for one's neighbor. As Gustavo Gutiérrez says:

> To know God is to do justice, is to be in solidarity with the poor person. And it is to be in solidarity with that poor person as he or she actually exists today—as someone who is oppressed, as a member of an exploited class, or ethnic group, or culture, or nation. At the same time, a relationship with the God who has loved me despoils me, strips me. It universalizes my love for others and makes it gratuitous too.[3]

Self-satisfaction with job, status, and family must not be allowed to blind us to injustice or demobilize our responsibility to assume the task of eliminating it. Christians are called not only to pray for justice but to become actively involved in establishing it.

Black churches have a special responsibility for the world, because we claim that Christ died to redeem it. We are thus called to bear witness to God's redemption of the world through what we do and say. When others give up in despair, feeling overwhelmed by the enormity of the evil that engulfs us, black churches continue to preach hope, because "when a people has no visions, it perishes."

What visions do we have in 1984? Are we going to continue to preach the same old sermons, pray the same old prayers, and sing the same old songs as if that alone would be enough for the establishment of freedom in the twenty-first century? Are we going to continue with the same old church meetings and conferences—electing officers and bishops, holding revivals and hearing charismatic speakers, buying old white churches and constructing new ones, appointing and calling pastors on the basis of a superficial emotional appeal, shouting and testifying for the saints, while the world around us continues toward destruction? Is that all that we have to offer our black people in 1984?

How can we sing "Glory Hallelujah" when our people's blood is flowing in the streets and prisons of this nation? What do we blacks have to shout about when our families are being broken and crushed by political, social, and economic forces so complex that most of us do not know what to do to resist them. This is the paradox, the contradiction, that makes *faith* necessary if we are to survive oppression and *analysis* necessary if we are to overcome it. To pray for justice without analyzing the causes of injustice is to turn religion into an opium of the people. The time has come for the black church to take a critical look at its vision with the intention of radically changing its priorities.

I realize, of course, that we cannot expect most African-American Christians to take the initiative to effect radical changes in the vision pursued by the churches. But there are many pastors, bishops, and lay leaders who can take the initiative, because they know what is wrong with the churches and they have the talent for leadership to effect significant change in the entire black community. Such persons will need to incorporate pro-

phetic self-criticism into their ministry and to be open to a divine
call that is not limited to or controlled by a denominational black
church hierarchy. They will not use the apostasy of the white
church as a way of justifying the growing opportunism among
black church leaders.

Although we must criticize the white church (and I have done
my share of that!), it is important to remember that the black
church will have credibility only to the degree that we acknowledge our own shortcomings and truly seek to overcome them.
They include: our lack of ecumenical spirit with each other, the
unbridled egotism and dishonesty among black preachers, and
more concern for raising money for the pastor's anniversary or to
build a new building than to house, feed, and assist the poor.

Although there are many shortcomings that are obvious to any
observer of the black church, few persons on the inside say or do
anything about reclaiming the integrity of the faith maintained by
the church. My concern is not to indict any one specific group—
whether bishops, pastors, or lay leaders. All of us are responsible,
and it is essential not to evade responsibility or to make excuses
for evil. Excuses for evil serve only to justify its continued existence.

Bishops, pastors, and other church leaders have a special accountability to the people whom they serve and to the God in
whose name they claim the right to serve. In God's name and in
the name of human decency, the people must demand accountability from those in authority over it or it will be enslaved by them.
The church will never become an instrument of liberation as long
as its leaders enslave the ones they are supposed to serve. Black
church persons must rise up and claim the right to fashion church
structures that are humane and liberating. We must demand a
new vision from our leaders or get new leaders who believe the
gospel that the church preaches.

Black theologians also have a special accountability. We
created a prophetic black theology during the 1960s that called
on black churches to remember their liberating heritage. We
reinstated the memory of our ancestors—their stories, songs, and
sermons that subverted a social order that exploited and dehumanized blacks. But today we black theologians seem to have

forgotten our own theological history. Black theology is in danger of becoming respectable in a corrupt church and in seminaries that favor the privileged. It is in danger of becoming nothing but a means of guaranteeing our professional status in white academic circles. We have not remained on the cutting edge of history but have turned the revolution we started into a church social and cocktail party among black and white academic elites. We must remember that the vast majority of our people "are not fighting for ideas, for things in anyone's head. They are fighting to win material benefits, to live better and in peace, to see their lives go forward, to guarantee the future of their children."[4] Therefore they are not interested in our cute academic games. They are in need of new ideas about their liberation.

Although some black theologians returned to the black church, most dropped the prophetic critique of the black churches that gave birth to black theology in the 1960s. In this context, black theology is in danger of becoming nothing but the justification of the churches as they are. How can black churches renew themselves without a black theology of renewal? How can the churches read the signs of the time if there are no prophetic theologians who can distinguish truth from heresy? Too many black theologians are overly concerned about "making it" in the system. Success in the system never created true prophets—only false ones. The fate of the theologians will be the same as that of the churches that gave birth to them.

The lack of vision in the churches is mirrored in the civil rights movement because the two have been and are closely related. It is symbolized particularly in the internal bickering that destroyed the SNCC, seriously weakened CORE and SCLC, creating PUSH (People United to Save Humanity) from the latter, and also seriously damaging the public image of the NAACP. With many persons wanting to be leaders and few wanting to follow, and with many leaders more concerned about their media image than about creating the structures for the liberation of the poor, it becomes clear why there have been no new visions.

It is not my intention to question the integrity of any black civil rights leader or public official, but we do have the right (indeed the responsibility) to put certain questions to all those who say that they serve the people. Why is it that so many of our leaders' actions bespeak concern about their own personal success rather than radical commitment to the black poor? Why can they not think new thoughts—for example, political alternatives not presently available in the Democratic and Republican parties?

There is no better symbol of the failure to think new thoughts than the twentieth-anniversary observance (August 27, 1983), of the historic march on Washington. Much has been said about the event, negatively and positively, and I do not deny its symbolic value for those who are fighting for justice. But after twenty years, we should have had more to offer our people than simply a memorial of a dream, especially inasmuch as the black poor today are worse off economically than they were in 1963. The chief thing that has changed for the better is the social status and financial rewards of the black middle class who organized the memorial march and the white ruling elites who financed it.

Again, the purpose of my comment is not to question the integrity of our civil rights leaders, many of whom have given of themselves in a sacrificial way for the cause of black liberation. But it should be emphasized that we need more than integrity and sacrifice among our civil rights leaders if freedom is going to be a fact. We need political intelligence that is sophisticated enough to move beyond the dream of integration into a decaying capitalist economy. No human being should want to integrate into a structure that systematically destroys the poor and enriches the rich. Civil rights leaders seem to be more concerned about appealing to the white public and the black middle class than they are about speaking the truth from the standpoint of the black poor.

Civil rights leaders fight among themselves for power and vie for exposure in the white media in order to mouth the next irrelevant idea that pops into their heads—and meanwhile the black poor are dying of hunger, drugs, and police brutality, in prisons and overcrowded, rat-infested ghettoes. The time has come for us to move beyond the dream of the integration of a few middle-class blacks in white institutions and government positions. We need to dream about *radically new* possibilities for the future or our people will perish, not only of racism and capitalism, but of our own neglect and illusions. We have the resources and the talent for creating radically new ideas about the political economy. The question is: Do we have the will and the determination to do it? Or are we too fearful of those in power or too satisfied with our own professional status?

What I am talking about will not be easy to accomplish, nor will it happen without careful analysis and intelligent planning. If we are to build a genuine black future, it will take the Talented Tenth that W.E.B. DuBois advocated, the mass involvement that Martin King demonstrated, and the integral solidarity with the grassroots that Malcolm X embodied in his life and death. Physical and mental energy, firm discipline, courage and commitment—all these are crucial ingredients for the creation of a new black future. If we believe that the present political economy must be radically changed before freedom can become a reality for all, then it is our duty to participate in the creation of a vision designed for the humanity of all.

The vision of a new social order that we need should not be taken from any one person (a university professor, politician, civil rights activist, or preacher) and should not be dependent upon the charism of Martin King or Malcolm X or any current aspirants to the mantle. The vision should be the result of a group of committed persons whose love for freedom is deep and broad enough to embrace and consider many viewpoints. The members of the team should include persons who represent a cross section of the total black community, including community grassroots activists and scholars, scientists and politicians, artists and lawyers, teachers and preachers, men and women, youth and senior citizens, Christians and non-Christians, artists and doctors. The chief requirement should be *commitment* to the freedom of all and a willingness to suppress one's ego in view of the needs of the community.

The initiative for the new vision and the creation of the team should come from the black church, because it is the only institution with the power and the resources to do the job. The financial resources for the program must come from the black community, with absolutely no help from the white community. White control through financial contributions and other fringe benefits has already rendered our civil rights organizations too much accountable to the white capitalists who are responsible for black oppression. It is as ludicrous to expect white capitalists to finance black freedom as to expect criminals to prosecute themselves.

This does not mean that there are not decent, well-meaning whites concerned about justice. Decency is not the point. The issue is black independence in thought and action, and that cannot happen if what we think and do is dependent upon those who have not shared our history of oppression. No oppressed people has ever had its freedom given as a gift or financed by its oppressor. Freedom must be taken against their will, and it involves risk, struggle, and a commitment to stand against those who deny it. We must not let our leaders trick us into thinking that African-Americans will get freedom by gearing the civil rights movement to the moral values of white liberals. As long as we permit whites to finance our organizations, they will control them. And they will decide what our leaders say, and how, when, and where.

The black church is the only major institution we have that is owned and operated by blacks with no appeal to white money. It is the only institution that is relatively free to act independently of the white ruling class. The black church, therefore, should take the initiative in the creation of a team of committed persons who are prepared to think and to act independently of both white liberals and black middle-class interests.

Although the team should determine its own immediate and long-range goals, I should like to conclude with a few suggestions regarding some elements in the new vision of freedom, some of which have been dealt with in earlier chapters.

1. The new vision will need to include an emphasis on black unity through an affirmation of the value of black history and culture. This is the strength of the nationalist tradition in our history. There will be no freedom for blacks without black unity. Whites have been able to divide and conquer us, because we have not had a deep knowledge and appreciation of our past. Those who do not know and love their history and culture cannot possibly love themselves.

To love our people does not mean hating whites. Indeed, we cannot love anybody unless we love who we are as blacks—that is, the culture and history that has sustained us through centuries of slavery and second-class citizenship. The enduring message of black power has nothing to do with hate. Rather black power "teaches love. But it teaches us that love, like charity, must begin at home; that it must begin with ourselves, our beautiful black selves."[5] Whatever vision of the new black future is created, it must be derived from and include at its center black love of self— the history and culture of an African people in white America.

Lack of knowledge of one's past leads inevitably to self-hate, and self-hate leads one to love the oppressor's values, and thus to act against one's own freedom. Malcolm X recognized and expounded this truth far more clearly than anyone else in our history. That is why he was so severely criticized during his lifetime and is seldom remembered today.

Any new vision that African-Americans create should be built upon the best in our past history, so that our children will proudly affirm their blackness.

2. After black unity has been achieved, the new vision will need to include the best in the integrationist tradition as articulated by Martin Luther King, Jr., in his dream of the "beloved community." Black unity and nationalism are the prerequisites of coalition, lest the beloved community turn out to be a pious front for white or middle-class interests.

Coalition is also crucial. To think that blacks could achieve their freedom through complete, permanent separation is nationalistic romanticism. The world is too small and complex for that sort of logic to have any credibility now. No, freedom will come only through the building of a society that respects the humanity of all, including whites. The Christian faith requires it, and human decency demands it. We blacks must not be so naive as to think that we will achieve our freedom by denying it to whites. The greatness of Martin King was his embodiment of this truth in his life and thought—from the beginning of his public advocacy of black freedom in 1955 to his tragic death in 1968.

3. The vision of the new social order must be antisexist. Many black men will be slow to accept this aspect in the new black perspective. The movement for black freedom in the churches and civil rights organization is male-dominated, which merely contributes to the retardation of freedom. Half the members of the

team must be women with diverse dimensions of a feminist consciousness. There can be no compromise on the idea that justice means the true equality of all, with mutual sharing of responsibility in all areas of the decision-making process. A truly liberated social order cannot have men dominating women.

4. The new social order should be democratic and socialist, including a Marxist critique of monopoly capitalism. It must also be a socialism that is critical of the authoritarian state socialism in Soviet Russia. Just as we should not reject Christianity because churches carry its name but do the opposite of what the faith stands for, likewise we should not reject socialism just because Soviet Russia adopted the name but does the opposite.

The new social order must view the necessities of life—food, shelter, work, play—as rights inalienably linked with membership in society. No one, absolutely no one, should control the wealth of a nation or community through the private ownership of property.

The socialist vision must be democratic, protective of individual liberties, and involving all persons in the community in its creation. That is why the team should include a wide representation of interests in the black community.

5. The new black perspective must be a global vision that includes the struggles of the poor in the Third World. African-Americans are linked in countless ways with their brothers and sisters in Africa, the Caribbean, Latin America, Asia, and the Pacific. Jesse Jackson is right. We must create a "rainbow coalition" that includes all the disadvantaged in the U.S.A. and throughout the globe. There will be no freedom for anybody until all are set free.

6. Any new vision of a just social order must affirm the best in black religion and embrace the creative elements in the religions of the poor who are struggling for freedom throughout the globe. Any social order that excludes religion or ignores it is doomed to failure from the start.

The life and thought of Martin Luther King, Jr., and Malcolm X are the best examples in the black community of the creative role that religion can play in the transformation of society. They combined their religious vision with their political commitment, but they refused to allow either their politics or their faith to separate them from other persons struggling for justice even though those persons held different views. Both men always remained open to be taught by the experiences of others in their struggle for justice. Although Martin King was a Christian preacher of the black Baptist tradition and Malcolm X was a minister in the religion of Islam, the distinguishing mark of their thought and practice was their commitment to justice for the poor and their willingness to die for it. Though they held sharply different views regarding religion and politics, they were *one* in their rejection of religious and political dogmatism. Both realized that an inflexible attitude was detrimental to the creation of coalitions among the poor and their supporters—coalitions that are indispensable for the establishment of a just society.

The members of these alliances should, like Martin King and Malcolm X, take their stand for the truth and refuse to be sidetracked by their fear of religious and secular authorities who would prevent them from speaking and doing what truth demands. It was Martin King's religious commitment that empowered him to say, "If you are twenty-five and have not found something that is worth dying for, then you don't deserve to live." Malcolm X made a similar comment in the language of his ghetto origins. He said that if you are not prepared to die for freedom, "you ought to get off the planet."

The creation of a just social order must be grounded in the hopes that have been engendered by the poor as they have emerged from their encounter with God in their fight for freedom. No society that is based merely on the intellectual reflections of university professors, professional politicians, or any other privileged analysts can be just. A just social order is one that takes seriously the prereflective visions of the poor as defined by their political struggles and celebrated in their religious life.

Although I am a Christian theologian, I contend that a just social order must be accountable to not one but many religious visions. If we are going to create a society that is responsive to the humanity of all, then we must not view one religious faith as absolute. Ultimate reality, to which all things are subject, is too mysterious to be exclusively limited to one people's view of God. God is found not only among blacks in North America but also in Latin America; not only among Christians in Africa but also

among the devotees of African traditional religions on that continent. God is found not only in European history but also in the
history of Asia long before the arrival of European missionaries.
Any creation of a just social order must take into account that
God has been known and experienced in many different ways,
and no single expression of God's identity in worship or theology
should be regarded as the final truth. As the Apostle Paul said,
"Now we see in a mirror dimly" (1 Cor. 13:12, RSV) and thus
cannot possibly have a perfect understanding of ultimate truth.
Because we have an imperfect grasp of divine reality, we must not
regard our limited vision as absolute. Acknowledging the imper-
fections of our own vision and the truth in other religions has
always been difficult for Christians, who have often talked and
acted as if they had the whole, pure truth. Today such a view must
be firmly rejected. God's truth comes in many colors and is revealed in many cultures, histories, and unexpected places.

Because, however, I am a Christian whose theological and political perspective has been defined by the black church tradition,
my view of a just social order cannot be understood apart from
my faith in God's liberating presence in Jesus. The importance of
God and Jesus for black Christians is best explained when we
consider the preponderance of suffering in black life and blacks'
attempt to affirm their humanity in spite of it. When we consider
slavery, lynching, ghettoes, and Ronald Reagan's vicious attack
upon the rights of the poor, how can we explain blacks' mental
and physical survival? How was it possible for black slaves to
hope for freedom when a mere empirical analysis of their situation of servitude would elicit despair? How is it possible for
blacks today to keep their sanity in the struggle for freedom when
they consider the continued exploitation of the poor in a world of
plenty?

I belong to a Christian community whose members believe that
we blacks have come "this far by faith," leaning on the God of
our slave grandparents. We have survived slaveships, auction
blocks, and chronic unemployment because the God of black
faith has bestowed upon us an identity that cannot be destroyed
by white oppressors. It is the knowledge that we belong *only* to
God that enables black Christians to keep on fighting for justice
even though the odds might be against us. We firmly believe that

Jesus heals wounded spirits and broken hearts. No matter what trials and tribulations blacks encounter, we refuse to let despair define our humanity. We simply believe that "God can make a way out of no way." Black Christians do not deny that trouble is present in their lives; we merely insist that "trouble does not last always" and that "we'll understand it better by and by." In the words of Charles Tindley:

> Trials dark on every hand,
> and we cannot understand.
> All the ways that God would lead us
> to that Blessed Promised Land.
> But God guides us with God's eye
> and we'll follow till we die.
> For we'll understand it better by and by.
>
> By and by, when the morning comes,
> All the saints of God are gathered home.
> We'll tell the story how we overcome.
> For we'll understand it better by and by.

The eschatological hope found in black faith is not pie-in-the-sky religion. It is not an opiate. Rather it is born of struggle here and now because black Christians refuse to allow oppressors to define who we are:

> O, nobody knows who I am,
> Till the judgment morning.

Notes

Chapter I

1. In Gayraud S. Wilmore and James H. Cone (eds.) *Black Theology: A Documentary History, 1966-1979* (Maryknoll, N.Y.: Orbis, 1979), p. 26. Some material in the chapter that follows here was first presented, under the title "Black Theology: Its Origin, Methodology, and Relationship to Third World Theologies," to the EATWOT conference held in Geneva, Switzerland, January 5-13, 1983. All the papers related to the Geneva conference—constituting the sixth EATWOT volume of analysis and commentary—will be published by Orbis Books under the title *Doing Theology in a Divided World*.

2. The Southern Christian Leadership Conference (SCLC) was founded in 1957 by Martin Luther King, Jr., and a group of southern black ministers. See the excellent essay of Adam Fairclough, "The Southern Christian Leadership Conference and the Second Reconstruction, 1957-1973," *The South Atlantic Quarterly*, vol. 80, no. 2, Spring 1981, pp. 177-94; also "Southern Christian Leadership Conference: 'The Ultimate Aim is the Beloved Community,'" in August Meier, Elliott Rudwick, and Francis L. Broderick (eds.), *Black Protest Thought in the Twentieth Century* (New York: Bobbs-Merrill, 2nd. ed., 1971), pp. 302-6. Unfortunately, there is not, to my knowledge, any detailed book-length, published study of the SCLC comparable to several excellent studies of the National Association for the Advancement of Colored People (NAACP), the National Urban League (NUL), the Congress of Racial Equality (CORE), and the Student Non-Violent Coordinating Committee (SNCC). Since the philosophy and activity of the SCLC were defined almost exclusively by Martin Luther King, Jr., biographies of his life and reflections on his thinking tell us much about the SCLC, especially until his death on April 4, 1968. Two important Ph.D. dissertations are Eugene P. Walker, "A History of the Southern Christian Leadership Conference, 1955-1965: The Evolution of a Southern Strategy for Social Change," Duke University, 1979; and Rose Mary Sloan, "Then My Living Will Not Be in Vain: A Rhetorical Study of Dr. Martin Luther King,

Jr., and the Southern Christian Leadership Conference in the Mobilization for Collective Action Toward Nonviolent Means to Integration, 1954–1964,'' Ohio State University, 1977. The best biography of King is Stephen Oates, *Let the Trumpet Sound: The Life of Martin Luther King, Jr.* (New York: Harper & Row, 1982); David Garrow's biography is expected to be the definitive study of King's life and of SCLC: *Bearing the Cross:* Martin Luther King, Jr., and The Southern Christian Leadership Conference, 1955–1968 (New Haven: Yale University Press forthcoming 1985).

3. The NCBC was originally called the National Committee of Negro Churchmen (NCNC). The name of the NCBC has been changed several times, with the initials "NCBC" remaining constant: National *Committee* of Black Churchmen, National *Conference* of Black Churchmen, and most recently, according to several members, National Conference of Black Christians. Because the NCBC has played an important role in the development of black theology, I shall later go into its origin in some detail and give the reasons for the changes in its self-identity.

4. The Interreligious Foundation for Community Organization (IFCO) was founded in 1967 as "a cooperative venture to fund locally-based organizations upgrading the conditions of the poor and offering participation and self-determination to people shut out of power" (Robert S. Lecky and H. Elliot Wright [eds.], *Black Manifesto* [New York: Sheed and Ward, 1969] p. 7). See also Lucius Walker, "IFCO and the Crisis of American Society," ibid., pp. 133–39; Gayraud S. Wilmore, *Black Religion and Black Radicalism* (Maryknoll, N.Y.: Orbis, 2nd ed., 1983), pp. 202–7.

5. I have found no detailed study of the origin and meaning of black caucuses in white denominations. Some references are made in Wilmore, *Black Religion*, chap. 8; "Identity Crisis: Black in Predominantly White Denominations," Second Annual B. Moses James Colloquium on Black Religion, March 13, 1976 (pamphlet); "The Black Church at the Crossroads," *Renewal*, Spring 1974; Wilmore and Cone, *Black Theology: A Documentary History*, parts 1 and 2.

6. With the rise of the Moral Majority and its attempt to impact political decisions, many conservative white Christians no longer champion the separation of religion and politics. Indeed Jerry Falwell said to a group of Chicago black ministers, "Dr. King was a true saint. . . . I confess I was wrong." He was referring not to King's goal of black freedom but the use of the church as a "base for political action." See James S. Tinney's excellent article, "The Moral Majority: Operating Under the Hood of Religious Right," *Dollars and Sense*, special issue, vol. 7, no. 2, June/July 1981, pp. 68–73.

7. It is really amazing that so many liberal white theologians and

ministers remained mute regarding the relationship between the Christian gospel and justice for African-Americans. Involvement of liberal white churches in the problems of religion and race may be dated with the holding of the National Conference on Religion and Race, Chicago, Jan. 14–17, 1963. See an account of the conference in Matthew Ahmann (ed.), *Race: Challenge to Religion* (Chicago: Henry Regnery, 1963). With the march on Washington (Aug. 1963), liberal white Christians became deeply involved. See Robert W. Spike, *The Freedom Revolution and the Churches* (New York: Association Press, 1965). The most notable exceptions of white theologians who before 1963 dealt with the race issue are: Kyle Haselden, *The Racial Problem in Christian Perspective* (New York: Harper, 1959); Liston Pope, *The Kingdom beyond Caste* (New York: Friendship Press, 1957); Paul Ramsey, *Christian Ethics and the Sit-in* (New York: Association Press, 1961); James E. Sellers, "Love, Justice, and the Non-violent Movement," *Theology Today*, Jan. 1962.

8. For Martin Luther King, Jr.'s, account of the bus boycott, see his *Stride toward Freedom* (New York: Harper & Row, 1958). For a critical account, see Oates, *Let the Trumpet Sound*; and David L. Lewis, *King: A Biography* (Urbana: University of Illinois Press, 2nd ed., 1978). For the story of the contemporary civil rights movement, see Robert H. Brisbane, *Black Activism: Radical Revolution in the United States 1954–1970* (Valley Forge: Judson, 1974); Vincent Harding, *The Other American Revolution* (Los Angeles: Center for Afro-American Studies, 1980); Harvard Sitkoff, *The Struggle for Black Equality, 1954–1980* (New York: Hill and Wang, 1981); Howell Raines, *My Soul is Rested* (New York: Putnam, 1977).

9. During the 1950s and '60s, Karl Barth, Rudolph Bultmann, Paul Tillich, and the death-of-God theology dominated the theological scene in seminaries and theological societies. There was hardly any discussion on the relationship between the black revolution and Christian theology. Almost all the theological issues for American theologians were defined by European theologians or by the death-of-God fad. See the *Time* cover story, "Is God Dead?" April 8, 1966.

10. An account of the life of Richard Allen and the founding of the African Methodist Episcopal (AME) Church is found in Carol V. R. George, *Segregated Sabbaths* (New York: Oxford University Press, 1973); and Charles H. Wesley, *Richard Allen: Apostle of Freedom* (Washington, D.C.: Associated Pub., 1935). Richard Allen's own account of his life is found in *The Life Experience and Gospel Labors of the Rt. Rev. Richard Allen* (Nashville: Abingdon, 1960).

11. See esp. Earl Ofari, *"Let Your Motto Be Resistance": The Life and Thought of Henry Highland Garnet* (Boston: Beacon, 1972). Henry H. Garnet is best known for his famous "Address to the Slaves of the

United States of America" in 1843, reprinted, with David Walker's "Appeal to the Colored Citizens of the World," by Arno Press, New York, 1969.

12. See esp. Herbert Aptheker, *Nat Turner's Slave Rebellion* (New York: Grove, 1966); Wilmore, *Black Religion,* chap. 3; Vincent Harding, *There is a River* (New York: Harcourt Brace Jovanovich, 1981), chap. 4.

13. See Edwin S. Redkey (ed.), *Respect Black: The Writings and Speeches of Henry McNeal Turner* (New York: Arno, 1971), p. 176. See also Redkey's *Black Exodus* (New Haven: Yale University Press, 1969).

14. Black preachers began to read old texts on the black church. These included Carter G. Woodson, *History of the Negro Church* (Washington, D.C.: Associated Pub., 1921); Benjamin E. Mays, *The Negro's God* (New York: Atheneum, 1969) [originally published in 1938]; Benjamin E. Mays and Joseph W. Nicholson, *The Negro's Church* (New York: Institute of Social and Religious Research, 1933); W.E.B. DuBois, *The Negro Church* (Atlanta University Press, 1903); E. F. Frazier, *The Negro Church in America* (New York: Schocken, 1974) [originally published in 1964].

15. Carol George's *Segregated Sabbaths* (n. 10, above) is an excellent account of Methodist independent churches; for the Baptists, see Mechal Sobel, *Trabelin' On: The Slave Journey to an Afro-Baptist Faith* (Westport, Conn.: Greenwood, 1979).

16. See esp. Albert J. Raboteau, *Slave Religion: The "Invisible Institution" in the Antebellum South* (New York: Oxford University Press, 1978).

17. See Woodson, *History of the Negro Church.*

18. This view was advanced by E. Franklin Frazier and the opposite view was promoted by Melville Herskovits. See the latter's *The Myth of the Negro Past* (Boston: Beacon, 1958) [originally published in 1941], and the former's *Negro Church* and his *The Negro Family in the United States* (University of Chicago Press, 1966) [originally published in 1939]. One of the best recent discussions of the issue of African survivals among African-Americans is in Raboteau, *Slave Religion,* pp. 3–92.

19. *Black Religion: The Negro and Christianity in the United States* (Boston: Beacon, 1964), p. 143.

20. See Martin E. Marty's review of it in the *New York Herald Tribune Book Week*, also reprinted in the paperback edition of Washington's *Black Religion.*

21. I have found no favorable responses to Washington's view in the black scholarly or church community. Carlton L. Lee's comment is representative: "There is a strong suggestion that [Washington] has not

thought carefully about many of the facts of the Negro American community, nor does he interpret the facts with the understanding or depth that the subject deserves. Moreover, he is not as careful when dealing with a moot and complex subject as one has the right to expect a responsible observer to be. . . . There is much wrong with the book. . . . It is unfortunate that the author . . . was unable to do what he most certainly wanted to do: say something relevant and significant about religion in the Negro-American community" (review in *The Christian Scholar*, Fall 1965, pp. 242–47). See also Jerome Long's review in *Foundations*, Oct. 1964, p. 380–82; Jefferson P. Rogers, "Black Worship: Black Church," *The Black Church*, vol. 1, no. 1, 1972.

22. Regarding the impact of Washington's *Black Religion* on the black church and the rise of black theology, see G. S. Wilmore, "Black Theology: Its Significance for Christian Mission Today," *International Review of Mission*, vol. 63, no. 250, April 1974, pp. 211ff. Referring to Washington, Wilmore says, "the term 'black theology' emerged just prior to the rise of black power . . . [as] a sharp reaction to the allegation that the black church was devoid of theology as such" (p. 211). Although my research does not confirm Wilmore's contention that the term "black theology" emerged prior to black power, but rather *after* it, yet it is true that black theologians and preachers felt compelled to respond to Washington's negative evaluation of the absence of theology in the black church.

23. An excellent study of black nationalism is that by Alphonso Pinkney, *Red, Black, and Green: Black Nationalism in the United States* (Cambridge University Press, 1976); see also E. U. Essien-Udom, *Black Nationalism* (New York: Dell, 1964); John Bracey, Jr., August Meier, and Elliott Rudwick (eds.), *Black Nationalism in America* (New York: Bobbs-Merrill, 1970). The best source for an introduction to Malcolm X's nationalist views is *The Autobiography of Malcolm X* (New York: Grove, 1964).

24. For the impact of the urban riots on the civil rights movement, see Harding, *The Other American Revolution*, chap. 28. For a moving account of Malcolm X's impact on the SNCC and its move toward black power, see esp. Julius Lester, "The Angry Children of Malcolm X," in Meier, Rudwick, and Broderick, *Black Protest Thought*, pp. 469–84.

25. The best interpretation of black power is still that by Stokely Carmichael and Charles V. Hamilton, *Black Power: The Politics of Liberation in America* (New York: Random House, 1967). The best interpretation of the SNCC and the events that led to the rise of black power is that by Clayborne Carson, *In Struggle: SNCC and the Black Awakening of the 1960s* (Cambridge: Harvard University Press, 1981), esp. pp.

215ff. For Martin Luther King, Jr.'s, response to black power, see his *Where Do We Go From Here? Chaos or Community?* (Boston: Beacon, 1967), chap. 2.

26. The entire text of this statement is found in Wilmore and Cone, *Black Theology*, pp. 23–30.

27. Before the rise of black theology, black churches accepted uncritically the theology of white churches, using their doctrines and creeds as if the racist behavior of whites had no impact upon their view of the gospel. The radical challenge of white religion occurred among the black nationalist-oriented religions of the urban ghettoes (Marcus Garvey, Nation of Islam, etc.).

28. For an interpretation of the role of the NCBC, see esp. Wilmore, *Black Religion,* chap. 8; see also his interpretation in *Black Theology: A Documentary History,* parts 1 and 2; Leon Watts, "The National Committee of Black Churchmen," *Christianity and Crisis*, special double issue, Nov. 2 and 16, 1970.

29. Wilmore and Cone, *Black Theology*, p. 23.

30. Ibid., pp. 23–24.

31. See his introduction, ibid., p. 16.

32. Ibid.

33. Ibid., pp. 43–47, gives the entire text of this document. For an interpretation of the significance of this document, see Wilmore, *Black Religion,* chap. 8; and also his interpretation in Wilmore and Cone, *Black Theology*, pp. 18ff.

34. Wilmore and Cone, *Black Theology*, p. 44.

35. Ibid., p. 45.

36. Ibid.

37. Ibid., p. 46.

38. Ibid.

39. "Our Heritage and Our Hope," an address given on the tenth anniversary of the NCBC; excerpts are included in the NCBC *Newsletter,* Fall 1981, pp. 3–4.

40. Interpreting the significance of the origin of the NCBC, Leon Watts wrote that "the group's very existence sought to say in clear and indisputable terms that black religion stands in contradistinction to the white American Christian establishment" ("The National Committee of Black Churchmen," *Christianity and Crisis*, Nov. 2 and 16, 1970, p. 239). Wilmore also suggests the emergence of a similar theological consciousness when he says that NCBC clergy "launched the first attempt since Garveyism to separate mainline black Christianity from the theology of the white churches and conceive liberation in the context of the legitimate use of ethnic consciousness and power" (Wilmore and

Cone, *Black Theology*, p. 4). See also Preston N. Williams "The Ethical Aspects of the 'Black Church/Black Theology' Phenomenon," *The Journal of Religious Thought*, vol. 26, no. 2, Summer Supplement, 1969, pp. 34–45; and J. Deotis Roberts, "The Black Caucus and the Failure of Christian Theology," ibid., pp. 15–25. An informative discussion of the significance of the NCBC and the rise of black theology is found in C. Eric Lincoln, *The Black Church since Frazier* (New York: Schocken, 1974). According to Lincoln, "The 'Negro church' that Frazier wrote about no longer exists. It died an agonizing death in the harsh turmoil which tried the faith so rigorously in the decade of the 'Savage Sixties,' for there it had to confront under the most trying circumstances the possibility that 'Negro' and 'Christian' were irreconcilable categories. . . . The black church is not the 'Negro church' radicalized; rather it is a conscious departure from the critical norms which made the Negro church what it was. The Negro church died in the moral and ethical holocaust of the black struggle for self-documentation because the call to Christian responsibility is in fact first and foremost a call to human dignity and therefore logically inconsistent with the limitations of Negroness" (pp. 105–6). Although one may question whether Lincoln's judgment on the death of the Negro church is still accurate today, he correctly expressed the consciousness of NCBC clergy during the 1960s.

41. New York, Sheed and Ward.

42. p. 78.

43. Gayraud S. Wilmore, "The Theological Commission Project of the National Committee of Black Churchmen (Fall 1968)," in Warner R. Traynham, *Christian Faith in Black and White: A Primer in Theology from the Black Perspective* (Wakefield, Mass.: Parameter, 1973), appendix D. This document is most informative in giving the theological basis for the origin of black theology. See also Patricia Culverhouse, "Black Religion: Folk or Christian," *Foundations*, Oct.-Dec. 1970, pp. 306–15.

44. New York, Seabury Press. My use of the term "black theology" was directly influenced by NCBC documents and the BMCR, a black caucus in the United Methodist Church. The latter held its formational meeting in Feb. 1968, which I attended.

45. Boston, Beacon, 1969.

46. Ibid., chap. 5.

47. Included in C. Eric Lincoln (ed.), *Is Anybody Listening to Black America?* (New York: Seabury, 1968), pp. 3ff.

48. Wilmore, "The Theological Commission Project," p. 83.

49. Ibid.

50. Ibid., p. 84.

51. Ibid.

52. Ibid., p. 85.

53. Ibid., pp. 85–86.

54. See Donald R. Cutler (ed.), *The Religious Situation: 1968* (Boston: Beacon, 1968), pp. 3–38. Although Vincent Harding was not an active participant in the NCBC, this essay, and many others, had a profound effect upon the creators of the new black theology. Another influential article was his "Black Power and the American Christ," *Christian Century*, Jan. 4, 1967 (reprinted in Wilmore and Cone, *Black Theology*, pp. 35–42). Harding's "No Turning Back?" in *Renewal*, Oct.-Nov. 1970, was particularly influential in the NCBC in that it was his critical reflections on some NCBC documents and will be referred to later. See also his influential "Religion and Resistance among Antebellum Negroes, 1800–1860," in August Meier and Elliott Rudwick (eds.), *The Making of Black America*, vol. 1 (New York: Atheneum, 1969), pp. 179–97.

55. See *Church in Metropolis*, Fall 1968, pp. 18–22; also published in Hart M. Nelsen, Raytha L. Yokley, and Anne K. Nelsen (eds.), *The Black Church in America* (New York: Basic Books, 1971), pp. 324–34.

56. See *Andover Newton Quarterly*, Nov. 1968, pp. 112–23. Preston Williams's writings played an important role in the development of NCBC theological consciousness and he also served as the chairman of the NCBC theological commission following Gayraud Wilmore.

57. *Foundations*, April-July, 1968, pp. 99–109. Henry Mitchell also played an influential role in the NCBC and in the development of black theology. He was the first occupant of the significant Martin Luther King, Jr., Memorial Professorship in Black Church Studies at Colgate-Rochester Divinity School. He is also the author of *Black Preaching* (Philadelphia: Lippincott, 1970).

58. Richard I. McKinney, "Reflections on the Concept 'Black Theology,' " *Journal of Religious Thought*, vol. 26, no. 2, Summer Supplement, 1969, p. 12.

59. Ibid., p. 13.

60. Ibid.

61. Ibid.

62. See Roberts, "The Black Caucus and the Failure of Christian Theology," ibid., pp. 15–25; Williams, "The Ethical Aspects of the 'Black Church/Black Theology' Phenomenon," ibid., pp. 34–45.

63. "Ethnic Pluralism or Black Separatism," *Social Progress*, Sept./Oct. 1969, pp. 32–39.

64. Roberts, "The Black Caucus," p. 21.

65. Edited by James J. Gardiner and J. Deotis Roberts (Philadelphia: Pilgrim, 1971). In addition to Johnson's essay, the other essays were: Albert Cleage, "The Black Messiah and the Black Revolution"; Joseph

Washington, "How Black is Black Religion?"; Walter Yates, "The God-Consciousness of the Black Church in Historical Perspective"; J. Deotis Roberts, "Black Consciousness in Theological Perspective"; Preston Williams, "The Ethics of Black Power."

66. The entire text of this statement is given in Wilmore and Cone, *Black Theology*, pp. 100–102.

67. Gayraud Wilmore, "The Theological Commission Project" of NCBC (1968) in Traynham, *Christian Faith,* p. 84.

68. *NCBC Newsletter*, June 1968, p. 5. Also quoted in J. Deotis Roberts, "The Black Caucus," p. 20.

69. See his general introduction in Wilmore and Cone, *Black Theology*, pp. 4ff.

70. For the entire text of this statement, see Wilmore and Cone, *Black Theology*, pp. 108–11.

71. See the bylaws of the SSBR, article I, section 2. See also "Black Religious Scholarship," *Addresses at the Tenth Annual Meeting of SSBR* (Oct. 22–24, 1981). Charles S. Rooks has reminded me that the revolt of black seminarians began in stage I and not in stage II as implied in my discussion. He is correct on this point. The revolt of black students began at Colgate Rochester Theological Seminary in the Spring of 1969. As Rooks pointed out to me, this takeover led to the calling of the Howard University conference on "The Black Religious Experience and Theological Education." See a fuller explication of this conference in note 73 below.

As Gayraud Wilmore was the acknowledged leader of the revolt of black clergy radicals, Rooks was the leader in the seminaries. See his "Implications of the Black Church for Theological Education," *The Voice*, Bulletin of Crozer Theological Seminary, vol. 61, no. 1, Jan. 1969, pp. 3–22. On page three of the article he writes, "Nothing that has happened in American theological education up to this very moment helps me to believe that white seminaries will ever regard black Christianity as something central to their main interests." Rooks was prophetic. Although some white seminaries have made some adjustments by hiring a few black faculty, allowing a few more black students to matriculate, and permitting a few courses in "black studies" to be taught, Rooks's statement is still true. The only white seminary that has shown genuine signs of regarding black Christianity as central to its mission is Union Theological Seminary in New York. Several denominational white seminaries have what are sometimes called "black studies" programs or "black church" courses, but they are usually for *black* students and are not *required* of *all* students.

72. I have discussed these issues in some detail in "An Interpretation

of the Debate among Black Theologians'' in Wilmore and Cone, *Black Theology,* pp. 609–23.

73. Under the leadership of Charles Shelby Rooks, then executive director of the Fund for Theological Education and later president of Chicago Theological Seminary, an important conference on the theme ''The Black Religious Experience and Theological Education'' was sponsored by the American Association of Theological Schools at Howard University, Feb. 20–22, 1970. Addresses and reports were given by C. Shelby Rooks, Charles Copher, Vincent Harding, Henry Mitchell, Robert Bennett, Charles Long, Archie Hargraves, and myself. They were published in *Theological Education*, Spring 1970. C. Shelby Rooks also chaired a special AATS (American Association of Theological Schools) committee on ''Black Experience and Theological Education.'' Its findings were published in *Theological Education,* supplement, Spring 1970. In theological education, no one has done more than Rooks in getting seminaries to take seriously the black religious experience. In his role as the director of the Fund for Theological Education and as the first president of the SSBR, he has had a profound impact upon increasing black presence (students and faculty) in seminaries and also in introducing the subject of the black experience in all aspects of the curriculum.

74. In a conversation with Gayraud Wilmore about this concern, he said: ''I think it was because of professional fear as much as professional jealousy. But also because many lacked the depth of alienation the clergy radicals had—thus the failure of most of the members of *SSBR* to produce anything in writing that can be considered a contribution to black theology. The movement was let down by 'reluctant scholars.' '' I think Wilmore is right on this. And it is unfortunate that so few black scholars have done anything since the original interpreters of black theology of the 1960s and early '70s. Many are enjoying the luxury of tenure and salary at white seminaries and universities, and they often defend the white oppressors' values more strongly than their white colleagues.

75. My critique of black professors is based on twenty years of teaching experience and participation in professional societies. Perhaps this critique, as well as others, is too harsh, but I do not think so. However Wilmore's observation should be noted: ''I think it ought to be acknowledged that membership in the white-dominated 'guild' of theological academics was much more difficult and hazardous professionally than anything radical pastors and church executives faced.'' That may be true, but I am not convinced. Even if it were true, the conservative posture then and now of black seminary and university professors of religion is too obvious to remain silent about it. Our education should enable us to analyze the gospel and the conditions of oppression in such a way that

poor blacks are empowered by our analysis. What is most disheartening is that tenured black professors are often more conservative than are the untenured ones. I think that we blacks often become so enamored by the white world and our desire to succeed in it that we forget what the gospel demands of us. If we are not prepared to define our lives by the *cross* of Jesus, then the Christian ministry is not our vocational calling. Martin Luther King, Jr., was even more radical: "A man who won't die for something is not fit to live." What are we prepared to die for? That is the question that every concerned human being, especially those in the Christian ministry, must answer.

76. For the entire text of this document, see Wilmore and Cone, *Black Theology*, pp. 340–44.

77. See Wilmore's discussion in his general introduction and his introduction to part 4, ibid., pp. 8–10, 253–54. The significance of the Black Theology Project and Theology in the Americas will be discussed in greater detail in chap. 8.

78. A detailed discussion of this and other related aspects of black theology will be taken up later. It should be said here that several black theologians have claimed that black theology went up a blind alley and lost itself in a general concern for "the oppressed of the world." I strongly disagree. To limit black theology to the exposition of the particularity of the black church in the U.S.A. not ony separates African-Americans from other blacks of the world but also negates the *universal* note of the Christian gospel. The central definition of the Christian gospel is inseparably concerned with the salvation of *all* persons and not just blacks in the U.S.A. The only way that black theologians can demonstrate this point is by using their own particularity as a window for accenting the universal emphasis of the gospel. We must not fall into the same trap as whites, that is, say that the gospel is universal but limit our interpretation of it to our own experience. See Louis-Charles Harvey, "Black Theology and the Expanding Concept of Oppression," *Journal of Religious Thought*, vol. 38, no. 2, Fall-Winter, 1981–82, pp. 5–15.

79. Wilmore and Cone, *Black Theology*, p. 91. There will be further discussion of the impact and significance of James Forman's *Manifesto* in later chapters.

80. The entire texts of both documents are found in Wilmore and Cone, *Black Theology,* pp. 345–59.

Chapter II

1. Cited in G.S. Wilmore and J.H. Cone, *Black Theology: A Documentary History* (Maryknoll, N.Y.: Orbis, 1979), p. 106.

2. Ibid., p. 322.

3. J.H. Cone, *Black Theology and Black Power* (New York: Seabury, 1969), p. 38. See also my *A Black Theology of Liberation* (Philadelphia: Lippincott, 1970).

4. See J. Deotis Roberts, *Liberation and Reconciliation: A Black Theology* (Philadelphia: Westminster, 1971), p. 21.

5. I did not deal with the problem of the relationship between black power and the biblical witness of Jesus Christ until I wrote *God of the Oppressed* (New York: Seabury, 1975), esp. chap. 2, pp. 30ff.

6. Later I did address the problem of ideology in some detail. See my *God of the Oppressed*, chap. 5, "Black Theology and Ideology."

7. Albert Cleage, *The Black Messiah* (New York: Sheed and Ward, 1968), p. 37.

8. Quoted in Alex Poinsett, "The Quest for a Black Christ," *Ebony*, March 1969, p. 176.

9. Ibid., p. 174.

10. Ibid., p. 176.

11. Nathan Wright, Jr., *Black Power and Urban Unrest* (New York: Hawthorn, 1967), p. 136.

12. *Concern*, vol. 9, no. 16, Oct. 1, 1967, p. 22.

13. For an account of the conference, see Chuck Stone, "The National Conference on Black Power," in Floyd B. Barbour (ed.), *The Black Power Revolt* (Boston: Extending Horizon, 1968), pp. 189-98. See also *Life*, Aug. 4, 1967, pp. 26-28.

14. "The Ethical Aspects of the 'Black Church/Black Theology' Phenomenon," *Journal of Religious Thought*, Summer Supplement, 1969, p. 35.

15. *Black Religion and Black Radicalism* (Maryknoll, N.Y.: Orbis, 2nd ed., 1983), p. 199.

16. I have a mimeographed copy of this important statement.

17. *Findings of Black Methodists for Church Renewal*, Service Center, Board of Mission, United Methodist Church (7820 Reading Rd., Cincinnati, Ohio), p. 4.

18. Ibid., p. 5.

19. Of course, as Wilmore reminded me, we could have chosen the language of African emigrationism or Garveyism. Bishop Henry M. Turner of the AME Church and Marcus Garvey of Jamaica were the most prominent advocates. It belongs to the tradition of black nationalism. During the 1960s, it was the language of a few urban cults. Maulana Karenga's "Kawaida faith" came close to it and was strongly supported by the influential Congress of African Peoples, founded by Amiri Baraka. It is significant that black clergy radicals chose the language of black power and thus remained in the mainline of black tradition. Even

the acceptance of black Christian nationalism (Cleage) or the Kawaida faith of Karenga would have made it difficult for the radical black Christians to stay within the churches. The isolation of Cleage is evidence of that fact.

The influence of Maulana Karenga during the 1960s and after has been enormous among black cultural nationalists. See excerpts from his "The Quotable Karenga," in Floyd B. Barbour (ed.), *The Black Power Revolt* (Boston: Extending Horizons Books, 1968), pp. 162–70; *Kawaida Theory* (Inglewood, Calif.: Kawaida Publications, 1980). The most important book of Karenga is his *Introduction to Black Studies* (Kawaida Publications, 1982).

20. See his "Toward Black Liberation," in Robert L. Scott and Wayne Brockriede (eds.), *The Rhetoric of Black Power* (New York: Harper & Row, 1969), pp. 101–2).

21. See Imamu Amiri Baraka (LeRoi Jones) (ed.), *African Congress: A Documentary of the First Modern African Congress* (New York: Morrow, 1972).

22. The relationship of the NCBC to the *Black Manifesto* and James Forman will be discussed later in this chapter.

23. For a comprehensive study of the riots, see *Report of the National Advisory Commission on Civil Disorders* (New York: Bantam, 1968).

24. According to Leon Watts and Gayraud Wilmore, both of whom were present at the Dallas convocation, the issue of the name was discussed. Some of the chief actors in NCNC "felt that they had to be careful not to panic some of the more conservative brothers and compromise on the more radical title" (Wilmore). However, I think that the ambiguity reflected in whether to use "Black" or "Negro" in the name of the new organization is much deeper and more complex than suggested in Wilmore's comment. Black clergy radicals were making a move away from Martin King and toward Malcolm X, away from an emphasis on love of whites to an accent on love of blacks, and that created an identity crisis in their Christian identity. I am sure that Watts and Wilmore made the move from "Negro" to "Black" without much difficulty. But their easy movement to black does not negate the deeper cultural and theological crisis, which they also must have experienced. A careful reading of the documents of black radical clergy cannot fail to reveal that all of us were involved in this crisis.

25. For an excellent account of black clergy radicals' rebellion in white churches, see Alex Poinsett, "The Black Revolt in White Churches," *Ebony*, September 1968, pp. 63–68. Among the black United Methodists, no one shook up the white church more than my former classmate at Garrett Theological Seminary (now Garrett-Evangelical), Archie

Rich, who was the pastor of Berea Methodist Church in Detroit, Michigan. See his "The Black Power Revolt" in *Concern*, Oct. 1, 1967, pp. 17–18. See also "Black Power Shakes the White Church," *Look Magazine*, Jan. 7, 1969; Clayton E. Hammond, "Black Power and Methodism," *Christian Advocate*, Aug. 24, 1967.

26. No other event made a greater impact on the white religious establishment than did this document. The full text is found in Wilmore and Cone, *Black Theology*, pp. 80–89.

27. Ibid., p. 84.

28. For a summary of church responses to the *Black Manifesto* demands, see John Haughey, "The Forman Box Score," *America*, June 14, 1969. The best account of the events surrounding the manifesto is found in Robert S. Lecky and H. Elliott Wright (eds.), *Black Manifesto* (New York: Sheed and Ward, 1969). It includes essays by James Forman, William Stringfellow, Harvey Cox, Stephen Rose, Dick Gregory, Robert Brown, and James Lawson. Also important is Arnold Schuchter, *Reparations* (Philadelphia: Lippincott, 1970). See also James Forman, *The Making of Black Revolutionaries* (New York: Macmillan, 1972). See esp. the important response by Ernest T. Campbell, then pastor of Riverside Church, "The Case for Reparations," *Theology Today*, Oct. 1969.

29. See "The National Committee of Black Churchmen's Response to the Black Manifesto," in Wilmore and Cone, *Black Theology*, p. 90.

30. "A Black Churchman's Response to the Black Manifesto," ibid., pp. 93–99. This article is an excerpt from a longer paper originally written for the Department of Evangelism, United Presbyterian Church. It was distributed to the staff of the denomination's Board of National Missions on June 30, 1969. See also his "Reparations: Don't Hang Up on a Word," *Theology Today*, Oct., 1969, pp. 284–87.

31. Wilmore and Cone, *Black Theology*, pp. 105-6.

32. Ibid., p. 106.

33. In a conversation with me, Wilmore has questioned my judgment on this matter. He says: "We never believed they would accede voluntarily. We did not wish to break with them completely—and we bluffed." I am sure that others would make similar comments *looking back* on that time. But the documents that black church radicals wrote and my own reading of that period seem to say the opposite. Perhaps a few, including Wilmore, were bluffing, but *not all*. Some really believed that whites would change their racist ways if they were shown how *sinful* they were. As I look back on my own writings and experiences of that time, I must admit that I had similar expectations. The belief that a persuasive presentation of the Christian gospel alone would rid whites of racism and create

the "beloved community" is deeply embedded in the black religious tradition.

34. Wilmore and Cone, *Black Theology*, p. 95, italics added.

35. Again Wilmore has provided another important angle of vision for an analysis of this period. He said in a conversation to me: "We relied too much on white friends within the establishment—the quasi-radical whites who might be able to deliver some concessions. It was the nineteenth-century abolitionist movement all over again when some black clergy persons finally had to break with William Garrison and white abolitionists."

36. Wilmore and Cone, *Black Theology*, p. 111.

37. New York: Random House, 1970.

38. See Bishop Joseph A. Francis's comments on this theme in *America*, March 29, 1980, pp. 256f. The whole issue is devoted to the theme: "Black Catholics and their Church."

39. The BCCC statement is found in Wilmore and Cone, *Black Theology*, p. 322. It also appeared in *Freeing the Spirit*, vol. 1, no. 3, Summer 1972, pp. 25–28. For an interpretation of the silent reaction of the Catholic hierarchy, see Joseph M. Davis, "Reflections on a Central Office for Black Catholicism," ibid., pp. 31–38. See also his "The Position of the Catholic Church in the Black Community," ibid., pp. 19–24. See also the essay by Sister M. Martin de Porres Grey, "The Church, Revolution, and Black Catholics," in *The Black Scholar*, Dec. 1970, pp. 20–26.

40. Publication Office, United States Catholic Conference (1312 Massachusetts Ave., N.W., Washington, D.C.), p. 1.

41. *America*, March 29, 1980, p. 256.

42. See Sister M. Shawn Copeland's statement on this, ibid., p. 270.

43. Bishop Joseph Francis, ibid. p. 256.

44. See Brother Cyprian Rowe's essay, ibid., pp. 262–63; Brother David Spalding, "The Negro Catholic Congresses 1889–1894," *Catholic Historical Review*, vol. 55, no. 3, Oct. 1969, pp. 337–57.

45. "The Resolutions of the National Convention of Black Lay Catholics," in *Freeing the Spirit*, p. 42. Many blacks left the Catholic Church during the black power movement because they could not reconcile being black and Catholic. See esp. Saundra Willingham, "Why I Quit the Convent," *Ebony*, Dec. 1968, pp. 64–74. She says, "Four months ago, I left the convent. . . . I left because I am black, they are white and 'ne'er the twain shall meet' " (p. 64).

46. *Freeing the Spirit*, p. 42.

47. At the recent Voices for Justice Conference on "The Challenge of

Being Catholic and American in the 1980s," held in Baltimore, July 21–23, 1983, I was invited to speak on how a black Protestant theologian views the attitude of the Catholic Church toward justice. My presentation was published in *The Tablet*, July 30, 1983 (pp. 12–13), under the title "A Frank Challenge to the Catholic Church on Racism."

48. Edited by Thaddeus J. Posey. The black revolt in the Catholic Church has been initiated more in worship than in theology, and Clarence Joseph Rivers has been the leading advocate. See his *The Spirit in Worship* (Cincinnati: Stimuli, 1978); *Soulful Worship* (Washington, D.C.: NOBC and Stimuli, 1974). An excellent collection on black worship is *This Far by Faith* (Washington, D.C.: NOBC, 1977).

49. See his "What Is 'Black Theology,' Anyway?," *The Critic*, Winter 1977, pp. 64–70; "Toward a Black Catholic Theology," *Freeing the Spirit*, vol. 5, no. 2, pp. 2–6; "The Church and Black Theology," in *The New Catholic Encyclopedia*, vol. 17; "Black Theology: Potentially Classic?" in *Religious Studies Review*, vol. 4, no. 2, April 1978, pp. 85–90; "Reflections from a Theological Perspective" in *This Far by Faith;* see also his essay on black theology in *America*, March 29, 1980, pp. 274–77. His most important book is *The Wisdom Community* (New York: Paulist, 1980).

Chapter III

1. G. S. Wilmore and J. H. Cone, *Black Theology: A Documentary History* (Maryknoll, N.Y.: Orbis, 1979), p. 101.

2. Martin King's dream that the "beloved community" could be accomplished through nonviolent direct action was shared by most black Americans, including younger members of the SNCC, even though many of the latter did not share its Christian orientation. It is necessary to know the depth of the commitment of young blacks to the achievement of justice through nonviolence and their perceived betrayal by white liberals and the federal government if one is to understand why they turned to black power. See esp. Clayborne Carson, *In Struggle: SNCC and the Black Awakening of the 1960s* (Harvard University Press, 1981). Julius Lester's "The Angry Children of Malcolm X" (in Meier, Rudwick, and Broderick, *Black Protest Thought* [New York: Bobbs-Merrill, 1971]) is required reading. Vincent Harding's *The Other American Revolution* (Los Angeles: Center for Afro-American Studies, 1980) is also important. An excellent autobiographical account is that by James Forman, *The Making of Black Revolutionaries* (New York: Macmillan, 1972). See also the illuminating essay by Emily Stopher, "The Student Nonviolent Coordinating Committee: The Rise and Fall of a Redemptive Organiza-

tion," *Journal of Black Studies*, vol. 8, no. 1, Sept. 1977, and the important book by Howard Zinn, *SNCC: The New Abolitionists* (Boston: Beacon, 1964). Lerone Bennett, "The Rise of Black Power," *Ebony*, Feb. 1969, pp. 36–42, is also useful. For an interpretation of the SNCC's move from Martin King's ideas to black power, see Gene Roberts, "The Story of SNICK: From 'Freedom High' to Black Power," *The New York Times Magazine,* Sept. 25, 1966. An excellent interpretation of the need for black power is Stokely Carmichael, "What We Want," *New York Review of Books,* Sept. 22, 1966.

3. For interpretations of the events surrounding the continuation of the Meredith march, see esp. Harding, *The Other American Revolution*, chap. 28; Robert Brisbane, *Black Activism* (Valley Forge: Judson, 1974), chap. 6; Harvard Sitkoff, *The Struggle for Black Equality* (New York: Hill and Wang, 1981), chap. 7; Paul Good, *The Trouble I've Seen* (Washington, D.C.: Howard University Press, 1975), pp. 247–72; Carson, *In Struggle*, chap. 13 and 14.

4. Harding, *The Other American Revolution*, p. 186.

5. Ibid., pp. 186–87.

6. Perhaps I should say a word about the differences between Albert Cleage and myself. There are many, but they all stem from one central difference: the theological value of skin color. I do not believe that God has created blacks with more propensity toward the good than whites or any other people. All persons were created in the image of God and all have sinned against creation, claiming for ourselves more than we ought. Furthermore I do not share Cleage's historical judgment about the "Black Nation of Israel" or of the African origins of Jesus. Even if his interpretation were based on factual evidence, the theological conclusion must point to a God concerned about the salvation of all, including whites. Cleage's Black Christian Nationalism is such a reaction to white racism, as was Elijah Muhammad's Nation of Islam that influenced him, that he fails completely to recognize the *oneness* of all human beings. Whatever else we may say about the methods that Martin Luther King, Jr., used in the civil rights movement, his "beloved community" is the goal of every genuine Christian, for without this element the gospel is no longer the gospel. It is Cleage's inordinate focus on the particularity of blackness that has led him to place the universalism of the gospel in jeopardy, turning it into an ideology. That is also why he rejects the letters of Paul and Jesus' resurrection as essential elements in his theological perspective. What black Christian can take Cleage seriously when he appears to show no respect for genuine biblical Christianity?

Despite my differences with Cleage's theology, our similarities were and still are much more significant, the most important of which is the centrality of blackness and its connection with liberation in the definition of the gospel for the black community. This agreement between us made us allies in our common effort to make the Christian faith relevant to the black struggle for freedom.

7. Sojourner Truth is best known for her speeches against slavery in the abolitionist movement, and Harriet Tubman has been called the "Moses" of her people because of her liberation of herself and more than three hundred other blacks to freedom. See chap. 6 in this volume for an analysis of Sojourner Truth's involvement in the fight for women's rights. See also *Sojourner Truth: Narrative and Book of Life*, Ebony Classics (Chicago: Johnson, 1970); Jacqueline Bernard, *Journey Toward Freedom: The Story of Sojourner Truth* (New York: Dell, 1967); Hertha Pauli, *Her Name Was Sojourner Truth* (New York: Camelot/ Avon, 1962). The best and most comprehensive treatment of Harriet Tubman's life is that by Earl Conrad, *Harriet Tubman* (New York: Paul E. Eriksson, 1969); see also Sarah Bradford, *Harriet Tubman: The Moses of Her People* (Secaucus, N.J.: Citadel, 1974) [originally published in 1869].

8. Richard Allen was the founder and first bishop of the AME Church (1816); see chap. 1, note 10. Daniel Alexander Payne was also a bishop and is best known for his emphasis on education and his initiative in purchasing and later serving as president of Wilberforce University, the oldest black university in the U.S.A. See his *Recollections of Seventy Years* (New York: Arno, 1969); *History of the African Methodist Episcopal Church* (New York: Arno, 1969). George Leile was a significant participant in organizing the First Baptist Church in Silver Bluff, South Carolina, in the 1770s, and Andrew Bryan of Savannah was also a significant Baptist of the late eighteenth century. See James M. Washington, "The Origins and Emergence of Black Baptist Separatism, 1863–1897" (Ph.D. dissertation, Yale University, 1979). James Varick and Christopher Rush were significant participants in the founding of the AMEZ Church (1821). See Carol George, *Segregated Sabbaths* (New York: Oxford University Press, 1973), and Bishop William J. Walls, *The African Methodist Episcopal Church: Reality of the Black Church* (Charlotte, N.C.: AMEZ Publ. House, 1974).

9. See Herbert Aptheker, *American Negro Slave Revolts* (New York: International Publ., 1943); idem, *Nat Turner's Slave Rebellion*; Arna Bontemps, *Black Thunder: Gabriel's Revolt, Virginia 1800* (New York: Macmillan, 1936); John O. Killens, *The Trial Record of Denmark Vesey* (Boston: Beacon, 1970); Robert S. Starobin (ed.), *Denmark Vesey: The Slave Conspiracy of 1822* (Englewood Cliffs, N.J.: Prentice-Hall, 1970). Particularly significant for black theologians was Vincent Harding's re-

search, "Religion and Resistance among Antebellum Negroes, 1800–1860," in A. Meier and E. Rudwick (eds.), *The Making of Black America*, vol. 1, pp. 179–97; see also his more recent publication *There Is a River* (New York: Harcourt Brace Jovanovich, 1981). Gayraud Wilmore's "Three Generals in the Lord's Army," chap. 3 in his *Black Religion and Black Radicalism*, captured the emphasis of our concern and research. Although we rejected Joseph Washington's claim that black churches had no theology, we did agree with his emphasis (in *Black Religion*) that black faith had identified the gospel with the struggle for freedom. His book was often quoted with approval on this point. He served as a corrective to the widely held contention that black religion was primarily otherworldly and compensatory. This view is strongly emphasized by Benjamin Mays in his *The Negro's God*.

10. Walker's "Appeal" and Garnet's "Address" had an enormous impact on the thinking of the early interpreters of black theology. They were quoted more often than any other leading figures of the nineteenth century; see chap. 1, note 11.

11. The impact of the rise of black consciousness made Henry M. Turner especially important for the young black clergy. He was a bishop in the AME Church, and the only mainline black churchman whose radicalism was competitive with that of Garnet and Walker. He was a major critic of Booker T. Washington and was even isolated in his own denomination; see chap. 1, note 13.

12. New York, Praeger, 1969. This book had a profound impact on black theologians, and Mbiti, despite his conservative Western approach to theology, emerged as the most quoted and influential of all African theologians. See his controversial essay "An African Views American Black Theology," *Worldview*, Aug. 1974, reprinted in Wilmore and Cone, *Black Theology*, pp. 477–82. See my response to Mbiti, "A Black American Perspective on the Future of African Theology," in *Black Theology*, pp. 492–502, and that of Desmond M. Tutu, "Black Theology/African Theology—Soul Mates or Antagonists?" ibid., pp. 483–91. Mbiti does not like the stress on race and color in North American black theology.

13. London, Oxford University Press, 1971.

14. London, Longmans, 1962.

15. London, Oxford University Press, 1965.

16. London, Lutterworth, 1968. Harry Sawyerr, an older African theologian, has not been friendly to black theology either; like Mbiti, he does not like the emphasis on race and color. Sawyerr wrote one of the earliest essays on African theology: "What Is African Theology?," *African Theological Journal*, no. 4, Aug. 1971, pp. 7–24.

17. London, Longman, 1970.

18. London, Lutterworth, 1969. The collection of essays in this book was often referred to by young African-American members of the clergy because of its influence in the development of an African theology.

19. Long was particularly influential as a teacher and lecturer on African religions in the Society for the Study of Black Religion. His most influential essay was "Perspectives for a Study of Afro-American Religion in the United States," *History of Religions*, vol. 2, no. 1, Aug. 1971, pp. 54–66. This essay and his active participation in the SSBR provided the most challenging critique of the dependence of black theology on Western theology. See also his "Myth, Culture, and History: An Inquiry into the Cultural History of West Africa" (Ph.D. thesis, University of Chicago, 1962), and "The West African High God: History and Religious Experience," *History of Religions*, vol. 3, no. 2, Winter 1964.

20. Nashville, AMEC, 1975.

21. I have referred to this debate in several places. See esp. my interpretation of the debate among black theologians in Wilmore and Cone, *Black Theology*, pp. 615–20. See also Wilmore, *Black Religion*, chap. 8 and 9.

22. Especially useful in this regard is Miles Mark Fisher, *Negro Slave Songs in the United States* (New York: Citadel, 1953), and John Lovell, Jr., "The Social Implications of the Negro Spiritual," *Journal of Negro Education*, Oct. 1939, and his definitive study *Black Song: The Forge and the Flame* (New York: Macmillan, 1972). These works provided significant counterinterpretations of the typical view that the slave songs were exclusively otherworldly. The research of many black historians also aided our this-worldly view of the spirituals and black religion. See esp. Vincent Harding's "Religion and Resistance" (note 8, above), and his "Beyond Chaos: Black History and the Search for the New Land," Black Paper no. 2, Aug. 1970, Institute of the Black World, and his "The Afro-American Past and the Afro-American Present," in Mitchell Goodman (ed.), *The Movement toward a New America* (New York: Knopf, 1970). No popular writer on the subject was more influential than the senior editor of *Ebony*, Lerone Bennett. See esp. his *Before the Mayflower: A History of the Negro in America, 1619–1964* (Chicago: Johnson, 1966) and *Confrontation: Black and White* (Chicago: Johnson, 1965). The writings of W. E. B. DuBois are particularly useful, esp. his classic *The Souls of Black Folk* (New York: Fawcett, 1961) [originally published in 1903]; see also his *The Gift of Black Folk* (New York: Washington Square, 1970) [originally published in 1924]. Another influential essay on the spirituals was that by Sterling Stuckey, "Through the Prism of Folklore: The Black Ethos in Slavery," in Jules Chametzky

and Sidney Kaplan (eds.), *Black and White in American Culture* (University of Massachusetts Press, 1969). My *The Spirituals and the Blues* (New York: Seabury, 1972) was written in the light of this emphasis on *black* rather than "Negro" history.

23. According to Richard Randall, "Once in America when we owned other men as chattels, Negro slaves chanted thinly-disguised songs of protest, set to the meter of spirituals—'Go Down Moses,' the fighting song of Harriet Tubman who came like Moses to redeem her black kinsmen from the 'Egypt-land of the South'; 'Steal Away,' which invariably meant a summons to sneak off to the woods for a slave meeting; and the militant 'Follow the Drinking Gourd,' which meant following the Great Dipper to the Ohio River and freedom" ("Fighting Songs of the Unemployed," *The Sunday Worker Progressive Weekly*, Sept. 3, 1939, p. 2). Earl Conrad made a similar interpretation of the spirituals: "Song, or the spiritual, as a means of communication, was a definite part of each of Harriet's campaigns. The spiritual, with its hidden meaning, was employed usually when the situation was the most dangerous. The idea of song was, in itself, disarming; thus, when the Negro sang he pampered his master's understanding of him as a 'loyal, satisfied, slave.' With a melody on his lips to cloak words which held an important and immediate significance, it was possible to dupe the slaveholder" (*Harriet Tubman*, p. 76). Interpretations such as these gave us the perspective on the spirituals and black religion we black theologians needed to ground black theology in the Bible and black history. It is true that we were often not as careful in our interpretation as we perhaps should have been, but we achieved the *militant* reading of the Bible our times required and our own history suggested.

24. According to Douglass: "We were at times remarkably buoyant, sang hymns, and made joyous exclamations, almost as triumphant in their tone as if we had reached the land of freedom and safety. A keen observer might have detected in our repeated singing of 'O Canaan, sweet Canaan, I am bound for the land of Canaan,' something more than a hope of reaching heaven. We meant to reach the *North*, and the *North* was our Canaan" (*Life and Times of Frederick Douglass* [New York: Collier, 1962], p. 159; a reprint of the 1892 edition).

25. A fuller exposition of my views on the black Christ is found in *God of the Oppressed* (chap. 6), *A Black Theology of Liberation* (chap. 6), and *Black Theology and Black Power* (chap. 2). For a description of the controversy and a variety of views on the subject during the 1960s, see Alex Poinsett, "The Quest for a Black Christ," *Ebony*, March 1969. Albert Cleage was the most controversial with his emphasis on the literal blackness of Jesus as a historical fact. See also Gayraud Wilmore, "The

Black Messiah: Revising the Color Symbolism in Western Christology,"
Journal of the Interdenominational Theological Center, vol. 2, no. 1,
Fall 1974, pp. 8–18; J. Deotis Roberts, *Liberation and Reconciliation: A
Black Theology* (Philadelphia: Westminster, 1971); *The Black Messiah*,
chap. 6; Vincent Harding, "Black Power and the American Christ," in
Wilmore and Cone, *Black Theology: A Documentary History*, pp.
35–42. For an exposition of the idea of a "black God," see chap. 4, "God
in Black Theology," in my *A Black Theology of Liberation*. However,
my *God of the Oppressed* is the most detailed explanation of my views.

26. See Sterling Brown, *Negro Poetry and Drama and the Negro in
American Fiction* (1937; repr., New York: Atheneum, 1969), p. 71. For
an interpretation of Cullen's poem, see also Jean Wagner, *Black Poets of
the United States,* trans. K. Douglas (Urbana: University of Illinois
Press, 1973), pp. 283–347.

27. It should be emphasized that the development of Christianity in
both the New World and Africa among blacks was inseparable from
internal and external rejection of slavery. Black religions are unthinkable
without this background since the sixteenth century. Hence whether the
term "liberation" was used or not, black church history has been about
liberation.

28. New York, Harper & Row.

29. See esp. his *Theology of the World* (New York: Herder and
Herder, 1969).

30. See the book that resulted from the Duke University consultation,
"The Task of Theology Today," April 4–6, 1968, in which the major
paper was given by Jürgen Moltmann: *The Future of Hope: Theology as
Eschatology*, Frederick Herzog (ed.), (New York: Herder and Herder,
1970). Major responses to the Moltmann essay were by Harvey Cox,
Frederick Herzog, Langdon Gilkey, John Macquarrie, and Van A. Har-
vey. Another conference was held in New York City, Oct. 8–10, 1971,
and a book was published with the title *Hope and the Future of Man*,
Ewert H. Cousins (ed.), (Philadelphia: Fortress, 1972). Major speakers
(whose essays were published) included Jürgen Moltmann, Wolfhart
Pannenberg, Johannes B. Metz (all from Germany), John B. Cobb, Jr.,
Daniel Day Williams, Schubert M. Ogden, Carl E. Braaten, and Philip
Hefner (all from the U.S.A.). More than a thousand persons turned out
to hear the European theologians.

31. The influence of Moltmann's *Theology of Hope* and later his *Religion, Revolution, and the Future* (New York: Scribner's, 1969) was
great. I read and then reread him: "The man who hopes will never be able
to reconcile himself with the laws and constraints of this earth, neither
with the inevitability of death nor with the evil that constantly bears

further evil. The raising of Christ is not merely a consolation to him in a life that is full of distress and doomed to die, but it is also God's contraction of suffering and death, of humiliation and offense, and of the wickedness of evil. Hope finds in Christ not only a consolation *in* suffering, but also the protest of the divine promise *against* suffering. . . . Peace with God means conflict with the world. . . . If we had before our eyes only what we see, then we would cheerfully or reluctantly reconcile ourselves with things as they happen to be. That we do not reconcile ourselves, that there is no pleasant harmony between us and reality, is due to our unquenchable hope. This hope keeps man unreconciled, until the great day of the fulfillment of all the promises of God. . . . This hope makes the Christian church a constant disturbance in human society" (*Theology of Hope*, pp. 21–22). As I read this and so many other passages like it, I concluded that this is exactly what hope in the spirituals means.

32. Nashville, Abingdon, 1971. Note esp. chap. 1, "Introduction: The Case for a Black Theology of Hope," and chap. 7, "The Implications of a Theology of Hope for the Black Community." In both chapters, Jones quotes liberally from Moltmann's writings.

33. See esp. his "Black Consciousness in Theological Perspective," in J. Gardiner and J. D. Roberts (eds.), *Quest for a Black Theology* (Philadelphia: Pilgrim, 1971), esp. pp. 79–81; see also Roberts's *Liberation and Reconciliation* (chap. 2, note 4, above) and his *A Black Political Theology* (Philadelphia: Westminster, 1974). The title of the last book reflects Roberts's interest in hope theology, which was also called political theology.

34. J. Deotis Roberts was one of the first to note the problem with hope theology. That was why he asked: "How hopeful is the theology of hope?" (see his "Black Consciousness in Theological Perspective," p. 79). In most cases Roberts did not see much hope for blacks in hope theology: "Some who have been the most vocal advocates of a theology of revolution have not touched the racial crisis in the United States. I am highly suspicious when Paul Lehmann, who teaches on the fringe of the largest black ghetto in the world, can wax eloquent concerning revolutionary theology, which is his answer to the situation in Latin America. Surely a political theology to be meaningful must be applied to the local crisis situation. . . . Another American, Prof. Richard Shaull of Princeton Seminary, has spoken on 'Revolutionary Change in Theological Perspective,' but he has selected Latin America. A black theologian, aware of the suffering of his people . . . has the responsibility to speak *first* to the American situation" (ibid., pp. 79–80).

35. It was revealing that no black theologians were invited as major

232   *Notes to Pages 69–70*

participants in the conferences on hope; the issue of racism and the black struggle against it were almost completely ignored. Jürgen Moltmann raised this problem at the New York conference, "Hope and the Future of Man," in his response to papers by Carl Braaten, John Cobb, and Philip Hefner. He asked: "*Whose* future do we mean? . . . Whose hopes are we giving an account of ? . . . A future which does not begin in the transformation of the present is for me no geniune future. A hope which is not the hope of the oppressed today is no hope for which I could give a theological account. . . . If the theologians and philosophers of the future do not plant their feet on the ground and turn to a theology of the cross and the dialectic of the negative, they will appear in a cloud of liberal optimism and appear a mockery of the present suffering. If we cannot justify the theme of this conference, "Hope and the Future of Man," before the present reality of the frustration and oppression of man, we are batting the breeze and talking merely for our own self-satisfaction" (Cousins, *Hope and the Future of Man*, pp. 55, 59). Many American theologians were upset with Moltmann's response and some considered it inappropriate and in bad taste. But I was very pleased and thought his comments would help American theologians to recognize that one cannot speak of hope without grounding that speech in the struggles of blacks for freedom. But American white theologians simply returned to theology as usual, even though they claimed to be *personally* concerned about justice. It was really strange to me, not to say disgusting, to listen to American white theologians speak of hope and ignore the hopes of the victims in their situation.

36. *The Power of the Poor in History* (Maryknoll, N.Y.: Orbis, 1983), p. 101.

37. Roberts writes: "At the Duke conference on the theology of hope, I put the question to Moltmann . . . as to the meaning of his theology for an oppressed people. His answer at that time was not very hopeful" ("Black Consciousness in Theological Perspective," p. 80). When Moltmann spoke at the hope conference in New York a few years later and in his later writings, as Roberts acknowledges, he was more explicit about the connections between his theology and the oppressed. But his concreteness and his naming the enemy still left something to be desired. José Míguez Bonino's critique of Moltmann caused a great stir, especially from Moltmann. See Míguez Bonino's *Doing Theology in a Revolutionary Situation* (Philadelphia: Fortress, 1975), chap. 7, esp. pp. 144ff. See also Moltmann's response: "On Latin American Liberation Theology: An Open Letter to José Míguez Bonino," *Christianity and Crisis*, vol. 36, no. 5, March 29, 1976, pp. 57–63. To Moltmann's credit, he also went to Latin America and encountered Latin American theologians on their

own theological turf. One important meeting was held in Mexico (Oct. 1977), which I also attended. The issue between Moltmann and the Latin Americans focused on the use of Marxism—i.e., social analysis and the naming of one's enemies. It was a spirited exchange but with each learning from the other. See an account of the conference in Jorge V. Pixley and Jean-Pierre Bastien (eds.), *Praxis cristiana y producción teológica* (Salamanca: Sígueme, 1979).

38. *Power of the Poor*, p. 191; see also his "Two Theological Perspectives: Liberation Theology and Progressive Theology," in *The Emergent Gospel*, S. Torres and V. Fabella (eds.), (Maryknoll, N.Y.: Orbis, 1978).

39. *Power of the Poor*, p. 196.

40. *The Wretched of the Earth* (New York: Grove, 1963), p. 252.

41. Ibid.

42. Ibid., p. 255.

43. Although the NCBC and the AACC were similar, they were also quite different. The AACC was made up of official representatives of churches. The membership base of the NCBC was individuals.

44. On black theology in South Africa, see Basil Moore (ed.), *Black Theology: A South African Voice* (London: Hurst, 1973); Allan A. Boesak, *Farewell to Innocence: A Socio-Ethical Study on Black Theology and Power* (Maryknoll, N.Y.: Orbis, 1977); and John W. de Gruchy, *The Church Struggle in South Africa* (Grand Rapids: Eerdmans, 1979).

45. I have tried to demonstrate in this chapter that from its very origin black theology was defined as liberation theology. We did not borrow the word "liberation" from Latin America. But because the problem of white racism has played the central role in creating the need for a distinctively black theology, the word "black" has been more visible in describing our theological enterprise than has the term "liberation." The focus on "black" has provided many white North American and European interpreters with the option of identifying "liberation theology" as exclusively limited to Latin America, even though blacks started using the word "liberation" in relation to theology about the same time as did Latin American theologians. The focus on liberation in terms of class in lieu of color gave white North American theologians yet another occasion for ignoring the problem of racism and what it means in the history of North America and Europe. As we black theologians faced the problem of limiting our theological vision to issues of color, we felt that our perspective of the world, when seen in terms of the immediate, existential needs of blacks, required that we focus on color as our central starting point in theology, even though we recognized the obvious shortcomings in that initial point of departure.

46. For an introduction to the important theology of liberation movement in Latin America, see José Míguez Bonino, *Doing Theology in a Revolutionary Situation*. The classic and most important text on liberation theology in Latin America is still Gustavo Gutiérrez's *A Theology of Liberation;* see also his *The Power of the Poor in History*. For the best introduction to the variety of perspectives of the excellent theological work that is being done in Latin America, see Rosino Gibellini (ed.), *Frontiers of Theology in Latin America* (Maryknoll, N.Y.: Orbis, 1979).

47. The dialogue between Latin American and African-American theologians began in Geneva at the WCC in 1973; see *Risk*, vol. 9, no. 2 (1973). For my report on the history of our dialogue with Latin American, Asian, and African theologies, and important essays on the themes, see Wilmore and Cone, *Black Theology*, part 4, "Black Theology and Third World Theologies," pp. 445–608; see also my "From Geneva to São Paulo: A Dialogue between Black Theology and Latin American Liberation Theology," in Sergio Torres and John Eagleson (eds.), *The Challenge of Basic Christian Communities* (Maryknoll, N.Y.: Orbis, 1981), pp. 265–81, and *My Soul Looks Back* (Nashville: Abingdon, 1982), chap. 4.

48. Boston, Beacon, 1973, rev. ed. [originally published in 1961].

49. Boston, Beacon.

50. New York, Morrow.

51. New York, Schocken.

52. New York, Doubleday.

53. Boston, Beacon.

54. Boston, Beacon.

55. New York, Doubleday.

56. Nashville, Abingdon.

57. See my *God of the Oppressed* and my "Interpretation of the Debate among Black Theologians," in Wilmore and Cone, *Black Theology*.

58. New York, Doubleday. See my response to Jones in *God of the Oppressed*, chap. 8, and "Interpretation of the Debate among Black Theologians."

59. See my response to Cecil Cone in "Interpretation of the Debate."

60. Wilmore and Cone, *Black Theology*, p. 255.

61. See esp. his "Perspectives for a Study of Afro-American Religion in the U.S." and his "Structural Similarities and Dissimilarities in Black and African Theologies," *Journal of Religious Thought*, vol. 32, Spring 1976. See my response in "Interpretation of the Debate."

62. New York, Morrow.

63. Philadelphia, Lippincott.

64. New York, Harper & Row.

65. See esp. his "Black Churches in Historical Perspective," *Christianity and Crisis*, Nov. 2 and 16, 1970, pp. 226–28; "They Sought a City: The Black Church and Churchmen in the Nineteenth Century," *Union Seminary Quarterly Review*, vol. 26, no. 3, Spring 1971.

66. I have referred to several articles of Preston Williams in earlier chapters. His most influential articles included "Black Church: Origin, History, Present Dilemmas" (chap. 1, note 55, above); "The Ethics of Black Power" (chap. 1, note 64); "The Ethical Aspects of the 'Black Church/Black Theology' Phenomenon" (chap.1, note 40); "Shifting Racial Perspectives," *Harvard Divinity Bulletin*, Fall 1968, pp. 12–15; "Ethics and Ethos in the Black Experience," *Christianity and Crisis*, May 31, 1971; "Toward a Sociological Understanding of the Black Religious Community," *Soundings*, Fall 1971; "The Price of Social Justice," *Christian Century*, May 9, 1973. Herbert Edwards's most important and insightful essay was his "Racism and Christian Ethics in America," *Katallegete*, Winter 1971. See also his "The Third World and the Problem of God-Talk," *Harvard Theological Review*, vol. 64, no. 4, 1971. Carlton Lee played a major role in the origin of the NCBC. One of his most important essays was his "Religious Roots of the Negro Protest," in Arnold Rose (ed.), *Assuring Freedom to the Free* (Detroit: Wayne State University Press, 1964).

67. See his "Africa and the Biblical Period," *Harvard Theological Review*, Oct. 1971; "Biblical Theology and Black Theology," *Journal of the Interdenominational Theological Center*, Spring 1976.

68. Johnson's essay, "Jesus, the Liberator" was the most influential. See also his *The Soul of the Black Preacher* (1970) and his *Proclamation Theology* (Shreveport, La.: Fourth Episcopal District Press, 1977). Warner Traynham has also written an important text on black theology, *Christian Faith in Black and White: A Primer in Theology from the Black Perspective* (chap. 1, note 43, above). This text is valuable not only because of its interpretation of the meaning of black theology but also because of the important documents in the Appendices on the early development of black theology.

69. New York, Doubleday.

70. His most important written contribution to black theology is "Toward the Promised Land," *The Black Church*, vol. 2, no. 1, 1972, pp. 1–48.

Chapter IV

1. G. S. Wilmore and J. H. Cone, *Black Theology: A Documentary History* (Maryknoll, N.Y.: Orbis, 1979), p. 4.

2. Ibid.

3. Ibid., p. 104.

4. Ibid., p. 4.

5. I have already referred to Charles Long's important research on Africa and the religion of the African-American people, and also to Leonard Barret's *Soul Force* and Cecil Cone's *Identity Crisis in Black Theology*. Also important regarding the African origin of black religion is Albert Raboteau's *Slave Religion: The "Invisible Institution" in the Antebellum South* (New York: Oxford University Press, 1978) and Henry Mitchell's *Black Belief* (New York: Harper & Row, 1975).

6. See Wilmore's interpretation of these themes in his *Black Religion and Black Radicalism*, 2nd. ed. (Maryknoll, N.Y.: Orbis, 1983), chap. 9.

7. New York, Seabury, 1969, p. 114.

8. George Breitman (ed.), *Malcolm X Speaks* (New York: Grove, 1965).

9. Wilmore and Cone, *Black Theology*, p. 18.

10. Ibid., p. 18.

11. I have referred to all these statements in earlier chapters, and they are found in Wilmore and Cone, *Black Theology*.

12. *A Black Theology of Liberation* (Philadelphia: Lippincott, 1970), p. 23.

13. "No Turning Back?" in *Renewal*, Oct.-Nov. 1970, p. 7.

14. Ibid., p. 9.

15. Wilmore and Cone, *Black Theology*, p. 91.

16. Ibid., p. 104.

17. Ibid., pp. 105–6.

18. "No Turning Back?" p. 8.

19. Ibid.

20. I have discussed some of the reasons for the tension between Marxism and black churches in *My Soul Looks Back* (Nashville: Abingdon, 1982), chap. 5. I will also refer to Marxism in chap. 7–10, below. Regarding Marxism and the black community, see the important studies by Cedric J. Robinson, *Black Marxism: The Making of the Black Radical Tradition* (London: Zed Press, 1983); and Mark Naison, *Communists in Harlem During the Depression* (Urbana: University of Illinois Press, 1983). See also Philip S. Foner, *American Socialism and Black Americans: From the Age of Jackson to World War II* (Westport, Conn.: Greenwood, 1977); Robert Allen, *Reluctant Reformers: Racism and Social Reform Movements in the United States* (Garden City, N.Y.: Doubleday, 1975); idem, *Black Awakening in Capitalist America* (Garden City, N.Y.: Doubleday, 1970); Cornel West, *Prophesy Deliverance: An Afro-American Revolutionary Christianity* (Philadelphia: Westminster,

1982). The most provocative discussion of the relationships between Marxism and the black community is that by Harold Cruse, *The Crisis of the Negro Intellectual* (New York: Morrow, 1967).

21. See the important study by James A. Geschwender, *Class, Race, and Worker Insurgency: The League of Revolutionary Black Workers* (Cambridge University Press, 1977).

22. Wilmore and Cone, *Black Theology*, p. 105.

23. An account of this encounter is in *Risk*, Aug. 1973.

24. I will return to a discussion of this conference in chap. 8, below.

25. E. Franklin Frazier, *Black Bourgeoisie: The Rise of the New Middle Class in the United States* (New York: Collier, 1962), pp. 159, 194.

26. Ibid., p. 194.

27. See esp. Martin Luther King, Jr.'s, "The President's Address to the Tenth Anniversary Convention of the Southern Christian Leadership Conference, Atlanta, Georgia, August 16, 1967," in Robert Scott and Wayne Brockriede (eds)., *The Rhetoric of Black Power* (New York: Harper & Row, 1969), pp. 146–65. David Garrow has made the claim that Martin King was a Marxist near the end of his life. See his *The FBI and Martin Luther King, Jr.: From "Solo" to Memphis* (New York: Norton, 1981), chap. 6. See also his *From Reformer to Revolutionary* (Democratic Socialists of America, Suite 801, 853 Broadway, New York, NY 10003).

Chapter V

1. *Black Religion and Black Radicalism*, 2nd ed. (Maryknoll, N.Y.: Orbis, 1983), p. x.

2. This point has been made by many black scholars in religion. C. Eric Lincoln's comment is representative: "There is no disjunction between the black church and the black community. The church is the spiritual face of the black community, and whether one is a 'church member' or not is beside the point in any assessment of the importance and meaning of the black church" (*Black Church since Frazier* [New York: Schocken, 1974], p. 115).

3. Wilmore and Cone, *Black Theology*, p. 244.

4. Until Sept. 1982, Joseph H. Jackson was the president of the National Baptist Convention U.S.A., the largest independent black denomination in America. He was a strong opponent of Martin Luther King, Jr., and of the black theology movement. Jackson was replaced by T. J. Jemison who did much to move the denomination back toward King's image. For Jackson's views on black theology, see his "The Basic Theological Position of the National Baptist Convention, U.S.A., Inc.," in

Wilmore and Cone, *Black Theology*, pp. 257–61; *Unholy Shadows and Freedom's Holy Light* (Nashville: Townsend, 1967); and *Nairobi: A Joke, a Junket, or a Journey?* (Nashville: Townsend, 1976). Jackson's rejection of black theology or any form of ethnicity in religion has been expressed in this way: "A theology that substitutes pigmentation for divine principles is not sufficient to save any race or nation from their sins" (cited in Leon Calvin, "Christian Activism and the National Baptist Convention," *Dollars and Sense*, a special issue on the black church in America, June/July 1981, p. 38). Jackson's authoritarian leadership led to a split in the denomination that created the Progressive National Convention in 1961. For a brief account of this history, see Edward Wheeler, "Beyond One Man: A General Survey of Black Baptist Church History," *Review and Expositor*, vol. 70, no. 3, Summer 1973, pp. 295–319. For an account of Jackson's ouster as president of the National Baptist Convention, see Chester A. Higgins, Sr., "New Man Heads Six Million Baptists," *The Crisis*, special issue on the black church, Nov. 1982, pp. 34–35; see also excerpts from Jackson's and Jemison's speeches, ibid., pp. 37–41. For an uncritical account of the new directions of Jemison's leadership, see Susan M. Smith, "Born to Lead," *Black Family,* Oct. 1983. Articles like this may be useful in limited contexts, but they will not contribute to the kind of leadership that the black church needs. They remind me of the kind of articles that are found in the *A.M.E. Christian Recorder* and other black Methodist publications about bishops, general officers, and leading pastors. Uncritical praise leads to unaccountable authority.

5. Wilmore and Cone, *Black Theology*, p. 27.

6. Ibid., p. 68.

7. Ibid., p. 46.

8. Ibid.

9. Ibid., p. 47.

10. Ibid., p. 277.

11. Ibid., p. 278.

12. Ibid.

13. Ibid., pp. 278–79.

14. *Findings of Black Methodists for Church Renewal* (chap. 2, note 17, above), pp. 3–4.

15. Some of the most trenchant criticisms of the black church from the outside have been by black scholars, two of the most severe being E. Franklin Frazier and Kenneth Clark. According to Frazier, "The Negro church and Negro religion have cast a shadow over the entire intellectual life of Negroes and have been responsible for the so-called backwardness of American Negroes. . . . It is only as a few Negro individuals have been

able to escape the stifling domination of the church that they have been able to develop intellectually and in the field of art" (*The Negro Church in America* [New York: Schocken, 1974], p. 90). Although Clark recognized the power of the black church to attract the masses, he says that its failure is "inherent in the general pathology of the ghetto of which the Negro church is a part. Among its more flagrant weaknesses is the fact that its potential strengths can all too easily be dissipated by preoccupation with trivia, with competitiveness, suspiciousness, and a desperate struggle for the empty status, bombast, and show of the ghetto world" (*Dark Ghetto: Dilemmas of Social Power* [New York: Harper Torchbooks, 1967], p. 175). One of the most informative discussions of the black minister is that by Charles V. Hamilton, *The Black Preacher in America* (New York: Morrow, 1972). However, the most telling criticisms of the black church from the outside have not been from black scholars but rather black nationalists, especially Black Muslims. No one did it more convincingly than Malcolm X. It was the black nationalist's contention that "Christianity was the white man's religion and the black church the white man's representative" that forced the black clergy to develop a black theology. See *The Autobiography of Malcolm X* (New York: Grove, 1964), pp. 221–22.

16. Martin Luther King, Jr., often criticized the black church for failing to be involved in the civil rights movement. According to King: "Two types of Negro churches have failed to provide bread. One burns with emotionalism, and the other freezes with classism. The former, reducing worship to entertainment, places more emphasis on volume than on content and confuses spirituality with muscularity. The danger in such a church is that the members may have more religion in their hands and feet than in their hearts and souls. At midnight this type of church has neither the vitality nor the relevant gospel to feed hungry souls.

"The other type of Negro church that feeds no midnight traveller has developed a class system and boasts of its dignity, its membership of professional people, and its exclusiveness. In such a church the worship service is cold and meaningless, the music dull and uninspiring, and the sermon little more than a homily on current events. If the pastor says too much about Jesus Christ, the members feel that he is robbing the pulpit of dignity. If the choir sings a Negro spiritual, the members claim an affront to their class status. This type of church tragically fails to recognize that worship at its best is a social experience in which people from all levels of life come together to affirm their oneness and unity under God. At midnight men are altogether ignored because of their limited education, or they are given bread that has been hardened by the winter of morbid class consciousness" (*Strength to Love* [Philadelphia: Fortress

Press, 1963], pp. 62–63). See also Wyatt T. Walker's analysis of the weaknesses of the black church in *The Black Church Looks at the Bicentennial: A Minority Report*, by Harold A. Carter, Wyatt T. Walker, and William Jones (Elgin, Ill.: Progressive National Baptist Publ. House, 1976), pp. 65–71. See the important critique of the black church by Calvin B. Marshall III, "The Black Church—Its Mission Is Liberation," in *The Black Scholar*, vol. 2, no. 4, Dec. 1970, pp. 13–19. Marshall is the pastor of the Varick Memorial AMEZ Church in Brooklyn, and he was chairman of the board of the Black Economic Development Conference and, of course, was active in the NCBC. His essay is an excellent example of black church self-criticism.

17. "Our Heritage and Our Hope," *NCBC Newsletter*, p. 3.

18. *Black Theology and Black Power*, p. 115.

19. Ibid.

20. See esp. the account of the National United Methodist Convocation on the Black Church (Dec. 10–13, 1973) in James S. Gadsden (ed.), *Experiences, Struggles, and Hopes of the Black Church* (Nashville: Tidings, 1975). A similar emphasis on the black church by blacks in white denominations is found in William B. McClain, "The Genius of the Black Church," *Christianity and Crisis*, Nov. 2 and 16, 1970, pp. 250–52, and Reuben A. Sheares II, "Beyond White Theology," ibid., pp. 229–35. See also the *Social Progress* issue on "Black Life in Church and Society," Sept./Oct. 1969.

21. "Message to the Black Church and Community," in Wilmore and Cone, *Black Theology*, pp. 345–49.

22. Roberts has written a great deal on the black church. See his major study, *Roots of a Black Future: Family and Church* (Philadelphia: Westminster, 1980); also his essays, "A Black Ecclesiology of Involvement," *Journal of Religious Thought*, Spring-Summer 1975, pp. 36–46; "The Impact of the Black Church: Sole Surviving Institution," *Journal of the Interdenominational Theological Center*, Spring 1979, pp. 138–47.

23. C. Eric Lincoln has done extensive writings on the black church. I have already referred to his *Black Church since Frazier*. Other important essays include "Black Church in the American Society: A New Responsibility," *Journal of the Interdenominational Theological Center*, Spring 1979, pp. 83–93; "Black Church and Christian Liberty," *A.M.E. Zion Quarterly Review*, Oct. 1981, pp. 2–10; "The Black Church and a Decade of Change: Part II," *Tuesday at Home*, March 1976.

24. In a discussion of this concern with Gayraud Wilmore, he said that he "remembered the debate about that question in Benjamin Payton's office at the NCC. We really decided that more black folk would see it in the *New York Times* than in the *Amsterdam News* and would take it

more seriously in the former." The NCNC members were probably correct in their belief that more blacks would see it in a white newspaper rather than a black one. Because of this unfortunate situation, black leaders must develop a way of communicating with their constituencies that is independent of the white media. Therefore the fact that more blacks would see the statement in the *New York Times* did not relieve the NCNC persons of using the black media. Even today black leaders still depend upon the white media for communicating with their community, and that partly explains why the civil rights movement has faded from the public view.

25. James S. Tinney, "The Moral Majority: Operating under the Hood of Religious Right," *Dollars and Sense*, June/July 1981, p. 70.

26. Ibid.

27. See McCall's review of Allan Boesak's *Farewell to Innocence* in *Occasional Bulletin of Missionary Research*, vol. 2, no. 3, July 1978, p. 110.

28. Wilmore and Cone, *Black Theology*, p. 246. The most tragic example of blacks being confused by the religion of whites was the infamous Jonestown holocaust (Nov. 18, 1978). For an insightful interpretation of the Jonestown event in relation to the black church, see Archie Smith, Jr., *The Relational Self: Ethics and Therapy from a Black Church Perspective* (Nashville: Abingdon, 1982), chap. 8.

29. Valley Forge, Judson, 1976.

30. Cited in Charles V. Hamilton, *The Black Preacher in America* (note 15, above), pp. 92–93.

31. Ibid., p. 94.

32. Ibid., p. 95.

33. Cited in David Wood Wills, "Aspects of Social Thought in the African Methodist Episcopal Church 1884–1910," Ph.D. thesis, Harvard University, 1975, p. 128, note 68.

34. Howard University Divinity School and the Interdenominational Theological Center are prominent exceptions. They are black, and they have done solid work in training black persons for the ministry. Under the excellent leadership of Dean Lawrence Jones, Howard has emerged as one of the best places for the training of ministers in the black church. Although ITC, an ecumenical seminary, has not lived up to its promise because of perpetual leadership problems, it has made and continues to make a significant contribution toward training ministers for the black church. Though Howard and ITC are fine black seminaries, it is revealing to note that their excellence is not due to their support by black denominations. To be sure, individual clergy and congregations often make outstanding contributions to both seminaries, but the organizational

structure of black denominations gives either very little support or not nearly what it is capable of offering. For example, to know what AME churches think about the theological training of their ministers, it is necessary to inquire about their support of Payne Theological Seminary in Ohio or Turner Theological Seminary at ITC. The same is true of AMEZ support of Hood Theological Seminary in Salisbury, South Carolina. It has always been puzzling to me that black churches often provide more support for their colleges (like Morris Brown in Atlanta or Edward Waters in Florida) than they do for their seminaries. Their support of their colleges is often outstanding when compared with their financial resources. But it is very small when compared with the overall budget of the college. This means that the ability of black churches to effectively manage undergraduate education by themselves is a thing of the past. Why then don't black churches realize their limitations and devote most of their educational resources to the training of their ministers? If they could become much more ecumenical in the best sense and less concerned about church politics, black churches would have the resources to support one or two seminaries.

It is important to note that the problem of black seminaries was addressed during the 1960s in the context of the origin of black theology. C. Shelby Rooks provided the leadership and raised the hard, uncomfortable issues. At "The Consultation on the Black Church" sponsored by the black seminarians of the Boston area (Nov. 1968), he stated the issue sharply and provocatively: "Should black students and professors separate themselves from white theological schools and seek a place where together they can face creatively and imaginatively the specific questions and problems that confront them?" Rooks's answer was as provocative as was his question, and it demonstrates an educational crisis in the black church that is still with us today. He said: "The question really stands or falls on whether black people understand the need for black churches to develop a new style of life and the attendant need to develop a more viable and exciting process of education for those who would lead such churches. Even if somehow we could separate ourselves from all the white seminaries in the land, not much will actually have happened unless that action produces a more vital, viable and relevant relationship for black churches to the radical issues of life and death in the black community. What I am trying to ask, positively rather than negatively, is whether black students and professors can somehow be the catalyst for the emergence of a new religious community that will legitimately become partner with all forces involved in the re-birth of Black America—indeed of America itself. If the answer to that is 'Yes,'—and I think it is—the next is how and where it can best be done—whether in an all-black setting or in a supposedly or reluctantly integrated one.'' His answer was a severe indictment of the black church and reinforces the urgency of our need to face head-on the crisis in the black church. Rooks said: "If somehow all of us could withdraw to develop a new style black theological education, where could we go? One alternative is to go to an already existing black theological school. I am sorry to say, however, that I have seen little evidence there of any consuming passion or concern for the development of a theological curriculum that takes the black church and its problems in mid-twentieth century seriously—which in fact is not just a sometimes inadequate imitation of the curricula of white schools. I keep hoping that one or another of these schools will develop the kind of expertise that will suggest to anyone anywhere who has a question about Black American Protestantism to say, 'X School is the place to look for the answers.' I'm talking about the kind of expertise that the Howard Law School developed in Civil Rights Law back in the '40s and '50s. So far I have seen no evidence of that happening in theological education.

"Think for a moment! When was the last time you heard of a significant faculty appointment in one of the black schools? What books do you recall written by any of their faculty? What statements have you seen from faculty or students in the midst of all the upheavals of this decade? What programs do you know about that get at the concerns and interests expressed in this Consultation? . . . My impression—and I wish someone would prove me wrong!—is that the *locus for creative treatment of the black church is not black seminaries as they now understand themselves and their task*" ("Implications of the Black Church for Theological Education," *The Voice*, Bulletin of Crozer Theological Seminary, vol. 61, no. 1, Jan. 1969, pp. 3, 4, 5. Italics added). It is a sad fact that black seminaries, with the significant exceptions of Howard and ITC, have continued to decline. They are even less relevant today than they were in 1969, and this fact is due to the lack of support from the black denominations that manage them. It is a sad testimony of what black churches think about theological education as preparation for the ministry. While not everyone will agree with the way I express my concern for the black church's lack of concern for a trained ministry, most know that I speak the truth. Many persons remain silent because they would lose their appointment if they spoke the truth too forthrightly. Others remain silent because they believe that the black church has already rendered itself hopelessly obsolete. But I disagree with both observations. The black church is still relevant to the liberation of blacks because of the gospel that is still available to it and also because it is the only institution that we own and thus control. But it must be emphasized that *if* the black church does not create a climate that encourages persons to speak the truth and also supports a trained ministry, it will die as most institutions do when they cease to speak to the needs of the persons they claim to serve. Those who love the church will speak out, and those who are only in it for what they can get out of it (i.e., appointment to a significant pastorate, election to a bishop or general officer) will keep silent. The black church is in dire need of men and women, ministers and laypersons, who have the courage to speak the truth.

35. Regarding the importance of biblical scholarship for the black church, see the insightful essay of Vincent Wimbush, " 'Rescue the Perishing': The Importance of Biblical Scholarship in Black Christianity," *Reflection*, vol. 80, no. 2, Jan. 1983, pp. 9–11.

36. *The Power of the Poor in History* (Maryknoll, N.Y.: Orbis, 1983), p. 45. A convocation on national and international priorities for the black church was held in Washington, D.C., Feb. 7–10, 1984. The convocation was sponsored by the Black Theology Project (BTP) of TIA in cooperation with Howard University Divinity School, the Congress of National Black Churches (CNBC), and the NCBC. Over one hundred blacks gathered, along with Hispanic, Amerindian, and African National Congress (ANC) representatives. For the first time since the Black Theology Conference in Atlanta in 1977, I felt that a significant number of black clergy began to deal with concerns that transcended the politics of their denominations. I was greatly encouraged by the ecumenical spirit among clergy in the NCBC, the BTP, and the CNBC. They seemed prepared not only to work together but to do so on issues that focused on the liberation of all—here and abroad. The presence of representatives of other minorities in the U.S.A. and of South Africans prevented us from remaining too parochial in our analysis. The creativity of the convocation was centered in the workshops, which had excellent leadership. The person most responsible for the success of the convocation was Howard Dobson, the director of BTP. Important follow-up meetings have already been planned and promise to bear fruitful results. I firmly believe that black clergy must find ways to transcend the petty politics of their denominations or blacks will have to dismiss them as irrelevant and seek to create other instruments of liberation.

Chapter VI

1. *The Life and Religious Experience of Jarena Lee, A Coloured Lady*, in Dorothy Porter (ed.), *Early Negro Writing: 1760–1837* (Boston: Beacon, 1971), p. 503.

2. From a speech given at the Fourth National Women's Rights Convention, New York City, 1853, in Gerda Lerner (ed.), *Black Women in*

White America: A Documentary History (New York: Vintage, 1973), p. 568.

3. "Black Women and the Churches: Triple Jeopardy," in G. S. Wilmore and J. H. Cone (eds.), *Black Theology: A Documentary History* (Maryknoll, N.Y.: Orbis, 1979), p. 377.

4. "Black Theology and the Black Woman," ibid., p. 426.

5. See Benjamin Quarles, "Frederick Douglass and the Women's Rights Movement," *Journal of Negro History*, vol. 25, no. 1, Jan. 1940, pp. 35–44. See also the editorial by Douglass published in *The North Star*, "The Rights of Women" (text in Philip S. Foner [ed.], *The Life and Writings of Frederick Douglass* [New York: International Publishers, 1950], pp. 320–21).

6. Cited in Hertha Pauli, *Her Name Was Sojourner Truth* (New York: Camelot/Avon, 1962), p. 176. For other accounts of the same incident, see Jacqueline Bernard, *Journey toward Freedom: The Story of Sojourner Truth* (New York: Dell, 1967), pp. 175ff.; James Loewenberg and Ruth Bogin (eds.), *Black Women in Nineteenth-Century American Life* (University Park: Pennsylvania State University Press, 1976), pp. 253ff.; *Sojourner Truth: Narrative and Book of Life*, Ebony Classic (Chicago: Johnson, 1970), pp. 103ff. All these accounts are based on Elizabeth Cady Stanton, Susan B. Anthony, and Matilda Joseyn Gage (eds.), *History of Woman Suffrage*, vol. 1 (Rochester, N.Y.: Susan B. Anthony, 1881).

7. Cited in Loewenberg and Bogin, *Black Women*, p. 235.

8. Cited in Pauli, *Her Name Was*, p. 176.

9. Loewenberg and Bogin, *Black Women*, p. 236; and Pauli, *Her Name Was*, p. 177.

10. Loewenberg and Bogin, *Black Women*, p. 236.

11. Ibid., p. 238.

12. On the history of black women's struggles for freedom in the 19th and early 20th century, see Bell Hooks, *Ain't I a Woman* (Boston: South End Press, 1981); Angela Y. Davis, *Women, Race, and Class* (New York: Random House, 1981); Lerner, *Black Women in White America;* Loewenberg and Bogin, *Black Women*; Dorothy Sterling, *Black Foremothers* (New York: Feminist Press and McGraw-Hill, 1979); Bettina Aptheker, *Woman's Legacy: Essays on Race, Sex, and Class in American History* (Amherst: University of Massachusetts Press, 1982).

13. See her essay "Black Women and the Churches: Triple Jeopardy" in Wilmore and Cone, *Black Theology*, pp. 377–88.

14. Cited in Jualynne E. Dodson, "19th-Century AME Preaching Women," in H. F. Thomas and R. S. Keller (eds.), *Women in New Worlds* (Nashville: Abingdon, 1981), p. 287.

15. "The Life and Religious Experience of Jarena Lee: A Coloured Lady (1836)," in *Early Negro Writing 1760–1837*, selected and introduced by Dorothy Porter (Boston: Beacon, 1971), p. 503. The full text has been reprinted under the title *Religious Experiences and Journal of Mrs. Jarena Lee* (Philadelphia), a 125-page book. No publisher is indicated.

16. "Life and Religious Experience," p. 503.

17. "Elizabeth, A Colored Minister of the Gospel," in Loewenberg and Bogin, *Black Women*, p. 133.

18. An excellent treatment of the origin of the modern women's movement out of the civil rights and black power movements is that by Sara Evans, *Personal Politics: The Roots of Women's Liberation in the Civil Rights and the New Left* (New York: Vintage, 1980).

19. Regarding Ella Baker, see Ellen Cantarow, Susan G. O'Mally, and Sharon H. Strom, *Moving the Mountain: Women Working for Social Change* (Old Westbury, N.Y.: Feminist Press, 1980), pp. 52–93; Barbara Omolade, "Black Womanhood—Images of Dignity: Ella Baker and Miriam Makeba," *The Black Collegian*, April/May 1981, pp. 52–60; James Forman, *The Making of Black Revolutionaries* (New York: Macmillan, 1972), pp. 215–23. Forman is an exception in that he does indicate the important role that women played in the freedom movement. See esp. his tribute to "Strong Black Women" (ibid., pp. 198–202). On Ella Baker, see also her interview with Gerda Lerner in *Black Women in White America*, pp. 345–52; in regard to her role in the founding of the SNCC, see Howard Zinn, *SNCC: The New Abolitionists* (Boston: Beacon, 1964); and Clayborne Carson, *In Struggle: SNCC and the Black Awakening of the 1960s* (Harvard University Press, 1981). For information on Ella Baker, Anna Hedgeman, and Rosa Parks and their roles in the civil rights movement, especially the March on Washington, see Patrice Gaines-Carter, "Women Were Always There," *The National Leader*, vol. 1, no. 17, August 26, 1982, pp. 10f. An important interview of Rosa Parks, "Montgomery Bus Boycott," is found in Joanne Grant (ed.), *Black Protest: History, Documents and Analysis, 1619 to the Present* (Greenwich, Conn.: Fawcett, 1968).

20. On Anna A. Hedgeman, see note 39, below.

21. Most serious accounts of the Civil Rights Movement in the south refer to the dynamic leadership of Fannie Lou Hamer. See her "It's in Your Hands," in Lerner, *Black Women in White America*, pp. 609–14; and her interview with Howell Raines in his *My Soul is Rested* (New York: Putnam, 1977), pp. 249–55. An excellent account of the Fannie Lou Hamer story is found in *Sojourners* (Dec. 1982) with articles by persons who knew and worked with her in Mississippi. See especially the

articles by Danny Collum, "The Life of Fannie Lou Hamer," pp. 11–14; and Edwin King, "A Prophet from the Delta," pp. 18–21.

22. See her *The Long Shadow of Little Rock* (New York: McKay, 1962).

23. Regarding the roles of Ruby Doris Robinson and Diana Nash Bevel, see the studies of Carson and Zinn referred to in note 19, above. See also Diane Nash, "Inside the Sit-Ins and Freedom Rides: Testimony of a Southern Student," in Mathew H. Ahmann (ed.), *The New Negro* (Notre Dame: Fides, 1961).

24. Quoted in Bell Hooks, *Ain't I a Woman*, p. 97.

25. In LeRoi Jones and Larry Neal (eds.), *Black Fire: An Anthology of Afro-American Writing* (New York: Morrow, 1968), pp. 583–84. Since Baraka became a Marxist, he has repudiated his earlier nationalist views and his views regarding the subordination of women. See esp. his introduction in his (edited with Amina Baraka) *Confirmation: An Anthology of African American Women* (New York: Quill, 1983), pp. 15–26; and *The Autobiography of LeRoi Jones/Amiri Baraka* (New York: Freundlich Books, 1984), pp. 300f. In his *Autobiography,* Baraka says, "The women in those 60's and early 70's black nationalist organizations had to put up with a great deal of unadulterated bullshit in the name of revolution" (pp. 300–1). There is a lengthy discussion of his past errors, and it is to his credit that he admits to them in print.

26. Cited in Helen King, "Black Woman," *Ebony*, March 1971, p. 68.

27. Ibid., p. 70.

28. Ibid.

29. Ibid., pp. 70–71. Carolyn Robers is quoted as saying: "The feminist movement is one of middle-class white women. Of course these are women whose humanity has been destroyed by their husbands, their fathers, their sons. White women who are housewives have been allowed to remain girls, while the black 'girl' taking care of the house was indeed the woman. White women have been do-nothing dolls and one gathers now that they want to be white *men* or something else. White women with their private schools and summer camps and nursemaids for their children, and mechanical kitchen, want some satisfaction in being a woman. Black women *do* have problems with their men and we are also affected by some of the stereotypes that white women experience, but these are minor irritations when we compare them with our greatest problem—that being one of American apartheid" (ibid., p. 75).

30. Ibid., p. 71.

31. Two prominent exceptions were Congresswoman Shirley Chisholm and the well-known attorney Florynce Kennedy, both of whom were strong supporters of women's liberation.

32. Cited in Sara Evans, *Personal Politics* (note 18, above), p. 87. Like Baraka, Carmichael regretted that statement. In fact several black women testified to the opposite behavior from him. But despite Carmichael's "slip of the tongue," his comment does reflect the lack of seriousness that the women's issue received in the black movement. Today Carmichael heads the All-African People's Revolutionary party that explicitly affirms the equality of women. For a typical black male view of women's liberation, see William H. Banks, Jr., "Women's Lib: A New Cop-Out on the Black Struggle?" in *Liberator*, vol. 10, no. 9, Sept. 1970, pp. 4–5. My own lack of sensitivity to this issue can be seen in my silence about it in my early writings and the excessively patriarchal language that I used. It was the strong resistance of black women that convinced me of the evil consequences of sexism. Other black men have been convinced as well. See esp. Manning Marable, "Groundings with my Sisters: Patriarchy and the Exploitation of Black," in his *How Capitalism Underdeveloped Black America* (Boston: South End Press, 1983).

33. Toni Cade (ed.), *The Black Woman: An Anthology* (New York: New American Library, 1970).

34. Ntozake Shange, *For Colored Girls Who Have Considered Suicide/When the Rainbow is Enuf* (New York: Bantam).

35. New York, Dial, 1979.

36. There are many outstanding black feminist writers. They include: Alice Walker, *In Search of our Mothers' Gardens* (New York: Harcourt Brace Jovanovich, 1983); *The Color Purple* (New York: Washington Square, 1982); June Jordan, *Civil Wars* (Boston: Beacon, 1981); Gloria T. Hull, Patricia Bell Scott, and Barbara Smith (eds.), *But Some of Us Are Brave: Black Women's Studies* (Old Westbury, N.Y.: Feminist Press, 1982). I have already referred to B. Hooks, *Ain't I a Woman* and to Angela Y. Davis, *Women, Race, and Class*; also important is Claudia Tate (ed.), *Black Women Writers at Work* (New York: Continuum, 1983); see also Maxine Williams, "Why Women's Liberation Is Important to Black Women," and Pamela Newman, "Take a Good Look at Our Problems," published together as a Merit Pamphlet, New York, 1970. *The Black Scholar* has been the chief forum for issues regarding black women in the black community. See esp. the following: Dec. 1971; March/April 1973; March 1975; April 1978; May/June 1979; Nov./Dec. 1981; Summer 1982. On the relationship between Marxism, feminism, and race, see Gloria Joseph, "The Incompatible Menage à Trois: Marxism, Feminism, and Racism," in Lydia Sargent (ed.), *Women and Revolution* (Boston: South End Press, 1981), pp. 91–107.

37. According to James Tinney, "The first black denomination to ordain women was the AMEZ Church, which ordained its first elder, the

Rev. Julia A. Foote, in New York in 1898. But its sister body, the AME Church, did not follow suit until 1948, when it ordained the Rev. Martha J. Keys" ("Black Churches Slow to Ordain Women," *National Leader*, Sept. 2, 1982, p. 24). This essay is a good summary of the attitudes of black churches regarding the ordination of women. For black women ministers' accounts of their struggles in the black church, see "The Holy War of the Rev. Trudie Trimm," *Ebony*, Sept. 1969, pp. 72–77; Mary R. Johnson, "Black Women in the Ministry," *Dollars and Sense*, June/ July, 1981, pp. 96–101.

38. See Jeane B. Williams, "Letter to the Editor," *A.M.E. Christian Recorder*, Nov. 1, 1982. This letter was in response to Capt. C. R. Chambliss, "Do We Mean It?" ibid., June 14, 1982. Unlike most AME ministers, Chambliss wrote a strong, supportive letter regarding the equality of women in the ministry. It is unlikely that Capt. Chambliss would have written such a strong letter if he had been dependent on an AME bishop, instead of the U.S. Navy, for support of his family. The same applies to my writings. However, unless the AME Church and other black churches create structures of accountability for authority, especially regarding the power of bishops and other church leaders, then neither women nor anyone else under their jurisdiction will receive anything close to justice in black churches.

39. See her *The Gift of Chaos* (New York: Oxford University Press, 1977) for her interpretation of her involvement in the NCBC (pp. 152, 159, 162–63). See also her *The Trumpet Sounds* (New York: Holt, Rinehart & Winston, 1964).

40. According to several NCBC members, the name was changed at the 1982 fall convocation in St. Louis. However, the issue of sexism had been raised by several women much before that time. Indeed, according to the minutes of the Feb. 20–21, 1975, and the Nov. 17, 1975, board meetings (held respectively in New York and Atlanta), the issue of sexism was discussed. In New York Gilbert Caldwell reported on a consultation on black women in the ministry held at Yale Divinity School: "The women [are] interested in knowing what NCBC is and what it is doing to push issues relating to women's liberation. Sister Mary Kinnard, who attended the consultation, felt that the women raised some significant issues and that they are treated inhumanly in the black church in terms of roles and the way they are perceived. She expects to help them develop a relationship with NCBC." Virgil Wood and Bishop Charles Golden of the United Methodist Church "noted that the name of the organization could serve as a deterrent to attracting women and that the organization should again review the need for a name change." At the Atlanta meeting the issue of changing the name was discussed again: "The proposed name

change surfaced as an attempt to communicate that the organization is not just for church 'men' but for both sexes. [But] strong opposition was expressed by some to the word 'Christians' as a substitute for 'Churchmen' in our name since the original intent to be 'broadly ecumenical' has never been challenged.'' When one reads NCBC minutes and listens to black clergymen talk about the problem of sexism in the black church, there is little difference between such talk and that of white liberals on racism. Black clergymen could enhance greatly their insight on sexism by comparing its close similarity with racism. Of course, black men often strongly resist that comparison, and such resistance only discloses their own sexism.

At a recent convocation on national and international priorities of the black church (see chap. 5, note 37, above), an innovative step was taken by black male ministers regarding sexism in the black church and community. It was, to my knowledge, the first time that black male ministers openly expressed a willingness to listen to black women regarding the problem of sexism in the black church and community, even though it was not a subject area of the convocation. But in planning for the future, the issue of sexism received top priority on the agenda. A resolution was passed that urged the Black Theology Project and NCBC to plan a conference in which the only subject would be sexism in the black church and community. To my knowledge, not only did no one resist this resolution, but rather all supported it enthusiastically. I was greatly surprised but very pleased. Finally some black male ministers are beginning to recognize the importance of this issue and thus are willing to face it head-on.

41. See her ''Black Theology and Feminist Theology: A Comparative View,'' *Anglican Theological Review*, Jan. 1978, pp. 3–24; also reprinted in Wilmore and Cone, *Black Theology*, pp. 398–417.

42. See her ''Black Women and the Churches,'' in Alice Hageman (ed.), *Sexist Religion and Women in the Church* (New York: Associated Press, 1974), pp. 63–76; also reprinted in Wilmore and Cone, *Black Theology*, pp. 377–88.

43. New York, Harper & Row, 1968.

44. One of the best collections of feminist writings in religion is that by Carol P. Christ and Judith Plaskow (eds.), *Womanspirit Rising: A Feminist Reader in Religion* (New York: Harper Forum Books, 1979). See also the important writings of Rosemary R. Ruether, *Sexism and God-Talk: Toward a Feminist Theology* (Boston: Beacon, 1983); *New Woman/New Earth* (New York: Seabury, 1975); *Religion and Sexism* (New York: Simon & Schuster, 1974); Elizabeth Fiorenza, *In Memory of Her: A Feminist Theological Reconstruction of Christian Origins* (New York: Crossroads, 1983); Letty M. Russell, *Human Liberation in a*

Feminist Perspective: A Theology (Philadelphia: Westminster, 1974); Sheila Collins, *A Different Heaven and Earth: A Feminist Perspective on Religion* (Valley Forge: Judson, 1974); Isabel Carter Heyward, *The Redemption of God: A Theology of Mutual Relations* (Washington, D.C.: University Press of America, 1982); Beverly Harrison, *Our Right to Choose* (Boston: Beacon, 1983); Mary Daly, *Beyond God the Father* (Boston: Beacon, 1973).

45. See esp. *Sexism in the 1970s: Discrimination against Women*, report of a WCC consultation, West Berlin (1974); Constance F. Parvey (ed.), *The Community of Women and Men in the Church: The Sheffield Report* (Geneva: WCC, 1983); idem (ed.), *Ordination of Women in Ecumenical Perspective* (Geneva: WCC, 1980).

46. EATWOT, an organization of African, Asian, Latin American, Caribbean, and U.S. minority theologians, has been encouraging the development of theologies from the perspectives of women in these continents and regions. See esp. Amba Oduyoye, "Reflections from a Third World Woman's Perspective: Women's Experience and Liberation Theologies," in Virginia Fabella and Sergio Torres (eds.), *Irruption of the Third World: Challenge to Theology* (Maryknoll, N.Y.: Orbis, 1983); "Feminism: A Pre-condition for a Christian Anthropology," *Africa Theological Journal,* vol. 2, no. 3, 1982; Marianne Katoppo, *Compassionate and Free: An Asian Woman's Theology* (Maryknoll, N.Y. Orbis, 1977); *Women in Dialogue,* An Inter-American Meeting, Puebla, Mexico, Jan. 27–Feb. 13, 1979. In a secular context, Cherríe Moraga and Gloria Anzaldúa (eds.), *This Bridge Called Me Back: Writings by Radical Women of Color* (Watertown, Mass.: Persephone Press, 1981) is an excellent example of black women joining in coalition with other women of color.

47. It is unfortunate that so many black theologians continue to ignore the issue of the sexist orientation of black theology and the black church. One exception is James H. Evans, Jr., "Black Theology and Black Feminism," *Journal of Religious Thought,* vol. 38, no. 1, Spring-Summer 1981, pp. 43–53.

Chapter VII

1. From "The New Context of Black Theology in the United States," in G. S. Wilmore and J. H. Cone (eds.), *Black Theology: A Documentary History* (Maryknoll, N.Y.: Orbis, 1979), p. 604.

2. See the Introduction to Sergio Torres and Virginia Fabella (eds.), *The Emergent Gospel: Theology from the Underside of History* (Maryknoll, N.Y.: Orbis, 1978).

3. Ibid.

4. It is obvious that the term "underside" is to be contrasted with its opposite—"topside," the plane of "dominance," a term that Third World theologians use to characterize the role of European and white North American theologies.

5. Sergio Torres and Kofi Appiah-Kubi (eds.), (Maryknoll, N.Y.: Orbis, 1979).

6. Virginia Fabella (ed.), (Maryknoll, N.Y.: Orbis, 1980).

7. Sergio Torres and John Eagleson (eds.), (Maryknoll, N.Y.: Orbis, 1981).

8. Virginia Fabella and Sergio Torres (eds.), (Maryknoll, N.Y.: Orbis, 1983).

9. See also chap. 1, note 1, above.

10. An account of black theology in contact with Third World theologies is found in Wilmore and Cone, *Black Theology*, pp. 445–608. For an interpretation of the black theology dialogue with African, Asian, and Latin American theologies, see my "A Black American Perspective on the Future of African Theology" in *African Theology en Route*; "A Black American Perspective on the Asian Search for Full Humanity," in *Asia's Struggle for Full Humanity*; "From Geneva to São Paulo: A Dialogue between Black Theology and Latin American Liberation Theology," in *The Challenge of Basic Christian Communities*; "Reflections from the Perspectives of U.S. Blacks," in *Irruption of the Third World*.

11. Our first efforts to transcend the particularities of our respective continents and to create a Third World theology of liberation occurred at the New Delhi conference (1981). See esp. Fabella and Torres, *Irruption of the Third World*.

12. The classic description of this methodological point is found in Gustavo Gutiérrez: "Theology is reflection, a critical attitude. Theology *follows*; it is a second step. . . . The pastoral activity of the church does not flow as a conclusion from theological premises. Theology does not produce pastoral activity; rather it reflects upon it" (*A Theology of Liberation* [Maryknoll, N.Y.: Orbis, 1973], p. 11).

13. Black theology emerged as a reflection upon the civil rights and black power movements. The origin of African theology can be dated as early as the 1950s and it was inseparable from the movement toward nationhood on that continent. Something similar happened earlier on the continent of Asia. An analogous comment can be made about feminist and other forms of liberation theologies as well. The distinctiveness of Latin American theology is its careful formulation of this methodological point with the use of Marx's philosophy.

14. Again Latin Americans have been the most articulate in the formulation of this point. See Gutiérrez, *A Theology of Liberation*, p. 10.

15. Malcolm X, *By Any Means Necessary*, George Breitman (ed.), (New York: Pathfinder, 1970), p. 155.

16. Archie Epps (ed.), *The Speeches of Malcolm X at Harvard* (New York: Morrow, 1968), p. 133.

17. See esp. José Miranda, *Marx and the Bible: A Critique of the Philosophy of Oppression* (Maryknoll, N.Y.: Orbis, 1974) and his *Being and the Messiah: The Message of St. John* (Maryknoll, N.Y.: Orbis, 1977); Elsa Tamez, *Bible of the Oppressed* (Maryknoll, N.Y.: Orbis, 1982).

18. "Towards a Theology of Han," in Kim Yong Bock (ed.), *Minjung Theology: People as the Subjects of History* (Singapore: Commission on Theological Concerns of the Christian Conference of Asia, 1981), pp. 53–54. A further explication of this point is made by Cyris Hee Suk Moon, "An Old Testament Understanding of Minjung" and Ahn Byung My, "Jesus and the Minjung in the Gospel of Mark," ibid. A slightly revised version of *Minjung Theology* was published by Orbis Books in 1983. For the use of the Bible in black theology, see my *God of the Oppressed* (New York: Seabury, 1975), esp. chap. 4–7. For African theologians' views of the Bible, see Kwesi Dickson and Paul Ellingworth (eds.), *Biblical Revelation and African Beliefs* (Maryknoll, N.Y.: Orbis, 1969).

19. Questioning of the authority of the Bible was sharply expressed by several South African and feminist theologians at the EATWOT Geneva conference (Jan. 1983). Some North American feminists reject the Bible and Christianity as incurably sexist. For a variety of perspectives on white North American feminist theology, see Carol P. Christ and Judith Plaskow (eds.), *Womanspirit Rising: A Feminist Reader in Religion* (New York: Harper & Row, 1979). It is important to note that many Third World women theologians of Asia, Africa, and Latin America do not like the term "feminist" as a description of their theological work. They view it as Western and thus not fully accountable to their cultural and political aspirations. They do, however, affirm the importance of women's experience in making theology. See esp. Amba Oduyoye, "Reflections from a Third World Woman's Perspective: Women's Experience and Liberation Theologies," in Fabella and Torres, *Irruption of the Third World*, pp. 193–200. Black North American women do not reject the term "feminist," and they are not as negative in their attitude toward the Bible and Jesus as are many white feminists.

20. Howard D. Gregg, *History of the A.M.E. Church* (Nashville: Henry Belin, Jr., 1980), p. 494.

Chapter VIII

1. Cited in Sergio Torres and John Eagleson (eds.), *Theology in the Americas* (Maryknoll, N.Y.: Orbis, 1976), p. 360.

2. For information on the preparation and the conference process, see ibid., pp. 3–19.

3. Rosemary Ruether's and Gregory Baum's letters to Sergio Torres expressed the sentiments of most whites who objected to the process, and they also touched on the feelings of some minorities as well; see ibid., pp. 84–92. I have written about this conference in Wilmore and Cone (eds.), *Black Theology: A Documentary History* (Maryknoll, N.Y.: Orbis Books, 1979), pp. 451–52; "From Geneva to São Paulo," in Sergio Torres and John Eagleson (eds.), *The Challenge of Basic Christian Communities* (Maryknoll, N.Y.: Orbis, 1981), pp. 265–80.

4. See my interview during the conference in which this point was strongly emphasized ("Black is Different: An Interview with James H. Cone," in *The Witness*, Jan. 1976).

5. On the racist attitudes and actions of the white socialist left in the U.S.A., see Robert Allen, *Reluctant Reformers: Racism and Social Reform Movements in the United States* (Garden City, N.Y.: Anchor, 1975); Philip S. Foner, *American Socialism and Black Americans* (Westport, Conn.: Greenwood, 1977); Harold Cruse, *The Crisis of the Negro Intellectual* (New York: Morrow, 1967).

6. See the "Statement from the Coalition of U.S. Nonwhite Racial and National Minorities," in Torres and Eagleson, *Americas,* p. 359.

7. Ibid., p. 360.

8. See my presentation at Detroit II entitled "International versus National Oppression," in Cornel West, Caridad Guidote, and Margret Coakley (eds.), *Theology in the Americas: Detroit II Conference Papers* (Maryknoll, N.Y.: Orbis-Probe, 1982), pp. 41–42.

9. See her "A Learning Experience," *Commonweal*, Nov. 21, 1980, p. 655.

10. Gregory Baum, "Theology in the Americas: Detroit II," *The Ecumenist*, Oct. 1980, p. 92.

11. Ibid., p. 93.

12. Ibid.

13. See "Report from the Theology in the Americas First Inter-Ethic/ Indigenous Dialogue and Message from the Haudenosaunee Dialogue/ Retreat," in *Detroit II Conference Papers*, pp. 187–90.

14. For an account of the Puerto Rico Dialogue Retreat, see "Doing Theology in the Americas," *TIA Newsletter*, vol. 7, no. 2, June 1982; on

the Pacific/Asian American Inter-Ethnic/Indigenous Dialogue, see *TIA Newsletter*, vol. 8, no. 2, June 1983.

15. *The Power of the Poor in History* (Maryknoll, N.Y.: Orbis, 1983), pp. 90–91.

Chapter IX

1. From "The Negro and Socialism," *The A.M.E. Church Review*, vol. 17, Oct. 1896, pp. 196–97; 200. Ransom's essay is reprinted in the important volume by Philip S. Foner (ed.), *Black Socialist Preacher* (San Francisco: Synthesis Publications, 1983), pp. 282–89. See also the important study on Ransom by Calvin S. Morris, "Reverdy C. Ransom: A Pioneer Social Gospeler," Ph. D. diss., Boston University, 1982.

2. Black activists and scholars of the Socialist and Communist parties, especially during the 1920s and '30s, are prominent exceptions. A. Philip Randolph and Chandler Owen, founders and editors of the *Messenger*, a black socialist newspaper, advocated radical changes in the political economy. Randolph is best known as the leader of the Brotherhood of Sleeping Car Porters. See Jervis Anderson, *A. Philip Randolph: A Biographical Portrait* (New York: Harcourt Brace Jovanovich, 1972).

It should also be remembered that W. E. B. DuBois, the most outstanding black intellectual of the twentieth century, joined the Socialist party for a brief time, broke with the NAACP over the limitations of its integrationist position during the 1930s, and joined the Communist party shortly before his death in 1963.

3. See an account of President Reagan's address at the National Association of Evangelicals in Orlando, Florida, in James Wall, "Mr. Reagan Speaks Only to 'Believers,' " *Christian Century*, March 23–30, 1983, p. 259. It is important to point out that not all Evangelicals support President Reagan's irrational anticommunism or reduce the meaning of socialism to Soviet communism. In fact, some young Evangelicals are openly critical of U.S. capitalism and are searching for alternative ways of living. See esp. the writings of Jim Wallis, editor of *Sojourners* and author of *Waging Peace* (San Francisco: Harper & Row, 1982). For a detailed account of developments among Evangelicals, see Richard Quebedeaux, *The Young Evangelicals* (New York: Harper & Row, 1974); *The Worldly Evangelicals* (San Francisco: Harper & Row, 1973).

4. My interpretation of Marxism has been influenced by my colleague Cornel West. We have jointly taught a course on black theology and Marxist thought for several years, and his insights into the nature of Marx's thought and the subsequent interpretations of Marxism have

been important influences upon my perspective. His *Prophesy Deliverance: An Afro-American Revolutionary Christianity* (Philadelphia: Westminster, 1982) is a major contribution to the black theology movement. See also his "Black Theology and Marxist Thought" in Wilmore and Cone, *Black Theology: A Documentary History* (Maryknoll, N.Y.: Orbis, 1979), pp. 552–67; "Socialism and the Black Church," *New York Circus: A Center for Social Justice and International Awareness,* Oct.–Nov. 1979, p. 508; "Black Theology and Socialist Thought," *The Witness,* April 1980, pp. 16–19.

Although my perspective on Marxism has been influenced by my dialogue with Cornel West, my introduction to the importance of Marxism happened during my travels to Africa, Asia, and especially Latin America and in my encounters with Third World theologians on those continents. See chapter 7 of this volume; see also my "Black Theology and Third World Theologies" in Wilmore and Cone, *Black Theology,* pp. 445–62; *My Soul Looks Back* (Nashville: Abingdon, 1982), pp. 93–113 and 123–38. See also *The Black Church and Marxism: What Do They Have to Say to Each Other* (with comments by Michael Harrington), an occasional publication of the Institute of Democratic Socialism. For historical accounts of the black community's relation to Marxism and socialism, see chapter 4, note 20, in this volume. Also on this subject see especially P. S. Foner (ed.), *Black Socialist Preacher.*

5. Ludwig Feuerbach, *The Essence of Christianity* (New York: Harper & Row, 1957), p. 22.

6. Quoted in David McLellan, *Karl Marx: His Life and Thought* (New York: Harper & Row, 1973), p. 58; see also Saul K. Padover (ed.), *The Letters of Karl Marx* (Englewood Cliffs, N.J.: Prentice-Hall, 1979), p. 21.

7. "Contribution to the Critique of Hegel's *Philosophy of Right: Introduction,*" in Robert C. Tucker (ed.), *The Marx-Engels Reader* (New York: Norton, 2nd ed., 1972), p. 53.

8. Ibid.

9. Ibid., pp. 52–53.

10. "Theses on Feuerbach," in Tucker, *Marx-Engels Reader*, p. 145.

11. Quoted in Ernst Bloch, *On Karl Marx* (New York: Herder and Herder, 1971), p. 59.

12. See Marx's second thesis on Feuerbach, in Tucker, *Marx-Engels Reader*, p. 144.

13. Ibid., p. 145.

14. Quoted in Nicholas Lash, *A Matter of Hope: A Theologian's Reflections on the Thought of Karl Marx* (University of Notre Dame Press, 1982), p. 159.

15. Quoted in Vincent Harding, "Religion and Resistance among Ante-Bellum Negroes 1800–1860," in A. Meier and E. Rudwick (eds.), *The Making of Black America* (New York: Atheneum, 1969), vol. 1, p. 181.

16. Henry F. May, *Protestant Churches and Industrial America* (New York: Octagon, 1977), p. 6.

17. Ibid., p. 45.

18. Ibid., p. 44.

19. Ibid., p. 52.

20. Ibid.

21. In Tucker, *Marx-Engels Reader*, p. 54.

22. *A Matter of Hope*, p. 75.

23. Ibid., p. 141.

24. Ibid.

25. Ibid., p. 144.

26. Ibid., p. 145.

27. Political Writings, vol. 2, *Surveys from Exile* (Baltimore: Penguin, 1974), p. 174.

28. Lash, *A Matter of Hope*, p. 78.

Chapter X

1. In George Breitman (ed.), *Malcolm X. Speaks* (New York: Grove, 1965), pp. 68–69.

2. "The President's Address to the Tenth Anniversary Convention of the Southern Leadership Conference, August 16, 1967," in Robert L. Scott and Wayne Brockriede (eds.), *The Rhetoric of Black Power* (New York: Harper & Row, 1969), pp. 161–62.

3. *The Power of the Poor in History* (Maryknoll, N.Y.: Orbis, 1983), p. 51.

4. Amilcar Cabral, *Revolution in Guinea: Selected Texts* (New York: Monthly Review Press, 1969), p. 86.

5. John O. Killins, "Symposium on Black Power," *Negro Digest*, vol. 16, no. 1, Nov. 1966.

Index

Compiled by James Sullivan

259

Other Orbis Books . . .

CONE, James H. & Gayraud S. Wilmore
BLACK THEOLOGY
A Documentary History

"It would be hard to imagine anyone talking or writing about Black theology without using this book as a reference. The six sections, each introduced by one of the editors, cover every aspect of the origin, development, and significance of a theological revolution in the United States which is still not clearly understood nor appreciated by the great majority of Protestants and Catholics. This is not only a documentary record but an eloquent and scholarly presentation of the issues and implications of Black theology. An extremely important book." *The Christian Ministry*

ISBN 0-88344-041-5   *672pp. Cloth $19.95*
ISBN 0-88344-042-3   *Paper $12.95*

WILMORE, Gayraud S.
BLACK RELIGION AND BLACK RADICALISM
An Interpretation of the Religious History
of Afro-American People

"The most important textbook on the history of black religion and the black church ever written. No student of black history and theology should be without it in his or her library."   *James H. Cone*

"A landmark for all of us who seek both to understand and to transform the entire American experience."   *Vincent Harding*

ISBN 0-88344-032-6   *320pp. Paper $9.95*

ANSBRO, John J.
MARTIN LUTHER KING, JR.
The Making of a Mind

"Of the numerous books written on Martin Luther King, Jr., John Ansbro's will join the few enduring ones. Ansbro's major contribution is

his focus on King's philosophical, theological, and moral development. In a carefully documented manner, Ansbro demonstrates the rich inner consistency and systematic character of King's thought.''   *Choice*
ISBN 0-88344-333-3   *368pp. Cloth $17.95*

BOESAK, Allan
BLACK AND REFORMED
Apartheid, Liberation, and the Calvinist Tradition

''In this collection, Allan Boesak continues to raise for those of us outside South Africa the issue of liberation of all people in that country. He creatively relates the black struggle for freedom in South Africa to the liberating message of Jesus Christ without sacrificing the universal note of the gospel.''   *James H. Cone,*
Union Theological Seminary, New York
ISBN 0-88344-148-9   *192pp. Paper $8.95*

FAREWELL TO INNOCENCE
A Socio-Ethical Study on Black Theology and Black Power

''Boesak provides a framework of review of current black consciousness, black power, black theology, and liberation theology and then offers a helpful, evolving black ethic. All the major black American and African theologians are included in summaries of these issues and are treated in adequate fashion. Boesak indicates his knowledge of the issues and in a brief concluding essay probes a black ethic that arises from oppressed peoples (e.g. black) and urges a reversal of much 20th century materialism 'to recapture what was sacred in the African community long before white people came—solidarity, respect for life, humanity, community.' ''   *Choice*
ISBN 0-88344-130-6   *197pp. Paper $6.95*

ERSKINE, Noel Leo
DECOLONIZING THEOLOGY
A Caribbean Perspective

''Erksine gives a picture, disturbing because it rings so true, of that 'colonial theology' which so often has legitimized the subjugation of the Caribbean's blacks. At the same time, he is critical of attempts to apply a merely American black theology or a merely Latin American liberation

theology to people in a situation which has its own unique history and problems.''
Bulletin of the Congregational Library
ISBN 0-88344-087-3
144pp. Paper $6.95

HOPE, Marjorie & James Young
SOUTH AFRICAN CHURCHES IN A REVOLUTIONARY SITUATION

"A useful historical outline, from the first settlement of the Dutch East India Company in 1652, to the militant demonstrations by the Coloreds in 1980; a detailed *Who's Who* in the religious resistance to apartheid; brief but often frank and revealing interviews with a broad spectrum of church leaders and other activists. A modest but real contribution.''

The Kirkus Reviews
ISBN 0-88344-466-6
282pp. Paper $9.95

WALSHE, Peter
CHURCH VERSUS STATE IN SOUTH AFRICA
The Case of the Christian Institute

Dr. Walshe, a South African scholar and author long resident in the U.S., traces the development of the South African Christian Institute. It came as no surprise when the Institute, along with the remaining organizations of the black consciousness movement, was banned in 1977, having made a major contribution—and a lasting one—to the evolution of an indigenous liberation theology. This book, based not only on the ample documentary sources, but on personal interviews with all the leading participants, is likely to remain a definitive account of a short but immensely influential episode in modern South Africa's history.
ISBN 0-88344-097-0
250pp. Cloth $19.95